THE

OCEAN

ON

FIRE

PACIFIC STORIES FROM

NUCLEAR SURVIVORS

AND CLIMATE ACTIVISTS

THE

OCEAN

ON

FIRE

Anaïs Maurer

DUKE UNIVERSITY PRESS
Durham and London 2024

© 2024 DUKE UNIVERSITY PRESS. All rights reserved
Printed in the United States of America on acid-free paper ∞
Project Editor: Michael Trudeau
Designed by Courtney Leigh Richardson
Typeset in Portrait Text by Copperline Book Services

Library of Congress Cataloging-in-Publication Data
Names: Maurer, Anaïs, [date] author.
Title: The ocean on fire : Pacific stories from nuclear survivors and
climate activists / Anaïs Maurer.
Other titles: Pacific stories from nuclear survivors and climate activists
Description: Durham : Duke University Press, 2024. | Includes
bibliographical references and index.
Identifiers: LCCN 2023027207 (print)
LCCN 2023027208 (ebook)
ISBN 9781478030041 (paperback)
ISBN 9781478024866 (hardcover)
ISBN 9781478059059 (ebook)
Subjects: LCSH: Pacific Island literature—History and criticism. | Pacific
Island literature—Themes, motives. | Nuclear energy in literature. |
Ecocriticism in literature. | Climatic changes in literature. | BISAC:
LITERARY CRITICISM / Subjects & Themes / Nature | LITERARY
CRITICISM / Australian & Oceanian
Classification: LCC PN849.O26 M387 2024 (print) |
LCC PN849.O26 (ebook) | DDC 809/.89965—DC23/ENG/20231019
LC record available at https://lccn.loc.gov/2023027207
LC ebook record available at https://lccn.loc.gov/2023027208

Cover art: *Nuclear Hemorrhage: Enewetak Does Not Forget*, 2017. Watercolor,
thread on paper, 16″ × 12″. © Joy Lehuanani Enomoto. Courtesy of the artist.

À ma maman, qui m'a transmis et appris
ce qu'il y a de plus important

Here is a story of a people on fire—we pretend it is not burning all of us
—Kathy Jetñil-Kijiner, *Anointed*

Papatūānuku shudders under her mantle of ocean
—fire and sea do not mix
—Keri Hulme, "Te Rapa, Te Tuhi, Me Te Uira (or Playing with Fire)"

And your Great world Ocean
The Color of the Sky
Will now be called:
"SEA OF FIRE"
—Wanir Wélépane, "Mer de feu," in *Aux vents des îles*, 46–47

Contents

Note on Language

I call Pacific countries by the names chosen by local decolonial activists. I thus use Aelōñ in Ṃajeḷ rather than the Marshall Islands, Aotearoa rather than New Zealand, Guåhan rather than Guam, Kanaky rather than New Caledonia, Māʻohi Nui rather than French Polynesia, Rapa Nui rather than Easter Island, and ʻUvea mo Futuna rather than Wallis and Futuna. Some of these names are official designations, while others are used only in activist circles. I chose to use names promoted by pro-independence activists regardless of the legal nomenclature of each country, since, as Pacific studies scholar Linda Tuhiwai Smith argues in *Decolonizing Methodologies*, renaming the land after colonizers stripped it of its ancestral designations is a way to "rewrite and reright" history.

There are two possible scripts to transcribe Reo Tahiti, the Tahitian language. I use the script adopted by the Tahitian Academy Te Fare Vānaʻa; however, when quoting texts using the alternative transcription method popularized by Duro Raapoto and the Veʻa Porotetani publications, I have kept the original script. There are also two modes of transcribing kajin ṃajel, the Marshallese language. I use the most recent script created by Takaji Abo, Bryon Bender, Alfred Capelle, and Tony deBrum in 1976, while indicating the still widely used ecumenical spelling in parenthesis.

Terms in Indigenous Pacific languages are not italicized since those words are autochthonous to the region studied here.

When longer quotations in languages other than English are given, the original appears as an italicized block quotation, followed by the English translation. All translations are mine unless otherwise indicated.

Acknowledgments

Saying thank you is one of the best parts of writing this book, because I have so much to be thankful for. The people I have met while working on this project are amazing, and I wish I could write another book just about them.

First of all, all my heartfelt gratitude to the antinuclear, environmental, and decolonial writers, orators, and artists in Māʻohi Nui whom I was blessed to talk to over the course of writing this book. Titaua Peu, Chantal Spitz, Raʻi Chaze, Titaua Porcher, Moetai Brotherson, Moanaʻura Walker, Stéphanie Ariirau Richard-Vivi, Flora Devatine, Heinui Le Caill, Taimana Ellacott, Tafetanui Tamatai, Matahi Coulon, Libor Prokop, Rehia Tepa, Tevahitua Bordes, Béatrice Airuarii Mou Sang Teinauri, Tepa Teuru, Tuarii Tracqui, and Guillaume Gay, talking with you about your creative output and your dreams for the future has been immensely generative.

Many thanks also to the antinuclear activists in Māʻohi Nui for your courage and for taking the time to share some of your wisdom with me: Tea Hirshon, Léna Lenormand, Hinamoeura Morgant-Cross, Teriihinoiatua Joinville Pomare, Michel Arakino, Jean-Claude Teunu, Hinatea Marotau, Jason Man Sang, Father Auguste Uebe-Carlson, Eliane Tevahitua, Jean Kape, Tiare Tuuhia, and the dearly missed Bruno Barrillot: your work will remain a source of inspiration for generations.

Finally, gratitude and admiration for the newest generation of activists-academics retelling the story of nuclear colonialism and environmental racism in Māʻohi Nui: Vehia Wheeler, Mililani Ganivet, and Tamatoa Tepuhiarii, your brilliant scholarship will forever change how the next generations will think about Tahitian history.

Six thousand miles away from Tahiti, I am immensely grateful for the scholars in New York City who supported this book project at its earliest stage.

Souleymane Bachir Diagne, thank you for being the kindest and most inspiring mentor I could have hoped for. I treasure every discussion we have ever had. Madeleine Dobie, thank you for your patient and thoughtful critical insights at every stage of the writing process. Your writing and your mentoring have helped me so much to grow as a scholar. Kaiama Glover, I am so grateful for your enthusiasm for this project, and for sharing your immense knowledge to put this work in dialogue with other oceans. This project would not have been the same without your expertise. Bruno Saura, thank you so much for believing in this book since the beginning. It is a privilege to have gotten to study under your guidance and to spend time learning from you in Tahiti and New York. Finally, my warmest māuruuru roa to Mirose Paia and Jacques Vernaudon for your time and support in establishing the first joint examination of Reo Tahiti between the University of French Polynesia and Columbia University. May there be many more!

Many friends and colleagues have generously shared feedback to improve various sections of this manuscript. I am especially grateful to Raju Krishnamoorthy, who has always agreed to be the first reader of my roughest drafts, and to Rebecca H. Hogue, Noémie Ndiaye, Samia Rahimtoola, Jay Sibara, Chris Walker, and Vehia Wheeler for their insightful suggestions and thoughtful comments on earlier versions of this book. A special thank you to my wonderful editor, Courtney Berger, who saw potential in this project when it was still a very imperfect draft: I am so lucky for the opportunities I have had to discuss this work with Courtney over the course of the past two years. The kind suggestions and critiques from the anonymous reviewers at Duke University Press were immensely helpful in improving this book. I am especially grateful to the second reviewer: their thorough, inspiring, and generous feedback has transformed this project in most generative ways. Lastly, many thanks to everyone at Duke University Press who worked on this project, especially to Sheila McMahon and Michael Trudeau for their meticulous and enlightening editing work, and to Paula Durbin-Westby for her thoughtful indexing.

I would also like to extend my warmest gratitude to the friends and colleagues who have given me the opportunity to present excerpts of this work in progress at their institutions: Matteo Aria at Sapienza Università di Roma; Gabrielle Decamous at Kyushu University; Sémir Al Wardi and Jean-Marc Regnault at the University of French Polynesia; Benoît Pélopidas at the Nuclear Knowledges program in Paris; Sébastien Philippe at Princeton University; Rebecca H. Hogue at Harvard University; Abigail Perez Aguilera at the New School; Emlyn Hugues at Columbia University; Ben Hiramatsu Ireland at Texas Christian University; Renaud Meltz, Alexis Vrignon, and Éric Conte at the Maison des Sciences de l'Homme du Pacifique; Mathew Bolton, Volker Lehmann, and Neil Cooper at the Friedrich-Ebert Foundation; Kaliane Ung at University of Pittsburgh; Adeline Soldin at Dickinson College; Rudy Le Manthéour at Bryn Mawr College; and Sab Garduño and Mays Smithwick at New York University, as well as the French department faculty at Georgia Tech, the University of Washington, and Scripps College. Discussions with you, your colleagues, and your students have been very influential in shaping this manuscript.

I am thankful to have crossed paths with antinuclear activists and scholars far away from home, on both sides of the Atlantic Ocean. To Emlyn and Ivana Hughes of the K=1 Project, I am so grateful for your inspiring dedication to the antinuclear struggle and for your friendship. To the activists of the Nuclear Truth Project and the New York Campaign to Abolish Nuclear Weapons I had the delight to meet, and in particular to my dear friend Kathleen Sullivan, and to the scholars and activists Ray Acheson, Pam Kingfisher, Dimity Hawkins, Marco de Jung, and Mathew Bolton, thank you for simultaneously fostering antinuclear rage and a loving community. To the amazing scholars of the Fem-Nukes community, and in particular to Catherine Eschle, Vanessa Griffen, and Claire Slatter, many thanks for your dedication to create and nurture alternative academic spaces and to enlighten younger researchers with your wisdom. And to the French antinuclear scholars who stand up to the French State, Sébastien Philippe, Benoît Pelopidas, Tomas Statius, and Jean-Marie Collin: thank you for the inspiring example you have set and for your dedication to change the conversation in that country. Last but not least, a warm thank you to my former students Rose Sullivan and Lilly Hermann for taking up the antinuclear struggle in new and inspiring ways!

I also wish to thank my friends and colleagues at Rutgers University who have been supportive of my research and have consistently encouraged the development of Pacific Studies and nuclear justice in this part of the world. A particularly warm thank you to Jennifer Tamas, Shanna Jean-Baptiste Dolores, Carole Allamand, Jorge Marcone, Andy Parker, François Cornillat, Lorraine Piroux, Ana Pairet, Jimmy Swenson, Myriam Alami, Renée Larrier, Matt Matsuda, Julie Rajan, Karen Bishop, Nelson Maldonado-Torres, Ben Sifuentes-Jáuregi, Nicola Behrmann, Camillia Townsend, Asa Rennermalm, Chloe Kitzinger, Laura Ramirez, Fatimah Fisher, Nina Echevarria, and the late Alan Williams. The pandemic has unfortunately prevented me from spending as much time with all of you as I would have hoped to, and I look forward to changing this in the less hectic years to come.

Outside of Rutgers, I am very grateful to all the colleagues with whom I had the pleasure to share most generative conversations that greatly influenced this work. The following people have helped to shape this project: Julia Frengs, Nitasha Sharma, Jinah Kim, Shine Choi, Elizabeth DeLoughrey, Michelle Beauclair, Alexander Mawyer, Candice Steiner, Jeffrey Zukerman, Craig Santos Perez, Tiara Na'puti, Sudesh Mishra, Fuifuilupe Niumeitolu, Aimee Bahng, Christine Hong, Gelva Terooatea, Amber Hickey, Laura Fujikawa, John Walsh, Francesco Lattenzi, Matteo Gallo, Nina Morgan, Serge Tcherkézoff, Richard Watts, Goenda Turiano-Reea, Lee Elmrich, Nicolai Volland, Lorenz Gonschor, Bruno Jean-François, Sarah Mohammed-Gaillard, Shawn Skabelund, Jennifer Wenzel, Etienne Balibar, Emmanuelle Saada, Emma Ching. To all of you, my most heartfelt gratitude: getting to share time and thoughts with you, to benefit from your proofreading, or to collaborate with you has been a gift.

Thank you to the friends who agree to *not* talk about work when the time comes! Thérèse, Martin, Camille, Manon, and MC: thank you for opening your homes and your hearts to me when I go to France. Aaron, Phil, and Youssef, thank for having been havens of fun even in the darkest of times. Ariirei and Poe, thank you for your brilliance and the dance parties under the stars. Rebecca, thank you for your laughter and your generosity in friendship. Outsized gratitude to the friends who have been like family for more than a decade in the strange country that is the United States: Erin, who has been spared reading a single line of my work but has had to examine all the nooks and crannies of my soul. Noémie, the most fun genius to hang out with, the kindest soul with the biggest heart. Raju, words fail me to thank you for everything you have done for me. You are the kindest and most brilliant person, and I am so grateful that we are friends.

And most of all, māuruuru roa, with all my heart, to my family. You made me the person I am with your gift of constant, solid love. First, to Muti, my grandmother, thank you for being such an inspiring woman at all walks of your life. Hervé, Rose, Cathy, and John, thank you for being cheerful grandparents. To Pakau, so generous and smart, thank you for your healthy contrarianism, always guiding everyone around you to think outside the box. To my strong and talented brother Jules, thank you for taking me far, far away from my computer screen, on all the most beautiful mountains and passes of Tahiti that I couldn't reach without you. To Justin, the most loving man I know: thank you for having made me laugh every single day since I met you. To my baby Jolal, who brought me more joy in his few weeks of life than I could have imagined existed on this earth.

And to my mom—thank you for *everything*. This book is dedicated to you. Your kindness, your brilliance, and your sense of ethics taught me what really matters and showed me how to love fiercely. I hope that my child takes after you.

Introduction

"WE ARE NOT DROWNING —

WE ARE FIGHTING"

Saving the environment never means saving people who
come from environments like mine.
. . . .
Addressing climate means admitting that it starts and ends with us.
—TERISA TINEI SIAGATONU, "Layers"

Floating Islands, Doomsday Dreams

In 2008, in the midst of a financial crisis, two venture capitalists argued that
economic deregulation could be the solution to environmental collapse.
These two men were Patri Friedman, grandson of the late economist Milton
Friedman, and Peter Thiel, Facebook Inc. director and PayPal cofounder.
Together, they founded the Seasteading Institute, an organization aiming to
build artificial floating islands as sustainable refuges in the age of rising sea
levels. These "floating startup societies," as they dubbed them, were to function

as independent nation-states, with "innovative government models" offering their citizens an escape from taxation.[1] Backed by Thiel's personal fortune (estimated at nearly US$3 billion), this science-fictional solution to rising sea levels soon became a concrete proposal. In 2017, Seasteading partnered with the start-up company Blue Frontiers and signed a Memorandum of Understanding with French Polynesia, the country also known as Māʻohi Nui, to begin investigating potential partnerships. Engineers explored Tahiti's lagoon and selected a location for a floating island prototype.[2] The organization soon persuaded the Polynesian government of Tahitian president Édouard Fritch to commit to creating a "special governing framework" for an "innovative special economic zone"—in other words, a new type of tax haven for the wealthy residents of a small floating island.[3] With housing units estimated to sell at no less than US$5 million apiece, this doomsday prep project clearly catered exclusively to the world's financial elite.

Despite his fervent message of environmental concern, Thiel's donations to the campaign of the US president who called global warming "a Chinese hoax" speak to his indifference to climate collapse. This indifference stems from the fact that, for the worlds' richest entrepreneurs, the climate crisis is synonymous with lucrative opportunities—what Canadian journalist Naomi Klein has called "disaster capitalism."[4] Thiel and Friedman's conceptualization of the ocean as the next frontier of neoliberalism draws from a long capitalist tradition, water having long been seen by Western investors as an open space ideally suited to support the free circulation of capital.[5] What is unique about Thiel and Friedman's project is that they envisioned building their neoliberal utopia on lands and seas that have been a primary locus of Western utopianism for centuries. The floating island prototype was to be built nowhere other than in the Atimaono lagoon, in the district of Mataiea, a few miles away from the bay in which, more than 250 years ago, French circumnavigator Louis-Antoine de Bougainville popularized the idyllic myth of the South Seas. Seasteading capitalizes on the market value of the legendary tropical island of Tahiti, while endangering the Tahitian environment and barring Indigenous Māʻohi people from their traditional fishing grounds.[6] The project simultaneously commodifies and erases Pacific cultures.

Yet the systematic erasure of Pacific peoples at the heart of Seasteading's venture is also precisely what brought this project to its demise. As investors were negotiating with the government of French Polynesia, people of the Mataiea district organized an association, No tōʻu here ia Mataiea (Out of my love for Mataiea), to protest the environmental and social impact of the floating island. Its members were primarily local fishers and their families, as well as prominent figures of the pro-independence movement such as Tina Cross and Steve Chailloux. The association's president, Antoine Matetei, highlighted that the prototype would deprive fishers of their primary source of income and sustenance and would destroy the surrounding coral. Interviewed by the local state TV station, Matetei joked that the project should be transferred to Moruroa, the nearby atoll in which France conducted 178 nuclear and thermonuclear tests between 1966 and 1996.[7] The language used by the Seasteading Institute, promising that the floating islands project would have a low environmental impact, was indeed reminiscent of the tropes used by the French government, assuring Tahitians in the 1960s that the nuclear testing center presented "no danger" for the population and would bring modernity, economic development, and technological know-how to the island.[8] After 193 nuclear tests, French officials were still claiming that the bomb was so clean that "one can't even call this a bomb. It's nuclear physics."[9] The Seasteading Institute asking Mā'ohi people to relinquish their coastline so that people threatened by rising sea levels can "find a refuge in the future" was also disturbingly reminiscent of the United States government asking the residents of Pikinni Atoll (Bikini) to turn their island into a nuclear testing site "for the good of mankind and to end all world wars."[10]

The uncanny parallels to be made between the nuclear tests and the floating island projects rang true to many residents. On January 30, 2018, a hitherto little-known Tahitian man, Sam Amaru, posted a video on Facebook lambasting the complicit Polynesian government:

> Aren't you sick and tired of destroying the country? During the nuclear era…, you told everyone that nuclear testing was safe. We all know that nuclear fallout was nefarious. Many Polynesian people became sick.… And now, with the floating islands, you continue this destruction.… You talk about COP21, you talk about global warming. But the basis of the food chain rests on coral, and you want to build an artificial island here, in the lagoon? How much coral is it going to destroy? And can you imagine the scene? An immense floating island, right in front of our eyes, with rich people strutting in thongs and jewelry, with all their money…not paying taxes…, while people here are fucked?[11]

His video went viral. It marked a turning point in the campaign against the floating islands, as it was viewed within a few days by more than 100,000 people (more than a third of the population of the country).

All over the island, Mā'ohi antinuclear activists joined the fight against the Seasteaders. Later in 2018, Mā'ohi antinuclear writer-activist Chantal T. Spitz took a public and remarked stance against the floating island project. Spitz has a large audience in the country, having risen to fame in 1991 for becoming the first Tahitian to publish a novel—a best-selling book denouncing nuclear imperialism at a time when French bombs were still detonating in Moruroa and Fangataufa. Mobilizing her literary talents against this new assault on Tahitian lands, Spitz published a short story in French about the Seasteaders' project, titled "J'eus un pays" (I had a country). The title constitutes a dystopian parody of a famous poem in Tahitian by antinuclear activist Turo a Raapoto, "E fenua to ù" (I have a country), which proclaims the resilience of Māʼohi people whose land is "not yet conquered" (aore ā i riro).[12] In her work of science fiction inspired by current events, Spitz imagines the reality that would await Tahiti if the Seasteaders were to accomplish their plans. Her story begins in present times:

> des morceaux de lagons du pays sont sélectionnés par NoFrontiers avec l'aval du gouvernement
> protection contre la montée des eaux innovation technologique énergies renouvelables développement économique emplois assurés sont les atouts lancés en appât[13]

> bits of the country's lagoon are selected by NoFrontiers with the benediction of the government
> protection against rising sea levels technological innovation renewable energies economic development guaranteed employment are the assets thrown as bait

Renaming the aggressor "NoFrontiers," Spitz underscores the hypocrisy of the start-up launched by the Seasteaders, named "Blue Frontiers." Indeed, seeing the ocean as a frontier to be trespassed means continuing to refuse the idea of limits—the very ideology that led to the current environmental crisis in the first place and is condemning most of life on earth to cataclysmic suffering. As British marine biologist Helen Scales notes, "the frontier story has always been one of destruction and loss, and increasingly it's becoming a desperate tale of the race to grab what's left."[14]

Under Spitz's pen, the reader is invited to reflect on what "technological innovation" and "economic development" have brought to Māʼohi Nui:

> plus de la moitié de la population sous le seuil de pauvreté
> échec scolaire et illettrisme galopants
> addictions multiples alcool sucres drogues violences
> chômage massif

richesses bedonnantes pauvretés bouffies
violences physiques sexuelles contre les enfants les femmes
obésité morbide cancers diabètes maladies cardio-vasculaires en explosion
déracinement des populations
conséquences de trente années de bidouillage nucléaire de l'état d'invasion[15]

more than half of the population under the poverty line
school dropouts galloping illiteracy
multiple addictions alcohol sugar drugs violences
massive unemployment
paunchy wealth swollen poverty
physical sexual violence against the children the women
morbid obesity cancer diabetes cardiovascular diseases exploding
uprooting of the populations
consequences of thirty years of nuclear diddling by the invading state

This is the material reality behind the money and the technology brought by "nuclear diddling" done by the French Centre d'expérimentation du Pacifique (CEP, Pacific Experimentation Center). People throughout the country suffer from high incidences of cancers, leukemia, stillbirths, and other radiation-induced illnesses. The incidence of thyroid cancer and acute myeloid leukemia in Māʻohi Nui is the highest in the world.[16] Māʻohi women are particularly affected: a comparative study conducted in 2000 reveals that women in Tahiti are ten times more likely to contract thyroid cancer than women in Hawaiʻi.[17]

Yet it is very telling to see that Spitz places radiation-induced diseases at the very end of her litany of issues brought by the CEP. In addition to spreading death and diseases, the French nuclear testing program brought dramatic social changes that shook Māʻohi society to the core. While the CEP brought hefty contracts to private French enterprises and the Tahitian business elite, most Māʻohi people did not benefit from the economic windfall. After a brief period of economic boom during the construction of the nuclear bases (during which Māʻohi workers were still paid less than the French minimum wage), the nuclear economy soon left many families uprooted from their islands, isolated in insalubrious urban housing, without access to traditional fishing and farming. Māʻohi geographer Gabriel Tetiarahi denounces that Māʻohi people quickly became unable to afford buying land on which to maintain communal life since "land prices in central Papeʻete are higher than those on the Champs Élysées in the center of Paris."[18] With the weakening of traditional agricultural knowledge and the poisoning by irradiation of many food sources, most people became dependent on a wage economy that left many unemployed, underemployed, or exploited.

The French educational system in place in Mā'ohi Nui, far from offering social mobility, failed to respond to the educational needs of the country and still leaves 40 percent of the nation's youth without a high school diploma.[19] In fact, the French schooling system exacerbated the deculturation brought by nuclear money by foregrounding in its curriculum French language, literature, and history, at the expense of Pacific knowledges and epistemologies. France has also failed to provide the country with an adequate social safety net. While unemployment rates are skyrocketing (less than half of working-age people have an official job), Mā'ohi people do not have access to French unemployment benefits, nor to the French basic solidarity income (*revenu de solidarité active*, or RSA). The Tahitian, French, and Chinese political and business elite were able to benefit from France's millions in nuclear subsidies, but many working-class Mā'ohi families were impoverished by the new economy. "Our people are more and more divided between those who take advantage of the bomb's money and the others, more and more impoverished," denounced antinuclear activist John Taroanui Doom as early as 1971.[20] The islands' high rates of incarceration, substance abuse, teenage suicides, school dropouts, and domestic violence cannot be separated from France's nuclear program. This other facet of nuclear colonialism seeps deep into the hearts and souls of the Mā'ohi people born with the bomb. "Tormented and lost for having forgotten the very name of the moon that saw their birth. Shorn of their memory. Stupefied by abhorrent, foreign beliefs, they will wander, orphaned from the breast and the placenta that nourished them," accuses Mā'ohi novelist Titaua Peu.[21]

In an island thus already violently shook by nuclear imperialism, Spitz envisions a bleak future for the fight against the new stealers of land. Her story paints an apocalyptic scenario vividly reminiscent of recent history:

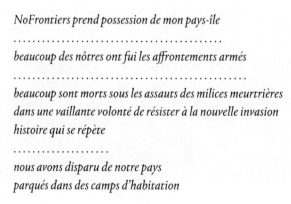

NoFrontiers prend possession de mon pays-île
....

beaucoup des nôtres ont fui les affrontements armés
....

beaucoup sont morts sous les assauts des milices meurtrières
dans une vaillante volonté de résister à la nouvelle invasion
histoire qui se répète
....

nous avons disparu de notre pays
parqués dans des camps d'habitation

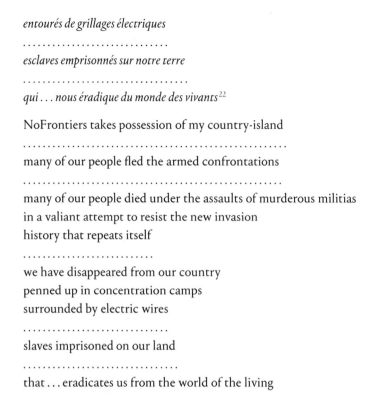

entourés de grillages électriques

. . . .

esclaves emprisonnés sur notre terre

. . . .

qui . . . nous éradique du monde des vivants[22]

NoFrontiers takes possession of my country-island

. . . .

many of our people fled the armed confrontations

. . . .

many of our people died under the assaults of murderous militias
in a valiant attempt to resist the new invasion
history that repeats itself

. . . .

we have disappeared from our country
penned up in concentration camps
surrounded by electric wires

. . . .

slaves imprisoned on our land

. . . .

that . . . eradicates us from the world of the living

Again, her story resonates with survivors of the nuclear testing era and their descendants. The "electric wires" separating Mā'ohi people from the parts of their islands seized by the French military are still standing today. The more than ten thousand Mā'ohi people diagnosed with a potentially radiation-induced cancer know in their bodies that the "invading state" will not hesitate to "eradicate [Indigenous people] from the world of the living." Spitz's not-so-fictional climate fiction simply notices that history "repeats itself": as Potawatomi philosopher Kyle Powys Whyte famously denounced, "some indigenous peoples already inhabit what our ancestors would have likely characterized as a dystopian future."[23]

And yet, despite its apocalyptic tone, Spitz's fiction tells a story of persistence and survival. While reminiscing about the nuclear apocalypse, Spitz's aesthetics are inspired by millennia-old Tahitian traditions. Her story's chant-like metrical units are rooted in the ancestral Tahitian art of 'ōrerora'a parau, a form of poetic and creative public speaking. Freed of punctuation marks and capital letters, her text lends itself to being performed orally, the speakers' tone and creativity advantageously substituting itself for written punctuation. The anaphoras ("many of our people"), the juxtaposed oppositions ("paunchy

wealth swollen poverty"), and the neologisms ("nuclear diddling") that structure her story are all additional markers of Indigenous oral aesthetic.[24] In sharing this story of past and future imperialist destruction, Spitz displays the
cultural resilience of Māʻohi people, who, even after a nuclear apocalypse, still
nurture transgenerational aesthetic and values. Spitz's story speaks of disaster,
but her style sings of survival, vitality, and regeneration.

And Māʻohi people won. In the wake of the Seasteaders' announcement
that they would build an island prototype in Tahiti's lagoon, activists simultaneously drew from their collective memory of the nuclear apocalypse and
the collective faith in Māʻohi culture's vitality and resilience. They multiplied
protests, in the streets, on the sea, and online. They denounced the latent
racism of the Seasteaders' techno-utopianism, pointing out that in Oceania,
scientific discoveries and technological experimentation have long been synonymous with environmental racism, dispossession, displacement, disease, and
death. Through speeches, stories, songs, and digital activism, Māʻohi people
also lauded the land they love and asserted their refusal to be erased from it.
Away from the world's mainstream media cameras, they performed what Candace Fujikane has called the "Indigenous economies of abundance" to oppose
"capitalist economies of scarcity": they reminded the world and each other
that the island was strong and bountiful and did not need to cater to a multibillionaire's anxieties.[25] In the face of this sustained grassroots opposition, Seasteading eventually abandoned its Tahitian project and was forced to search
for other locales in which to install its floating tax h(e)aven. A protest initiated
by a few fishers in the commune of Mataiea had defeated a capitalist venture
backed by one of the richest men in the world. The ousting of the Seasteaders
perfectly illustrates the slogan chosen by the Pacific Climate Warriors across
all of Oceania: "We are not drowning—we are fighting."

To better understand Pacific activists' attitude in the face of climate collapse, it is important to remember that the issues perceived as imminent
threats in mainstream climate discourse have already been experienced to their
fullest deadliness by Oceanians. Climate scientists warn of an apocalyptic future of climate refugees, global pandemics, and mass extinction. It is horrify-
ing to think of the deadliness that carbon-fueled capitalism is unleashing on
a global scale. But it is often forgotten that Pacific people have already undergone multiple occurrences of forced migration, massive waves of death and
diseases, and alienation from biodiversity. Since the sixteenth century, entire
islands were seized by colonizers, claimed for settlers, or wiped off the map
by thermonuclear blasts. Entire communities became sick due to introduced
viruses and radioactive fallout. And as fish and plants became overexploited,

then irradiated, the multispecies societies in which humans and nonhumans had been entangled were abruptly torn apart. Many Oceanians already live in an apocalyptic world—a world of ecosystem collapse, species loss, mass displacement, and cultural disintegration.[26] Without minimizing the scope of the devastation that an increasingly unstable climate will bring on a global scale, it is nevertheless important to point out that environmental collapse is not beginning only now that the West is becoming structurally affected by it. In the poignant words of American literary scholar Elizabeth DeLoughrey: "The apocalypse has already happened; it continues because empire is a process."[27]

In a context in which too many people throughout the world oscillate between climate apathy, apocalypse fatigue, and ecoanxiety, it is more important than ever to (re)discover Pacific (post)apocalyptic narratives. First, because this history deserves to be known and passed down from generation to generation, in Oceania and beyond. But also because Pacific (post)apocalyptic literature can help to apprehend climate collapse on a global scale. Indeed, these stories eschew the major pitfalls of the mainstream climate discourse on the intensifying environmental chaos. Pacific literature does not feature simplistic messages calling on individuals to go green, which so often seem futile in the face of military and industrial devastation and leads to widespread climate apathy. Rather, Pacific (post)apocalypse stories describe environmental collapse under nuclear imperialism and climate change in all their social and political complexity, as a consequence of racism, militarism, and carbon-fueled industrialization. Pacific (post)apocalypse stories' calls to action are calls to radical political change and testaments to the power of collective action.

Pacific stories also eschew the melancholic tales of dystopian loss that lead to the apocalypse fatigue trapping so many people into despair and climate inaction. While Pacific storytellers lament the devastation brought by colonial pandemics and nuclear fire, they also take great pains to highlight the "resilience and dignity of our communities" in the aftermath of pandemics, nuclear fallout, and king tides.[28] Samoan scholar Albert Wendt famously claimed that Oceanians "have performed and are performing one of the most heroic feats of survival in the history of colonized people,"[29] and Pacific people's fight against climate collapse is rooted in this transgenerational feat of survival through multiple apocalypses. Heeding these stories may fill readers with much-needed examples of the need to keep on mobilizing against environmental destruction, even after tipping points toward environmental chaos have already been reached.

Finally, Pacific (post)apocalyptic stories are also bereft of the tropes pervading blockbuster climate fiction, such as hyperviolent males fighting to survive through feats of physical strength and technological breakthroughs. These mainstream apocalypse narratives simply reiterate the myths that have enabled industrial capitalism in the first place: materialism, techno-utopianism, competition, individualism, and estrangement from other-than-human forms of life. They portray an environmentally and socially bleak future, spreading debilitating ecoanxiety.[30] Pacific (post)apocalyptic stories, by contrast, showcase "the enduring ties that hold people together" in times of catastrophic change.[31] They narrate (post)apocalyptic examples of mutual assistance, cultural resilience, and South-South transnational solidarities. They teach how to mourn for what has been lost and how to find the strength to keep fighting for that which remains. If the stories analyzed in this book carry some hope, it is the hope that the climate apocalypse may not necessarily take the form of the hopeless fight of all against all.

This does not mean that Pacific suffering should be instrumentalized by readers who are simply consuming it for entertainment or inspiration. The value of Pacific creative discourse does not lie in its ability to be appropriated and instrumentalized by global environmental movements. Rather, Pacific stories of (post)apocalyptic regeneration can function as a global moral compass—or star path—for the rest of the world. To put it in the words of Māʻohi antinuclear philosopher Richard Ariihau Tuheiava, the love that unites Pacific people and their land can radiate outside Oceania: "We should be able to promote it and affirm it on a universal scale." He asserts, "Our Indigeneity ties a geographic area to a spiritual connection. It ties the universal to a specific place; it lets our ancestors speak in the name of the universal."[32] Long marginalized, Pacific epistemologies should be recognized for their foundational contributions to human knowledge.

Pacific stories by nuclear survivors and climate activists are not modern instantiation of the noble savage narrative—this Western myth that elevates Indigenous peoples to a state of timeless purity by presuming that Indigenous communities are immobilized in an original state of nature. Indigenous peoples are sometimes idealized by ecoanxious foreigners as the last people living in Holocene conditions—what Kyle Whyte ironically calls "Holocene survivors."[33] Instead, Pacific people have long entered the twenty-first century era of man-made, militarized, global environmental collapse. As Indigenous people are claiming the world over, "our history is the future."[34] In this sense, Pacific stories of nuclear testing and climate change are (post)apocalyptic in the etymological sense of the word: they help *uncover* (αποκαλύπτειν) alternative modes of being in the world, beyond the hackneyed fetters of imperialism, capitalism, and petro-fueled modernity. Oceania was the first continent to see its environment destroyed by nuclear fire on a previously unimaginable scale. It is also the first continent to imagine a new world emerging from the ashes of the old one.

The Nuclearized Anthropocene

After the United States detonated the first nuclear bombs, very few people realized that humanity had entered a new era. The conventional bombing of German cities had generated more casualties than Hiroshima and Nagasaki, and the longer-term effects of radiation were not yet known to the wider public. The atomic bomb, presented to the public as the weapon that had put an abrupt end to World War II, led many people to hope that the mastery of the atom was going to bring the end of all wars.[35] Yet the invention of nuclear warfare, followed by the development of the thermonuclear bomb, brought the world into the era of the nuclearized Anthropocene.

For the first time, a handful of men had created the tools not only to destroy humanity but also to obliterate the whole planet. The destructive scope of the atomic bomb cannot be understated. The largest nonnuclear weapon in the contemporary United States arsenal, the Massive Ordnance Air Blast (MOAB) dropped on Afghanistan in 2017 to much international outrage, had a destructive power of "only" 0.009 kilotons.[36] By contrast, Castle Bravo, the largest US thermonuclear bomb detonated on Pikinni (Bikini) in 1954, had a yield of 15,000 kilotons. For the Pacific people whose lands were obliterated by the blast of the bombs, the difference between conventional and unconventional weapons is not a discursive abstraction. In addition to their sheer blast power, nuclear weapons also eradicate life through long-lasting nuclear fallout. Some irradiated areas, such as Pikinni Atoll, are off-limits for hundreds of thousands of years. Atomic bombs thus completely transformed the scope of (some) humans' power over the planet. While the beginning of modern ecology is often dated to 1962 and the publication of Rachel Carson's *Silent Spring*, it should really be dated back to the understanding of the interconnectedness of the world brought by the first nuclear bomb.[37]

Nuclear testing is also the starting point of a new age of imperialism. After World War II, the power of a country became more dependent on its nuclear strike capacity than on the size of its empire. But the nuclear industrial complex—the interconnected network of uranium mines, uranium shipping infrastructure, nuclear power plants, nuclear bombs, advanced army bases, and radioactive waste dumps—is transnational. Countries in search of a nuclear arsenal have always depended on other nations' resources: uranium is mined on foreign land, bombs are tested on colonies, and radioactive waste is dumped on poorer countries. As political science scholars Shine Choi and Catherine Eschle underscore, there is a "material colonial relationship at the heart of the global nuclear order."[38]

This type of colonialism, however, is different from pre-1945 forms of colonial oppression. When imperial powers began coveting strategic territories in which to deploy their nuclear strike capacity, large-scale colonialism was replaced by different structures of imperial oppression, taking the form of imperial webs of smaller nuclear colonies the world over. Amid international pressure to decolonize in the 1960s, nuclear colonizers went even further, negotiating for countries like Algeria or the Marshall Islands to become independent on the condition that their former colonizer would remain in control of circumscribed sites such as In Ekker or Kuwajleen (Kwajalein) to be used as nuclearized bases. These comparatively small areas of militarized lands in independent countries make up what American historian Daniel Immerwahr has called a "pointillist empire," which today extends all over the planet.[39] This forms the special basis of *nuclear imperialism*: the state-sponsored, systemic mode of oppression of current or former sites of empire through any use of the nuclear complex.[40] In fact, decolonization may have happened on such a wide scale after 1945 in large part because imperial countries got hold of smaller territories in which to develop their nuclear strike capacity.

Marking a new age in both ecology and imperialism, the nuclear bomb can therefore be seen as the starting point of the global environmental crisis that now threatens life on earth on an unprecedented scale. With the A-bomb, the whole world entered an era in which apocalypse became a permanent horizon — no longer a fantasized religious eschatology but rather the very real knowledge that the current social world (dis)order can collapse at any moment. It also marks the moment when (some hu)man(s) became convinced that it was possible to truly become master and possessor of nature. While I do not wish to contribute here to the heated debates about the starting point of the Anthropocene, it should be noted that the "bomb spike" that followed the dramatic increase in thermonuclear weapons testing in the 1960s has left a very tangible geological record in the planet's sedimentary layers. The appearance in the atmosphere, the soil, and the bodies of all living species of new man-made radioactive elements has led some scientists to suggest that a mid-twentieth-century boundary level is a possible benchmark to define the beginning of the historic period in which (some hu)man(s) have acquired the power to geologically alter the planet.[41]

In Western countries, antinuclear activists and climate activists tend to fight in separate trenches, barely talking to each other. In the United States and France, many environmentalists are in fact pronuclear, on the grounds that nuclear power is low carbon.[42] France's number one best-selling book in 2022 thus claims that nuclear power is the only technology standing between humanity and climate collapse.[43] Yet nuclear issues and climate issues are inextricably linked. Climate instability increases the chance of nuclear accidents and of an all-out nuclear war. Nuclear power plants are all located near water sources, such as rivers and oceans. As sea levels rise and rivers are more and more frequently subjected to droughts, it becomes clear that "the climate is antinuclear."[44] Conversely, the nuclear arms race itself has a tremendous carbon footprint and largely contributes to the environmental crisis.[45] Moreover, both nuclear imperialism (the outsourcing of nuclear pollution) and carbon imperialism (the outsourcing of the adverse consequences of CO_2 emissions) make racialized people bear the brunt of contemporary environmental devastation. And of course, both proponents of the atom and believers in fossil-fueled infinite growth believe in man's ability to control nature, and they trust that more technological breakthroughs can solve the issues created by technological innovation in the first place. Instead of conceiving of nuclear war and climate collapse as two distinct scenarios that could threaten most life on earth, it would be more generative to think of them as inextricably linked in the nuclearized Anthropocene—and to challenge them both simultaneously.

Oceania First

In the mad rush toward extinction of life that characterizes the past seventy-five years, Oceania has always been on the front lines. The Pacific Islands have been the site of the majority of nuclear weapons tests throughout history— a "nuclear playground," to use Australian political scientist Steward Firth's expression.[46] The United States, the United Kingdom, and France have all tested their nuclear bombs in the Pacific Islands: on Pikinni, Kalama (Johnston Atoll), Kiritimati (Christmas Island), Terapukatea (Malden Island), Amchitka, Moruroa, and Fangataufa. While these nuclear powers also irradiated other Indigenous lands on the continents, their most powerful and most dangerous weapons were all launched in the Pacific (see map I.1). The 106 American bombs detonated in the Pacific accounted for 73.5 percent of the yield of all 1,054 U.S. tests.[47] In the Marshall Islands alone, the bombs' blast represented the equivalent of 8,580 Hiroshima-sized bombs, or 1.47 Hiroshimas each day

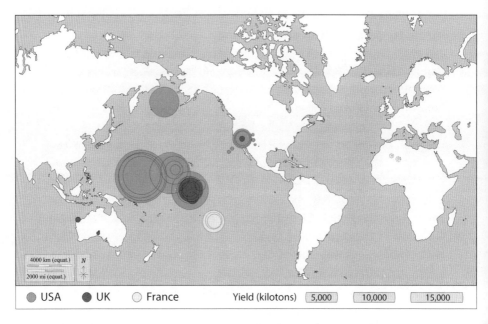

MAP I.1. Western nations' nuclear tests' yield. Map by Anaïs Maurer and Rose Sullivan.

over the twelve years of the tests.[48] The largest bomb detonated in Pikinni, Castle Bravo, would have killed 90 percent of the populations of the District of Columbia, Baltimore, Philadelphia, and New York City within three days if it had been detonated in Washington, DC.[49] Together, the United States, the United Kingdom, and France have detonated a blast equivalent to dozens of thousands of times that of Hiroshima in the skies and under the reefs of the great Pacific Ocean.[50]

The effects of nuclear imperialism did not stop with the last nuclear test in Oceania in 1996. The French, American, and British armies have left heaps of contaminated waste, both on the atolls where nuclear tests were conducted and on rear operating bases where nuclear experimentation centers had their headquarters.[51] Pacific waters have been used as toxic and radioactive waste dumping sites for decades, even after the United Nations' London Convention prohibited such practices in 1972. Japan still "outsources" 300 tons of water contaminated by its Fukushima nuclear plant daily.[52] The Pacific Islands are also targeted as dumping sites for nuclearized countries' radioactive waste—a phenomenon that American sociologist Valerie Kuletz has called "second order nuclearism."[53] While the global imperial mindset commonly associates nuclear devastation with the red buttons on desks in Washington, Beijing, and Pyongyang, it would be more accurate to recenter the nuclear apocalypse in the vast ocean where it actually took place.

After having been used as "natural" laboratories on which to experiment with radioactive weapons of mass destruction, the Pacific Islands are now being used as showcases of forthcoming climate change. Outsiders began referring to Oceania as the proverbial canary in the coal mine; not valuable in and of itself but rather in service to a larger (global) environmental purpose.[54] As British anthropologists Tony Crook and Peter Rudiak-Gould have argued, climate change as a discourse and steering concept has particular resonance in the Pacific "because here the discourse takes some of its most arresting and intense forms."[55] The Pacific Islands in general, and low-lying atolls in particular, evoke some of the most imminent and irreversible threats caused by climate change in the global public imagination. Coral ecosystems and atolls threatened by rising sea levels have been used internationally as symbols of the reality of climate change, through a form of climate porn that Australian geographer Carol Farbotko has identified as "wishful sinking."[56]

The archipelagoes most threatened by rising sea levels are often islands formerly used as nuclear testing sites because nuclear colonizers systematically located their testing sites in low-lying atolls (see map I.2). As a result, contemporary resistance to climate collapse benefits from an already established framework of pan-Pacific solidarities, developed in the past century during the fight for a nuclear-free and independent Pacific. Nuclear imperialism made some islands uninhabitable for the next hundreds of thousands of years. The climate crisis adds another cataclysm onto communities still struggling to recover from the last imperial assault on their lands.

It is in this context that Pacific environmental activists refuse to be reduced to the harrowing symbol of the drowning Islander, a word I capitalize throughout to emphasize its nature as a social construct. Pacific people's disappearance has been forecast by imperial observers for the past five hundred years. According to Western colonizers, Oceanians were to disappear in contact with the white race, wiped out by imported diseases. Pacific cultures were then to be annihilated by the "modern" lifestyle brought by nuclear imperialism. And today, the Pacific Islands are to be erased by rising seas. Yet, despite half a millennium of alleged imminent disappearance, Pacific cultures are still vibrant, and Pacific people continually reassert the vitality of the ever-regenerating Pacific seascape.

It is important to put the consequences of ecocide in historical perspective because these various forms of environmental aggression are underpinned

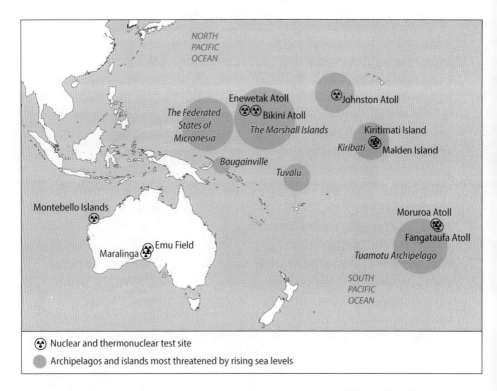

MAP I.2. Low-lying atolls and nuclear testing sites. Map by Anaïs Maurer and Rose Sullivan.

by the same ideology: annihilation racism. Annihilation racism, as defined by French anthropologist Alban Bensa, is an ideology that "presupposes not so much the inferiority of the colonized people but rather their inevitable disappearance as a prehistoric race."[57] Annihilation racism is the ideological backbone informing Westerners' continued legitimization of—and apathy toward—epidemiological, nuclear, and climate cataclysms in Oceania. Pacific opposition to climate collapse is grounded in a centuries-long history of struggle against this annihilation racism. Pacific stories of multigenerational resistance to biopolitical change can thus move mainstream environmental discourse from speculative narratives about climate collapse to historically informed reflections on environmental racism.

Positioning Pacific (Post)apocalyptic Stories:
Corpus, Methodology, Translation

The beginning of antinuclear art and literature in the Pacific is often dated to the publication, in 1959, of Māori poet Hone Tuwhare's antinuclear piece "No Ordinary Sun."[58] This poem marks the beginning of what Marjorie Tuainekore Crocombe has called a "creative revolution" in the 1970s, when Pacific activists fought for a nuclear-free and independent Pacific in widely diffused printed and visual works.[59] Yet the turn to oral tradition and multilingual archives shows that Oceanians have opposed nuclear technology in creative discursive practices *ever since the first nuclear bomb was detonated.* Consider, for example, the songs performed in 'Uvea, the largest island of the French colony of 'Uvea mo Futuna (Wallis and Futuna), as early as 1945. With no major transshipment infrastructure, no television, and radio access reserved to the island's elite, one could be tempted to assume that 'Uvea was far removed from the detonation of Little Boy on Hiroshima, thousands of miles away. Yet that year, a group of men interpreted a foi lau (traditional informational song) that would usher the island into the Atomic Age.

Koeni te pule-tau foou
Osi ina fakaosi te tau
Ko Tuluma ae ne'e na fau
Si'i foi pulu fakamataku

. . . .

Koeni te foi pulu ka oho
Kolo tona tatau mo te temonio
Au loto ke puli aupito
Saponia he e tau fakapo

Talavou tou fakafiafia
Kua tokalelei te Pasifika
Kua hiki nima lava Saponia
Ki te foi pulu a Amelika.[60]

Here comes the new war chief
The one who put an end to the war
It is Truman who built
This dreadful bomb

. . . .

Here is the bomb to be launched
It is like the devil

I want the complete annihilation
Of Japan, the ruthless fighter

Young people, let's rejoice
Peace is back in the Pacific
Japan signed the peace
Because of the Americans' bomb.

Uvean foʻi lau function as a collective news report, sharing contemporary events through ritualized singing.[61] Here, the message of this news report cannot be mistaken: nukes are bad news. Uveans immediately gauged in negative terms the impact of this "dreadful bomb" ("pulu fakamataku") from the moment its existence was revealed. The Uvean singer who composed the chant, Reverend Father Soane Vahai, learned about the nuclear bomb through Western propaganda relayed by the few dozen American military men present on the island at that time. Back then, the specifics of nuclear weapons were not yet fully understood by the global public, and their dangers were downplayed by politicians and journalists alike.[62] As a result, the news of Hiroshima and Nagasaki was first met in many places with "relief and jubilation."[63] The bomb is presented in this song through this American perspective as a device to bring back peace, while Japan is pictured as an evil enemy that should be annihilated ("puli aupito," translating literally as "very disappeared"). Nevertheless, Vahai managed to transcend American disinformation. While presenting it as a tool for peace, he also notes: "Kolo tona tatau mo te temonio" (It is like the devil).

The word *temonio* was introduced in the Uvean language in the 1830s by the French missionaries who established the first Catholic mission on the island.[64] Adapted from the French noun *démon*, temonio encapsulates the major antagonism structuring Christian faith, opposing God to the devil, heaven to hell, and salvation to damnation. The use of such a loaded comparison by a Christian composer like Reverend Soane Vahai is highly subversive and renders the whole stanza entirely oxymoronic. How can peace and salvation come from a weapon likened to the devil? This skepticism toward American propaganda must be analyzed in ʻUvea's larger historical context.

In 1945, ʻUvea had already been invaded twice in the name of peace and salvation. The first time was in 1837, when French missionaries settled on the island and began talking about saving the souls of Uveans. Within three years, a large-scale epidemic from a new virus brought by a European man wreaked havoc on the island. While French settlers could write in the 1830s that Uveans were in extraordinarily good health and that even "the elderly were not missing a single tooth," they would bemoan a few decades later that Uveans were "sickly, of poor constitution, prone to all sorts of diseases."[65] Taking advantage of the fact that the traditional religious and political elite was weakened by the epidemiological crisis, French missionary Father Bataillon pressured the islands' Aliki (leaders) and the Lavelua (high chief) to adopt a new legislation that would put traditional values under further stress. The code of laws that bears his name, adopted in 1851, forced Uveans to abandon their traditional houses to live in concentrated communities more easily surveilled by the Church, forbade people of opposite genders to socialize outside of church-sanctioned activities, and transferred the political power from the Lavelua and the Aliki to the Catholic mission.[66] The code was applied for 110 years, and the local police severely sanctioned and fined the people who tried to preserve precolonial practices well into the second half of the twentieth century.[67] As Uveans' first encounter with Western salvation discourse resulted in unprecedented death and destruction, Reverend Soane Vahai may have apprehended with caution the foreigners' claim that these new weapons of peace were any different.

As the island was beginning to recover from the major epidemiological and sociopolitical trauma of evangelization and colonization, it would soon face another threat. In 1942, the United States used the island as a military base for its Pacific theater, stationing massive contingents of American soldiers and quickly outnumbering the local population (without Uveans' consent). The American military instructed the entire valid population to dig trenches across the island (perpetuating a tradition of forced labor initiated by the French administration), recruited against their will hundreds of young Uvean men to participate in military operations in the Coral Sea, and impregnated numerous Uvean women who had to rely on communal networks to raise their unrecognized children.[68] When preparing to evacuate the island in 1944, the US Army destroyed its own military materiel, tanks, and cars by sinking them in 'Uvea's lagoon, durably polluting the island's waters.[69] Given that America had thus transformed the daily lives of Uveans, it is no surprise that the explosion of the most powerful American weapon was mentioned in circumspect terms in 'Uvea's oral literature. Even though American occupiers controlled the technological means of information, Vahai and his choir still interpreted the invention of the nuclear bomb in ambiguous terms, mobilizing the central binary opposition at the heart of Christianity to locate nuclear technology on the side of evil.

THIS BOOK ANALYZES PACIFIC (post)apocalyptic nuclear stories from the time of Vahai's choir's performance in 1945 to today. I define the word *stories* in its broadest sense, as print, oral, digital, embodied, and visual literature. Many of these stories defy genre classification. Literary scholar Caroline Sinavaiana-Gabbard suggests that given the problematic role Western literary categories have played in imposing hegemonic norms on Pacific orators, artists, and writers, it may be more adequate to avoid generic labels when analyzing Pacific creative discourse.[70] In all their diversity and fluidity, these stories are best described in the words of ri-Ṃajeḷ poet-scholar Kathy Jetñil-Kijiner as "the different ways in which we have expressed ourselves."[71] Sunnie Kaikala Mākua, Manulani Aluli Meyer, and Lynette Lokelani Wakinekona describe it as the act of "listening to the operating vibrational truth of one's own life, and then expressing it. This can take any form: writing, singing, speaking, praying, dancing, etc."[72] Thus understood, Pacific literature has been flourishing ever since Pacific people sailed to the islands on double-hulled canoes millennia ago.

While I focus on nuclear stories created from 1945 onward, this does not mean that World War II marked an aesthetic rupture in Pacific creative discourse. As literary scholar Brandy Nālani McDougall underscores, "our ancestral literature constantly informs and guides our contemporary literature and our contemporary selves."[73] My analyses of Pacific (post)apocalyptic stories consider the importance of transgenerational Indigenous aesthetics and practices as a source of inspiration for the antinuclear literature and visual art analyzed in this book. Following Craig Santos Perez's guidelines to Indigenize literary theory, I highlight how Pacific antinuclear literature draws from older and deeper Indigenous aesthetics—from both a rich oral tradition (encompassing cosmogonic stories, genealogies, and tales) and a vast visual tradition (from tattooing to weaving and dancing).[74] Retracing how customary Indigenous orature and visual technologies persist and flourish in the age of the atom reaffirms the strength of Pacific cultures in the face of past, future, and ongoing apocalypses. This is not necessarily to be celebrated as the power of storytelling; it is simply the current reality of the Pacific environmental movement. As Wendt notes, Pacific literature, anchored in multigenerational aesthetic practices through its content as well as its style, declares Pacific peoples' "marvelous endurance, survival, and dynamic adaptation" in the face of imperial violence.[75]

Since nuclear pollution and climate change issues know no borders, this book's analytical framework is transnational and multilingual. I explore literatures in English, French, Hawaiian, Spanish, Tahitian, and Uvean as well as visual arts by painters from across the region. Readers may find in these pages heretofore untranslated nuclear stories from the French-occupied Pacific, as I offer English translations of influential texts and songs from imperial and Indigenous languages of these archipelagoes. By discussing all these works in English, I hope to contribute to breaking down the linguistic boundaries threatening to compartmentalize environmental and decolonial movements in the Pacific. As American literary scholar Julia Frengs explains, literature from non-Anglophone Pacific countries has been significantly undertranslated, whether these works are in colonial or Indigenous languages. For example, only 3 percent of Oceanian printed novels written in French have been translated into English.[76] This creates linguistic boundaries between activists otherwise united by similar forms of colonization, militarization, deculturation, environmental racism, and/or calls for Indigenous sovereignty. It is important to make translations of these works into English available because English is an official language in the majority of Pacific countries and the most-taught foreign language in the region. It has long stopped being the language of colonizers and is now a language in which people throughout the Pacific communicate with each other.

There are, however, potential issues with discussing translated works. As Kanaka 'Ōiwi poet-scholar Jamaica Heolimeleikalani Osorio warns, a translator may "contain and domesticate" others' work and rob it of its subversiveness, its literariness, or its cultural referents. The translation of Indigenous languages is particularly problematic as it "leaves certain languages and people visible and recognizable, and others not."[77] While wary of these limitations, I am offering this modest contribution to multilingual dialogue because it responds to Pacific Francophone authors' expressed desires. The dozens of antinuclear writers and orators I consulted in current or former French colonies of the Pacific unanimously expressed a desire to be translated into English. When I interviewed the president of Mā'ohi Nui, Moetai Brotherson, about his antinuclear novel, *Le Roi absent* (The absent king), he joked that he wished he had written the book in English in the first place: "I would be much more read!"[78]

Despite their inevitable structural limitations, translations from French, Spanish, Tahitian, and Uvean respond to non-Anglophone Pacific writers,' singers,' and orators' explicit desires to have their stories put in conversation with those of English-speaking artists "who came with us on their great canoes, born of the same dream of freedom."[79] While many Pacific countries have been or are currently occupied by colonizers such as Spain, the United Kingdom, France, Germany, Japan, the United States, Chile, and Indonesia, imposing various languages onto the islands, my hope is to contribute to mitigate the ensuing linguistic compartmentalization. When translating Indigenous languages already shaken by centuries of settler colonialism and decades of nuclear imperialism, I grant them visible priority to the original text, situating the source text first and paraphrasing Indigenous concepts in my analyses. I hope that the stories translated here can contribute to facilitate dialogue between nuclear survivors and climate activists across linguistic boundaries, in Oceania and beyond.

Pacific countries are sometimes referred to as "the hole in the doughnut"— an ironic jab at the exclusive focus on Pacific Rim countries in mainstream political discourse and academic studies. While it is widely recognized that nuclear testing, overfishing, coral bleaching, microplastic biomagnification, extreme weather patterns, and rising sea levels have greatly impacted Pacific societies for more than half a century, local writers, singers, and artists are rarely acknowledged as leaders of twenty-first-century environmental movements. They are, rather, portrayed as the unfortunate first victims of the climate crisis. To put it in the words of CHamoru poet and scholar Craig Santos Perez, Pacific peoples are "the new polar bears: We sport a vulnerable-yet-charismatic-species-vibe, an endangered-yet-resilient chic, a survive-and-thrive swagger."[80]

This book participates in the growing movement calling for an analysis of Pacific arts from new disciplinary perspectives. For too long, Pacific cultures have been primarily analyzed by anthropologists and historians; and Pacific studies remained marginal in fields such as philosophy, literature, and art history. As denounced by Pacific studies scholar Teresia Teaiwa, Pacific literature in particular has remained "a global literary backwater."[81] The implicit assumption underpinning this hypervisibility in social sciences and underrepresentation in the humanities is that Pacific cultural production is a relic of the past. It is denied the quality of being pioneering artwork on a global scale, addressing the main cultural questions of the twenty-first century. In fact, the academic marginalization of Pacific art and literature correlates with the geopolitical marginalization of the Pacific Islands as expendable nuclear testing grounds and of the Pacific Ocean as expendable carbon-dumping grounds.

The origins of this problem in the field of Pacific studies can be traced back to its institutional beginnings after World War II. In the postwar decades, universities, wealthy donors, and secret services cooperated to create, fund, and develop various subfields of area studies. The stated objective was to study areas that the United States feared might succumb to communism to better control them. As American historian Agnes Quigg documented, the rare institutions to offer a degree in Pacific Islands area studies were structured by this Cold War agenda, which promoted social sciences at the expense of the humanities.[82] In Francophone universities, the field of Pacific studies was similarly initially created to serve the French imperial agenda. The main institution offering courses in Pacific languages and cultures, the Institut National des Langues et Civilisations Orientales in Paris, was founded to train imperial diplomats and businessmen. It took repeated interventions by Pacific Islands studies scholars such as Albert Wendt, Vicente M. Diaz, J. Kēhaulani Kauanui, Teresia Teaiwa, and Haunani-Kay Trask to challenge the disciplinary divisions and hierarchies instituted during the Cold War.[83]

Even when Pacific creative discourse is acknowledged as an important perspective on global environmental and sociopolitical issues, as has been the case in the field of environmental humanities, it is not always given the centrality it deserves. Consider, for example, Rob Nixon's 2011 canonical book, *Slow Violence and the Environmentalism of the Poor*. In this work, Nixon transformed the environmental humanities by underscoring the key role played by disenfranchised communities in the environmental movement. His book highlights how decolonial writer-activists have combined demands for racial, environmental, and economic justice by fighting against the environmental disasters that affect primarily the world's poorest communities. Making a compelling case to bridge environmental humanities and postcolonial studies, Nixon's groundbreaking book demonstrates that environmental movements are bound to remain inefficient if they exclude the voices of the poor. However, his central concept of slow violence is not corroborated by Pacific stories of environmental collapse. In fact, the nuclear narratives discussed in this book challenge the validity of the concept of "slow violence."

Nixon argues that nuclear contamination and climate change are emblematic of slow violence, "a violence that occurs gradually and out of sight, a violence of delayed destruction that is dispersed across time and space, an attritional violence that is typically not viewed as violence at all."[84] Yet for many Oceanians, the violence of nuclear imperialism and carbon imperialism is neither slow, nor delayed, nor out of sight. On the contrary, Pacific stories convey a sense of urgency, of baffling rapidity in the turn of events. Such is the narrative of the people of Roñḷap (Rongelap) and Utrōk (Utirik) who saw the light of the Bravo nuclear bomb on the morning of March 1, 1946. Within a few hours, they were burning, vomiting, and losing their hair and skin. Three days later, when a US military ship came to take them away (as objects of scientific study), they were stolen from their island without even having the time to realize it. Darlene Keju-Johnson, a ri-Ṃajeḷ antinuclear activist, recalls: "Some American soldiers came and said, 'Get ready. Jump in the ocean and get on the boat because we are leaving....' That's your home and you have to decide, with your husband and children, whether you are going to leave or not. But there was no time. People had to run fast."[85] Her sentences, made of a juxtaposition of monosyllabic words, and the staccato rhythm of her narrative underscore the rapidity of nuclear violence. Keju-Johnson would later develop two tumors within her lifetime. She died of cancer at forty-five years old. This radio-induced violence never seemed attritional or delayed to her, nor to anyone who loved her. Throughout her lifelong struggle as an antinuclear activist, she always highlighted the instantaneous brutality of nuclear imperialism.

As this book shows, contemporary Pacific climate activists often narrate the violence of climate collapse as a sequel to nuclear imperialism and mass epidemics, thereby emphasizing not only the immediacy of its devastation but also its historical continuities with older forms of environmental racism. The term *slow violence* fails to encapsulate this reality. This violence is neither slow nor dispersed across space. It is *slowed down* as it travels through space. It is slowed down as it moves from Roñḷap to the academic centers of nuclearized nations. It is slowed down as it is transformed from oral testimony to written scholarship. It should therefore be referred to as slowed violence.

The (post)apocalyptic stories analyzed in this book may therefore inspire environmental activists worldwide, particularly in other Indigenous-led front lines against petrocapitalism. Global environmental movements are bound to remain incomplete and polarizing if they continue failing to consider the perspective of the Pacific theorists, writers, artists, and activists who are among the most affected by, and the most active against, global climate collapse.

Listening to Pacific (post)apocalyptic stories may also help avoid repeating mistakes that were made in the past. Focusing on Pacific (post)apocalyptic stories today can help address the roots of the problems behind the current climate crisis, which remains, as Amitav Ghosh famously diagnosed, a crisis of imagination.[86] Nuclear colonizers not only ignored the pain and destruction they inflicted on Pacific land and people; they also never acknowledged the disjuncture between their worldviews and that of nuclear survivors. Nuclear colonizers extolled the ideal of becoming master and possessor of nature; nuclear survivors continued to feel connected to the land even after it was blasted by nuclear fire. Pacific (post)apocalyptic stories can help retrace these major differences in worldviews between those who think they can remove themselves from the land as they destroy it and those who nurture the land even after it has been destroyed. While the Pacific antinuclear movement was largely ineffective in putting an end to the proliferation of weapons of mass annihilation, it succeeded in reaffirming the importance of protecting a two-way nurturing relationship between people and the land that sustains them. This worldview resonates today louder than ever as this relationship continues to be under ever-growing stress on a global scale.

Personal Background

This book stems from my upbringing in the nuclear colony of Tahiti, the largest of the 118 islands of Māʻohi Nui (French-occupied Polynesia). Māʻohi Nui is one of the Pacific nations that stands out for its strength in the face of repeated imperial assaults. Despite an epidemiological apocalypse that killed 90 percent of Māʻohi people throughout the eighteenth and nineteenth centuries, and a nuclear apocalypse that brought deadly radiation-induced diseases to the archipelagoes in the twentieth and twenty-first centuries, Māʻohi Nui is still a Māʻohi country. While France prohibits statistics identifying people by race, it is generally understood that three-quarters of the population is Indigenous, identifying as either Māʻohi or "ʻĀfa" ("Demi" or mixed race), while Hakka Chinese and French settlers each make up about half of the rest. I belong to the latter category.

My family is a pure product of French imperialism. I grew up in Tahiti, yet this is only the latest stage in my family's journey through France's former and current colonies. My mother is a white woman born and raised in Senegal. My adoptive father is a white man born in Morocco. On my biological father's side, my forebears were settlers in French-occupied Algeria. My brother studied in the French-occupied Caribbean and in French-occupied Guyana before returning to Tahiti. This is characteristic of many French families, for which job opportunities in current and former colonies are provided by homogeneous institutions—what French journalist Léopold Lambert calls "the French colonial continuum."[87] This phenomenon transcends class divisions: my grandparents were waiters and railroaders, while my parents and I work in the privileged strata of academia. Regardless of their income, however, my family members were (and still are) able to move across France's sites of empire because their (neo)colonial institutions favor settler migration. Today, my family is still in Tahiti. I'm grateful to be able to spend several months every year with them on the island. We do not have strong ties to hexagonal France, in which none of us have lived for long; and we are profoundly attached to Māʻohi Nui. We have all supported the main pro-independence party for decades.

In Tahiti, a racially diverse minority benefits from the oppression and dispossession of a primarily Māʻohi majority. Nuclearized Tahiti is an extremely segregated place: the people who benefited from the nuclear center's economic fallout and those who lost everything under the CEP rarely mingle. I was raised among Tahiti's beneficiaries of the CEP, befriending mostly the Tahitian, Hakka, and French people for whom the nuclear center brought financial, professional, and romantic opportunities. This was the case for my mother and adoptive father, who both teach at the University of French Polynesia—an institution built in the 1980s with nuclear money by a pronuclear Tahitian government. But in my childhood, this was rarely talked about—especially in those circles. France only officially recognized that the tests could potentially have had any environmental impact on the country in 2010, a half century after the first French nuclear bomb. Nevertheless, growing up in a country contaminated by the fallout from 41 atmospheric tests and the irradiation from 152 underground tests, it was hard not to wonder about the potential impact of France's alleged "clean bomb." I saw many loved ones struggle with health issues. Some of our closest friends passed away from a generalized cancer at a wrongfully young age. I am still moved by their strength and their courage while they lived with the disease, and I still miss them. I frequently worry about my parents' health, wondering how the consequences of eating irradiated food will manifest in their senior years.

This background shaped my experiences when I left Tahiti to attend university in France and later in the United States. Throughout the past decade, I am infinitely grateful to have been welcomed back by family, friends, artists, scholars, and activists on each of my returns to the island. I share the antinuclear stories presented here with their guidance and their help, as they pointed me toward universities' collections, local bookstores, personal libraries, museums, archives, and digital activism, first in Mā'ohi Nui, then in other Pacific countries.

Throughout the writing of this book, I frequently returned to the question of ethical story sourcing. Who retells stories? To whom? And why? These are important questions, as story sourcing too often takes the form of the extraction of "raw material," to be profitably "processed" in Western academic centers without any benefit for the original storytellers.[88] Such an approach, as denounced by Potawatomi philosopher Kyle Powys Whyte, "treats Indigenous peoples as resources that can be used for better or worse purposes for the advancement of humanity."[89] The stories featured in this book are not the result of invasive fieldwork preying on Indigenous pain. They were made accessible because their authors wanted them to be known and shared.

In a groundbreaking article offering potential frameworks for conducting research on Mā'ohi Nui, Vehia Wheeler and Pauline Reynolds invite scholars working on French-occupied Polynesia to pay attention to "the value of hōro'a mai, hōro'a atu (to give and to receive)," foundational in the building of community and kinship in the country.[90] This book is immensely indebted to the value of hōro'a atu, as I have learned everything from the many activists, artists, and scholars who first challenged nuclear colonizers' narratives in Mā'ohi Nui and beyond. By translating, analyzing, and sharing some of these stories into English,

I offer my modest contribution to nurturing the transnational solidarity that has characterized the Pacific antinuclear movement since its inception. My wish is to help facilitate conversations on nuclear and climate justice across continents, disciplines, and languages. Writing between Tahiti and New York, I think of my role as a scholar as relational. My work seeks to highlight common tropes in (post)apocalypse narratives of Oceania, to help identify strategies of resistance that have been used across different cultural and linguistic contexts, and to put them in relation across languages, genres, and oceans.

This book is one of many calls for change coming from Māʻohi Nui, and I hope that it will contribute to building up international outrage at nuclear-armed and carbon-addicted countries. I particularly wish to inspire new readers to put pressure on the French, British, and American governments to provide meaningful reparations to all the people who developed radiation-induced cancers because of nuclear imperialism. Finally, by analyzing the complex role played by some Indigenous leaders in the nuking of their own land, I hope to foreground the importance of class struggle and feminist struggle within the movement for environmental justice so that the next generation of climate activists can learn, as I did, from its shortcomings as well as its victories.

Charting Chapters

This book honors Pacific Indigenous activists. The writers and artists discussed here identify as CHamoru, Fijian and i-Kiribati, Kanak, Kanaka Maoli, Māʻohi, Māori, ni-Vanuatu, ri-Maj̧el, Samoan, and Uvean.[91] There are many ways of analyzing such a vast corpus. One is to treat literary and artistic works as the product of creative geniuses at odds with their community's trends. Another is to envision bodies of literary work as sociological documents revelatory of a society's cultural preoccupations at any given moment. This book alternates between these two approaches. I foreground the work of trend-setting artists such as Julian Aguon, Alexandre Moeava Ata, Raʻi Chaze, Cronos, Bobby Holcomb, Witi Ihimaera, Kathy Jetñil-Kijiner, André Marere, Craig Santos Perez, Terisa Tinei Siagatonu, Chantal Spitz, Paul Tavo, Teresia Teaiwa, THS!, Soane Vahai, and Albert Wendt. But this book also presents general trends in a corpus understood as a sociological archive revealing of broad cultural tendencies. Analyzing transnational leitmotivs, I argue that these writers, artists, and activists all give voice to the collective trauma of nuclear imperialism and carbon imperialism.

Each chapter tackles a specific issue presented as an imminent threat in mainstream climate discourse. Mainstream environmentalists in overindustrialized countries tend to focus on imminent and looming threats: the threat of mass extinction, the threat that entire countries will become uninhabitable, and the threat that a changing climate will bring more deaths and diseases. I show that each of these threats has already been experienced by Pacific communities during the period of nuclear imperialism and that Pacific activists today draw from their experience of the nuclear apocalypse to mitigate each of these threats in times of climate collapse. Each chapter also analyzes how nuclear storytellers draw inspiration and strength from older and deeper Indigenous customary practices. Contemplating the loss of land in the wake of nuclear imperialism, the stories shared in this book all seek to (re)build multispecies community even after land, people, and other-than-humans have been violently separated from each other.

I begin by exploring "Isletism," the ideology that underpins the ongoing assault on Pacific peoples. For centuries, Westerners have seen the Pacific Islands as isolated islets, outside of modern history. Imagining the tropical island as marooned at the earliest stage of a supposedly unilinear path to "progress," Western narratives have denied Oceanians both the right to history (through claims of ahistorical primitivism) and the right to a future (through speculation about an inevitable annihilation in contact with the white race). Indigenous Pacific people were contaminated with viruses and irradiated by nuclear bombs because of this annihilation racism that considered Pacific cultures as always already doomed to disappear. Today, the very same imperial obliviousness structures Western nations' responses to the climate crisis, which range from compassionate apathy to downright indifference. The Pacific is still conceived as being outside history, outside the realm of the biopolitical, making it easy to downplay Westerners' responsibility in the Pacific epidemiological, nuclear, and climate genocides. While such ideological representations are pervasive among foreign writers, I highlight that they occur even in the works of progressive intellectuals invested in the struggle for racial justice and anti-imperialism in other contexts. Looking in particular at Denis Diderot's writings on Tahiti and Pablo Neruda's poetry on Rapa Nui (Easter Island), I show how even the best-intentioned foreigners who never lived in Oceania are likely to blindly perpetuate Isletist tropes when writing about the Pacific.

In the second chapter, I present the counterhegemonic ideology to Isletism: "Oceanitude." Coined in 2015 by ni-Vanuatu novelist Paul Tavo, Oceanitude refers to a literary, philosophical, and political current theorizing Pacific collective identity in times of nuclear imperialism and carbon imperialism. This chapter explores Oceanitude as a movement that challenges the Cartesian definition of humanity as the master and possessor of nature. When first defining

Oceanitude, Tavo suggests that in the Pacific, collective identity stems from the consciousness of sharing a genealogical relationship with the ocean, which can only be protected collectively. Exploring then the genealogy of Oceanitude itself, I highlight its links to the anti-Cartesian Black liberation movement known as Negritude. I show how Tavo's Oceanitude draws from concepts developed by Negritude philosophers Aimé Césaire and Léopold Sédar Senghor but goes further in its dismantling of Cartesian hubris. I also ask how the concepts underpinning the philosophy of Oceanitude illuminate a contemporary Pacific struggle: the fight against settler desecration on Mauna Kea. The political, philosophical, and artistic scope of Oceanitude suggests that this movement has the potential to reaffirm the importance of nurturing relationships between each other and the (is)lands that sustain us.

The subsequent three chapters shift from a theoretical analysis of ideologies to a close reading of Pacific (post)apocalyptic stories. I organized these three chapters according to what I perceive as the global urgency of the issue explored. The third chapter thus focuses on alienation from biodiversity, a problem already well underway on all continents. This sixth mass extinction is not the first instance of a collapse of multispecies relationships. Under nuclear imperialism, the relationships developed between humans and marine creatures were brutally shattered as fish became irradiated. Close-reading stories by Māʻohi writer Raʻi Chaze, Māori author Witi Ihimaera, and CHamoru poet Craig Santos Perez, this chapter analyzes what new solidarities may be forged in times of multispecies societies' collapse. Drawing from the ongoing relevance of customary oral and visual arts such as Māʻohi cosmogonic stories, the ancestral koru motif in Māori tattoo, and the CHamoru traditional lisåyo mourning prayer, all three writers find strength and inspiration in transgenerational customary practices to help them fight for the other-than-humans of the Pacific. While writing about the suffering and the disappearance of animals assaulted by atomic bombs and climate change, their style suggests the regenerative power of stories, visual motifs, and art forms honoring multispecies societies.

In the fourth chapter, I turn to the threat of increased deaths and diseases brought by climate change. New viral pathogens, global warming, and widespread pollution have begun to lead to the recrudescence of scores of diseases, particularly devastating in a Global South already weakened by neoliberal economic policies. In this respect, too, Pacific nuclear stories put in perspective the perceived novelty of the threat. Pacific nuclear victims have already experienced the spread of nuclear-induced diseases, threatening the living and their descendants for generations. Analyzing visual arts and fiction by Bobby Holcomb, André Marere, Cronos, THS!, Alexandre Moeava Ata, and Albert Wendt, this chapter explores how antinuclear artists and writers have addressed this plague from Tahiti to Samoa. Departing from the canonical antinuclear artists who have told the story of nuclear imperialism in tragic, doleful, and angered tones, these storytellers substitute acerbic irony to pathos. They stand out in their choice to talk about death and diseases by turning to humor, parody, and caricature. Drawing from traditional forms of Indigenous humoristic genres such as Ari'oi theater in Tahiti and fale aitu in Samoa, these creative artists and writers perpetuate an ancestral tradition to ridicule the myths propagated by people in power, thereby suggesting the cultural vitality of traditional clowning in the face of the apocalypse.

Finally, the last chapter analyzes the threat of mass displacement for climate refugees. Once again, it is important to remember that Pacific people have already experienced forced displacement and permanent exile as their islands became nuclear testing sites. Mā'ohi, ri-Majel, and i-Kiribati people can all testify to what it is like to see your home become off-limits for thousands of years. This chapter explores the forms of resistance and resilience developed in Oceania during periods of forced displacement, analyzing how songs and literature can help rebuild a home away from one's homeland. I analyze performances by ri-Majel spoken-word artist Kathy Jetñil-Kijiner, a novel by Mā'ohi writer Chantal Spitz, and songs by Teresia Teaiwa, who traces her lineage back to Fijian, Banaban, Tabiteuean, and African-American heritages. Once again, transgenerational Indigenous cultural practices such as aj (traditional Marshallese weaving), eorak (Marshallese funeral ritual), and papara'a tupuna (Mā'ohi genealogy) are central sources of inspiration for this literature. Together, Jetñil-Kijiner, Teaiwa, and Spitz present inspiring tales of solidarity in the face of forced migration, while offering a valuable contribution to the survival of dislocated cultures in contemporary arts.

To conclude this book, I wondered how to reckon with the threat that the fight against global warming may not succeed. The window to curb greenhouse gas emissions and limit catastrophic climate change is closing right now. How to keep on fighting when carbon-fueled capitalism keeps winning? Reflecting on the words of wisdom proposed by CHamoru human-rights activist Julian Aguon, the conclusion to this book interrogates the importance of mourning in the fight for climate justice. Perhaps the (post)apocalypse nuclear stories analyzed here deliver a most important lesson in the "arts of living on a damaged planet" and encourage us to search for love and beauty even in nuclear ruins.

I

$\sim$

ISLETISM

The Latest Stage of Orientalism

Observed in great numbers at the end of the 18th century, Polynesians almost went extinct at the turn of the 20th century, but they withstood the changes in the climate provoked by almost two centuries of colonialism and multiplied again.
—JEAN-MARC TERA'ITUATINI PAMBRUN, *L'Île aux anthropologues*

For those of us who are victims—one holocaust is as bad as another.... All indigenous people have endured some form of extinction by induced diseases, bombs or false treaties. Let the academics debate the terminology. I'm here to fight for my people.
—CATHIE DUNSFORD, *Manawa Toa*

Drowning our children with each mushroom cloud, love boat, fantasy island.
—SIA FIGIEL, *Where We Once Belonged*

Why were the world's most dangerous weapons of mass destruction tested primarily in Pacific islands? Western imperial powers all began their nuclear testing on continental grounds and subsequently moved their experiments to Oceania. In 1946, the United States moved its main testing facilities from New Mexico to Aelōñ in Ṃajeḷ (the Marshall Islands). In 1957, the UK moved its facilities from Australia to Kiribati. And in 1966, France left Algeria for Māʻohi Nui (French Polynesia). Governmental officials have attempted to justify this systematic transfer of nuclear testing facilities by making claims about the "isolation" of their Pacific testing sites, drawing upon the imagery of the remote, primitive, prelapsarian Pacific Island widely circulated in travel literature and Hollywood movies.

Nothing could be further from the truth. When the United States transferred its tests to Aelōñ in Ṃajeḷ in 1946, it first had to displace the entire population of two islands, Pikinni and Eniwetok. As the tests became increasingly powerful and dangerous, the United States also sent into exile all the inhabitants of the islands of Roñḷap (Rongelap) and Aelōñin Ae (Ailinginae) in 1954, and most of those of Kuwajleen (Kwajalein Atoll) in 1959. Great Britain enforced similar displacements, moving people hundreds of miles from Kiritimati (eastern Kiribati) to the Gilbert Islands (western Kiribati) and Wagina (Solomon Islands). France also displaced entire communities, forcing all the inhabitants of Tureia to leave their island repeatedly in the 1970s.[1] Recently declassified reports further show that France should have evacuated Mangareva mā (Gambier) after the first bomb critically contaminated the archipelago in 1966 but decided against it "for political and psychological motifs."[2] When Pacific peoples were not deported, they were barred access to lands that had previously been burial grounds, as well as sites for fishing and harvesting, such as Moruroa, Fangataufa, Marutea, and Woomera. The notion that the Pacific is "empty" emerges from a Western ideological discourse about the region, which, buttressed by a powerful military industrial complex, can create the reality that it purports to describe.

This ideology, presenting the Pacific Islands as an empty desert outside modernity, has had dramatic ramifications for Oceanian societies. Erasing an area from the map removes all its inhabitants from global public consciousness. Postcolonial scholars have shown how much treatment of a land and treatment of its people are intrinsically linked.[3] Presenting Oceania as an empty desert has led not only to the devastation of Pacific islands but also to the deportation and erasure of Pacific peoples. It leads to what French anthropologist Alban Bensa has called "annihilation racism": the presupposition not so much of the inferiority of the colonized people but rather of their inevitable disappearance.[4]

This first manifested in nuclear colonizers' medical racism. As soon as nuclear testing began in Oceania, colonial governments decided to use Pacific people as human experiments to study the effects of irradiation. In 1954, when Americans detonated their first thermonuclear bomb, ri-Ṃajeḷ were intentionally exposed to lethal nuclear fallout. The Bill Clinton administration declassified several documents in 1994, acknowledging that these studies were part of a plan devised in 1953, the Project 4.1, titled "Study of Response of Human Beings Accidentally Exposed to Significant Fallout Radiation" (Washington still claims that Project 4.1 was conceived of a posteriori, after an allegedly unpredicted shift in the wind's direction).[5] Great Britain and France conducted similar experiments on human beings, respectively on the islands of Kiritimati and in Algeria.[6]

When not left in radioactive fallout for scientific studies, Pacific people were abandoned in radioactive fallout out of pure and simple annihilation racism. As Henry Kissinger infamously said of ri-Majel near American nuclear testing sites: "There are only 90,000 people out there. Who gives a damn?"[7] This annihilation racism also creates the reality it purports to describe. Almost all the 539 Rongelapese and Utrikese living on the island at the time of the Bravo test contracted radio-induced diseases. Tureia, the inhabited atoll closest to Moruroa, buried one-third of its adult population between 1997 and 2002. The dead were nearly all victims of cancer.[8] Tureians and Mangarevians further report being unable to access their medical files and being denied access to the bodies of their relatives held by the army, and they had their stillborn babies confiscated by military doctors.[9] This is an especially violent form of annihilation racism since, in Māʾohi traditions, the bodies of the dead need to be handled according to specific customs to facilitate the journey of the varua (soul/spirit) from the Ao (connoting daytime, the world of the living, and the profane) to the Pō (connoting the sacred, generative darkness).[10] This traditional importance of performing rituals after a loved one's passing away persisted, in different ways, after the evangelization of the islands. Not every Māʾohi family adheres to these customs, but for those who do, being denied the right to bury their relatives in ancestral grounds constitutes a doubly violent confiscation of the deceased, excluded from both the realm of Ao and the realm of Pō. Nuclear colonizers' annihilation racism thus assaults Pacific peoples' physical, mental, and spiritual well-being.

The international community unanimously condemned the widespread use of unethical scientific experiments on human subjects throughout the 1940s. The Nazi regime, the Japanese empire, and the United Kingdom conducted scientific experimentation on Jewish, Chinese, and Indian people during World War II. Many other countries, including Australia, Canada, Sweden, the United States, and the USSR, used children, prisoners, sick, differently abled, and mentally ill people (often from poor, racialized minorities) to perform harmful and deadly medical experiments on human beings, without their subjects' consent and/or knowledge.[11] These atrocities conducted on the continents have become central historical narratives of the twentieth century worldwide. Yet the experiments conducted on Pacific peoples have been virtually erased from global public consciousness, just like the Pacific Islands are erased from most planispheres. My goal in highlighting these inconsistencies is not to hierarchize crimes against humanity, nor to compare their degree of violence, but rather to point out a discrepancy in the roles they occupy in mainstream historical narratives. The double standards applied to the suffering of continental victims and of "Islanders" suggest that the construction of these two "categories" of people is subtended by different instantiations of imperialist ideology.

Understanding the historical roots of annihilation racism is crucial in these times of climate collapse and will help avoid advocating for superficial solutions to contemporary environmental racism. This chapter explores the genesis, dissemination, and evolution of Isletism, the ideology that has permitted the rise of annihilation racism in the Pacific. I first explore the spread of theories about racial hierarchies at the turn of the eighteenth century, analyzing G. W. F. Hegel's writing as representative of wide-ranging trends. I then turn to the long literary history that has underpinned the spread of Isletist tropes, showing that progressive writers such as the anti-colonial Enlightenment philosopher Denis Diderot contributed to spread common Isletist myths when writing about Oceania. I conclude by analyzing the perpetuation of Isletist tropes in the age of the atom, by looking at Pablo Neruda's problematic collection of poems on Rapa Nui (Easter Island). Shaping geopolitics, literature, iconography, and the film industry, Isletism is an all-encompassing ideology. Opposing these Isletist myths is an ongoing battle.

Isletism: The Ideology behind Annihilation Racism

The invention of the West is commonly dated to the early sixteenth century. The expulsion of Muslims from Europe, the plundering of the Americas, and the maturation of the absolutist nation-state underpinned a new socioeconomic order, concomitant with a new ideological order through which Europe became the West.[12] Canonical European thinkers, from Hegel to Karl Marx, have conceived of history as a progress narrative, a universal evolution toward "modernity," with the West leading the rest of the world on this unidirectional path to progress.

Distance along the path of "progress" allegedly traveled by some portions of humanity could be measured only by the distance others lagged behind.[13] Therefore, theorizing the Western man as the apex of historical evolution must be contemporaneous with the construction of fantasized Others trailing behind the course of history. Western imperialism imposed its own conceptions of modernity on the rest of the world, forcing those who had supposedly become stranded in their historical development to follow the now unidirectional path to progress. Racialized people the world over were thus summoned to adopt first "Christianity," then "civilization," and now "development."[14]

Postcolonial theory has greatly contributed to deconstructing the mechanisms of this invention of the Western Self and exposed its dependence upon the simultaneous invention of a racialized Other. Many scholars, most notably Edward Said, led the way to theorizing this mechanism by analyzing two fantasized regions, the Orient and the Occident. However, looking at other geographic areas of the world reveals that Orientalism has taken many forms. Other postcolonial scholars have argued that tropical islands as geopolitical spaces were particularly influential for the construction of the Western collective fantasy of the Self.[15] The invention of the Pacific Islander, long represented as an ahistorical figure excluded from humanity's progress, has been a sine qua non to the invention of the Western Self as the epitome of modernity.

I propose to call this hegemonic discourse on Pacific islands "Isletism." For centuries, Westerners have seen Pacific islands as isolated islets far removed from modern history, too small to sustain civilization and too isolated to be integrated in networks of empire. I use the word *Isletism* to designate not a hypothetical geographic determinism that would characterize tropical islands but rather *the Western cultural construct* of tropical island cultures. Isletism is an ideology, a subset of Orientalism, that informs foreigners' representations of all of Oceania. Born in Europe, Isletism has now spread globally as Western worldviews permeated the world at large.

Orientalism presents the Orient as stranded at an earlier stage in historical development and as having become a declining and decadent civilization. Isletism, by contrast, imagines the tropical island as marooned at an even earlier stage of historical development. The tropical island is where the West turns to imagine its inception. The "Islander," a word that I capitalize throughout to emphasize its ideological character, has been constructed as frozen in time: not so much lagging behind the developments of civilization like the "Oriental" but rather outside of civilization altogether. Islanders from the Caribbean to the Pacific have been both feared as primitive cannibals still living in the Stone Age, and lauded as prelapsarian savages endowed with the nobility and wisdom that Westerners attributed to their own antiquity. But whether stranded in humanity's Golden Age or marooned in primitive savagery, the Islander has halted at the beginning of human history in Western narratives. Journeying away from Europe has often been associated with going back in time; the Pacific Islands, located at the antipodes of Europe's economic and intellectual centers, were seen as stagnating at the beginnings of historical development.

Isletism is properly understood as a subset of Orientalism because of its place in the history of racial constructions. Since the debate of Valladolid, many philosophers, politicians, and novelists contributed to popularize the hegemonic Western narrative that different races had different value. The influential German philosopher G. W. F. Hegel, for example, famously claimed in his Berlin *Lectures* that while sub-Saharan Africa allegedly had no history, he still believed that Africa could be brought back into the course of history by being colonized and modernized.[16] He did not uphold similar hopes for First Nations Peoples in the Americas and in tropical islands, which he deemed fated to natural extinction by contact with more "advanced races."[17] Hegel's ideas contributed to popularize discourses on decadent civilizations in the Orient, redeemable primitivism in sub-Saharan Africa, and irredeemable primitivism for Indigenous people.[18]

This hierarchization of races continued to inform geopolitics well into the era of decolonization. After World War I, for example, the League of Nations divided the former German and Ottoman empires among the war's victors according to the mandated territories' alleged level of "development." Class A mandates, located in the Middle East, were considered sufficiently "advanced" to have their provisional independence recognized. Class B mandates, mostly located in Africa, obtained independence in the early 1960s. Class C mandates were predominantly the Pacific Islands. They were deemed best administered under colonial power, and they are the countries of the mandate era to acquire independence the most belatedly.

For centuries, racial hierarchies and progress narratives fantasized by the West have thus continued to inform global geopolitics. The fact that Western countries tested their nuclear weapons exclusively on Indigenous lands can also be directly traced back to such theories.[19] Indigenous people were irradiated because they were considered outside the realm of humanity, at the very bottom of the Western hierarchization of races and doomed to disappear. As American geographer Sasha Davis put it, nuclear powers thought that Oceanian lives could be sacrificed "not because the people there are enemies but because, politically, they are not even recognized as fully human."[20] This form of annihilation racism is the logical conclusion of centuries of hegemonic Isletist narratives about Pacific peoples.

Imperial Obliviousness, or How Not to See a Genocide

It is worth taking a moment to discuss the use—or absence thereof—of the term *genocide* to describe the history of the Pacific. Mā'ohi novelist Chantal Spitz once noted, "There may not have been a will to make us disappear, but there was a will to not give a damn about what could happen to us."[21] Can genocide be defined by this oxymoron, as the "will to not give a damn"? Genocide is a controversial concept, and it is not reducible to a simple numerical definition. The exploitation of Africa under (neo)colonialism, resulting in staggering numbers of deaths, is rarely referred to as a genocide since it aims at exploiting rather than annihilating a group of people. Genocides are not always associated with racism either: the Cambodian genocide, which resulted in the extermination of almost two million people, did not stem from ethnic divisions. The term is shrouded in ambiguity and lends itself to a variety of interpretations.

Pacific colonial history is a history of extreme violence. From the sixteenth to the nineteenth centuries, colonial wars and imported diseases decimated Pacific peoples. Westerners enslaved Oceanians through indentured labor (Blackbirding), shelled villages, deported and enclosed communities in reservations, deprived Pacific peoples of their means of subsistence by stealing arable land, and massacred protesters when they rebelled. But most deaths occurred because of the introduction of lethal epidemics. The resulting demographic collapse was staggering, as 70 to 95 percent of the population across Oceania was killed by the end of the nineteenth century.[22] "We lost 90 percent of our population due to disease," explains Kanaka 'Ōiwi poet and academic Jamaica Heolimeleikalani Osorio. "Ninety percent of our population just died. That's an apocalypse."[23]

And yet, despite the deadliness of Westerners' presence in the Pacific, most scholars have been reluctant to use the word *genocide* to describe Oceania's history. The rare intellectuals who have described Indigenous mortality in such terms have been attacked, and even censored, by the establishment. For example, Māori politician Tariana Turia, who described Māori people's treatment at the hands of Pākehā settlers as a holocaust in 2000, was publicly censored by her prime minister, who instituted an all-out ban on using this terminology to refer to non-Jewish histories.[24]

Some scholars explain the widespread reluctance to refer to this period as a genocide by pointing out that epidemics were the main cause of mortality.[25] The argument posits that, while Europeans did introduce deadly diseases, their responsibility and culpability should be attenuated by the fact that it was not premeditated. Westerners' obliviousness in the Pacific is contrasted with their deliberateness to use epidemics as bacterial warfare against Native Americans.[26] I would contend, however, that the Pacific epidemiological crisis was dramatically exacerbated by Westerners' annihilation racism and their belief in Isletist narratives. Should intentionality matter when passivity has such deadly consequences?

Most colonial administrators were convinced that Pacific peoples would naturally go extinct in contact with the white race, and it is this ideological belief that prevented people in power from establishing adequate health services in their Pacific colonies. As Kanaka activist Kalama'okaina Niheu denounces, the epidemics were the result of *preventable* imperial activity: "The colonizers inadvertently introduced diseases . . . and *allowed them to spread*."[27] Consider, for example, the administration's behavior in Mā'ohi Nui—then the Établissements Français d'Océanie (EFO, French Establishments of Oceania). French social geographer Philippe Bachimon conducted a comprehensive study of health services in the EFO and found out that there were no civil doctors on the archipelago before the beginning of the twentieth century. The few military doctors stationed in the country only treated the white residents and the wealthy "mixed-race" ('āfa) community of the capital. The only hospital in Tahiti, built in 1843, was not open to Mā'ohi people unless a Catholic organization recommended them.[28] Moreover, French colonizers generally legislated only on diseases that could spread to the European community and mostly dealt with Indigenous patients by quarantining them. In Tahiti, for example, the main disease to which the administration reacted was syphilis. By the mid-nineteenth century, 222 of 430 Tahitian women tested had been infected, and syphilis was officially considered as a major threat for . . . visiting male Europeans! A free clinic was built in 1854 to isolate affected Mā'ohi women from marines. Nothing was done to slow the spread of diseases such as elephantiasis and tuberculosis, which affected primarily Tahitian people.

American colonizers do not have a better legacy. The example of their occupation of 'Uvea (Wallis) is particularly telling. Stationed in 'Uvea during World War II, the US military grew concerned about the possibility that Hansen's disease (leprosy) could spread to its troops. American officials decided to conduct blood tests on the entire local population and to exile every Uvean suspected to carry the disease to the leprosarium on the islet of Nukuatea. Alexandre Poncet, apostolic vicar on the island at the time, mentioned the event in his diary. Poncet was no advocate for Indigenous rights: he approved of Uvean forced labor and pledged allegiance to the Nazi Vichy government in France. Nevertheless, his diary makes mention of the "rumor" that many Uveans were exiled to Nukuatea under the mere suspicion of being contagious and that some healthy villagers were mistakenly sent to the leprosarium because the US Army "confused" some names.[29] This anecdote speaks volumes to Americans' annihilation racism: the spread of diseases in racialized communities only mattered inasmuch as it could potentially affect white colonizers. Epidemics among Pacific peoples were seen in a Hegelian perspective, as a natural consequence of contact with a "superior race."

To this administrative and medical negligence can be added the devastating impact of "Blackbirding" (the Pacific slave trade) on spreading epidemics, which greatly contributed to the depopulation of the islands. Consider the case of Rapa Nui (Easter Island) and the Rapanui (the Indigenous people of the island). As slave trade was gradually abolished in the Atlantic throughout the nineteenth century, slave merchants turned to the less closely monitored Pacific labor force.[30] Because no Western nation claimed monopoly over the exploitation of Rapanui labor, slave merchants preyed on its population with unprecedented rapacity. In just a few months, between 1862 and 1863, 60 percent of the island's men were coerced into indentured labor and sent to Latin America and Australia. Work conditions were atrocious, and 90 percent of these indentured laborers perished.[31] Only fifteen of the "recruits" were returned to their homes as promised by their employers. These laborers carried with them new diseases that subsequently caused thousands more deaths. Chilean colonization further degraded the situation by imposing a travel ban on the epidemics-stricken population, ensuring widespread contamination within the trapped community. By the late nineteenth century, only 130 people were still alive on the island.[32] Rapa Nui people's extermination was not premeditated. However, these epidemics were clearly exacerbated by man-made policies. Colonizers' alleged obliviousness of being disease carriers becomes irrelevant when one considers that annihilation racism clearly motivated capitalist slave owners and colonizers to ignore the deadly effects of their (in)action(s).

Michel Foucault has famously described the nineteenth century as marking the beginning of biopolitics.[33] He argued that while sovereign power used to let live or make die, biopolitical power, by contrast, has the capacity to make live or let die. Under biopolitical technologies of governance, "letting" a population die must be interpreted as a form of political will. The issue is that, while it is widely recognized that imperial nations were governed by biopolitical logic in the nineteenth century, the Pacific is still conceived as being outside this historical development—even while France, England, Spain, Germany, Japan, Chile, and the United States began controlling various governments in Pacific territories. If one fails to understand nineteenth-century Oceania as governed by the ethics of biopolitics, it becomes easy to downplay colonizers' responsibility in the Pacific genocide.

For half a millennium, European narratives have argued that Oceanians have no value. Pacific Islanders have been denied both the right to history (through claims of ahistorical primitivism) and the right to a future (through speculation about an inevitable annihilation). Isletist theories created the conditions for Westerners' unaccountability and ensured that they would remain innocent of the consequences of their own (in)action(s) despite knowing what these would be. This is not dissimilar to what Robert Fletcher has called "imperialist amnesia," defined as the disavowal of the legacy of European colonization to help efface the grim realities of the colonial enterprise.[34] But while imperial forgetting as defined by Fletcher tends to be a contemporary phenomenon that takes place *after* the imperial aggression took place, the imperial forgetting at work in Oceania happens *at the moment when decisions were made to act without accountability*. More than imperialist amnesia, Isletist theories triggered what would better be described as imperialist obliviousness. Conceptually related to "imperial agnosia" and "colonial unknowing" as defined by Jodi Byrd, Manu Vimalassery, Juliana Hu Pegues, and Alyosha Goldstein, imperial obliviousness is a mode of knowledge production and occlusion that requires the active participation of colonial agents at the time of its occurrence as well as in its aftermath.[35] Since Westerners began foraying into Oceania, they refused to acknowledge that their actions were introducing diseases and that their inaction was spreading death. Seeing Pacific islands as prehistoric or ahistoric presupposed that these spaces had no memory and therefore that there was no need to be accountable to history. Colonizers did not forget about the genocide they provoked; they actively refused to notice it.

Today, the very same imperial obliviousness structures Western nations' responses to the climate crisis. Pacific countries are among the most impacted by rising sea levels, ocean pollution, the massive industrial extraction of sea life euphemistically referred to as "fishing," increasingly challenging weather conditions, and the fast disappearance of reef ecosystems sustaining the nutritional and cultural needs of large communities. Yet the response to this ecological crisis by the leaders of overdeveloped nations ranges from compassionate apathy to downright indifference, betraying a contemporary instantiation of imperial obliviousness.

The United Nations' sustainable development goal to limit global temperature rise to "below 2 degrees" Celsius condemns low-lying Pacific Island nations to submersion. It also condemns all Pacific coral reefs to extinction, ensuring widespread disruption of cultural lifestyles and acute food shortages even in mountainous islands.[36] By refusing to even try to limit temperature rise to 1.5 degrees, the majority of the world's leaders have implicitly admitted to perceiving Pacific Islanders as sacrificial victims to the development of an unsustainable fossil-fuel economy. Furthermore, by refusing to even put down in writing that the 2 degrees goal is a death sentence for Pacific atolls, and refusing to make the implicit explicit, the UN delegates are adding insult to injury. Some Pacific activists, aware that discursive erasure enables actual erasure, have accurately begun calling the threat to their islands a "climate genocide."[37]

Given the ongoing prevalence of annihilation racism in contemporary political discourses, the history of colonialism in Oceania should be remembered as a genocide. Even if there wasn't an explicit *intention* to kill Pacific people, there was enough "will to not give a damn" to make the word meaningful. Māori novelist Cathie Dunsford eloquently summarizes the issue in one of her novels: "We must work together for our mutual survival—or we are doomed to suffer endless variations of the Holocaust. All indigenous people have endured some form of extinction by induced diseases, bombs or false treaties. Let the academics debate the terminology. . . . We will not be silenced or forgotten."[38]

This debate about the use of the term *genocide* to describe Pacific history emphasizes the importance of discussing the cultural production of ideologies. Isletism is an ideological discourse, illustrated in artistic production that has shaped and continues to inform geopolitics. Western literature, mythology, and film, to which I now turn, played an important role in propagating these Isletist tropes.

Morbid Erotica

In Western cultural discourses, the locus of humanity's Golden Age has always been projected outside Europe. In classical works, it was located southward in the mystical Mediterranean Isles of the Blessed, while in medieval texts it was imagined eastward in the Garden of Eden. When Europeans began invading distant continents in the fifteenth century, these mystical islands and the Garden of Eden underpinned their understanding of the regions they invaded. First, the Caribbean islands were endowed with the qualities of the legendary isles and gardens that filled these travelers' imagination, and they became associated with paradise and utopia.[39] However, as the Caribbean archipelagoes were gradually plundered and locked into the emerging networks of mercantile capitalism established through genocide and slavery, they lost their mystical and utopian appeal. The search for islands of fabulous wealth and eternal happiness simply moved westward, following the westernmost fringes of the expanding Western empire. It lingered briefly on the American continent (Europeans had long thought of America as a large island and searched for a westward passage to the mystical isle of California).[40] By the eighteenth century, the myth of the tropical island had moved from the Caribbean to the Eastern Pacific, and circumnavigators began to speculate that their insular utopias could be found in the antipodes of Europe. There, it flourished into the myth of the South Seas, still shaping the global collective imagination of Oceania to this day.

Europeans entered the Pacific in the sixteenth century. In 1521, Magellan's crew chanced upon on Guåhan (Guam), naming it Islas de los Ladrones (Islands of Thieves), becoming the first Westerners to shore on a Pacific island—and the first Europeans to murder Pacific Islanders. Spain and Portugal rapidly claimed possession of many Pacific archipelagos, from Aelōñ in Ṃajeḷ (the Marshall Islands) to Henua Enata (the Marquesas Islands) in the following decades. However, these early imperialists were not particularly laudatory when describing the region. The invention of the myth of the South Seas began in the late eighteenth century, contemporaneous with the so-called Enlightenment. French philosopher Jean-Jacques Rousseau's ideas particularly contributed to revive the ancient myth of the "noble savage": his writings about human nature, arguing that human beings were good by nature yet corrupted by civil society, were very influential, and the circumnavigators who left Europe in the eighteenth century were in search of the utopian Austral continent in which Rousseau's theories could be verified.[41] They did not find the Austral continent, but they landed in Tahiti.

And Tahitians were expecting them.

When French captain Louis-Antoine de Bougainville first anchored his ship in Tahiti's lagoon, he thought he had met Rousseau's men of nature in the last area of the globe preserved from the "civilizing" influence of Europe. But in 1768, Bougainville was not the first European to reach the region. Tahitians had most likely been told of Álvaro de Mendeña's 1595 fusillades in Fatu Hiva and of Jacob Roggeveen's 1722 massacre in Rapa Nui, two islands with which Tahitians were in contact. The arrival of foreigners in strange canoes with a taste for bloodbaths was theorized as a threat when tahu'a (high priest) Vaitā made a prophecy on the marae Taputapuātea in the neighboring island of Ra'iātea:

> *Te haere mai nei na ni'a i te ho'e pahi ama 'ore . . . e e riro teie nei fenua ia ratou. E mou teie ha'apaora'a tahito nei, e e tae mai ho'i te manu mo'a o te moana, e te fenua nei, e haere mai e ta'iha'a.*[42]

They are coming on a ship without an outrigger . . . and they will possess this land. There will be an end to our present customs, and the sacred birds of sea and land will come to mourn.

This prophecy would be crucial in shaping the first encounter between Tahitians and the French. "Contact did not happen at the moment of physical encounter," explains Māʻohi philosopher Richard Tuheiava. "It had already happened in the realm of the invisible. . . . It had already been interpreted."[43] Just a few months before Bougainville's arrival, when the Briton Samuel Wallis stopped in Tahiti and opened deadly fire on Tahitian warriors, Vāitāʻs prophecy became history.

Warned by Vāitāʻs prophecy and by the actions of previous foreigners, when Bougainville anchored his ship in the lagoon, Tahitian chiefs turned to a different strategy and attempted to tame Europeans by offering them the sexual favors of their youngest and highest-ranking women.[44] Charmed by this welcome, Bougainville named Tahiti the New Cythera, in reference to the island of Aphrodite, the Greek goddess of love. This would mark the beginning of the Isletist myth of the South Seas.

Bougainville's journal features all the tropes that would become characteristic of Isletism. First, Tahiti is presented as the last bastion unspoiled by European "civilization," ignoring the fact that Tahitians had long been aware of Westerners' presence in the region.[45] Second, the story's women voluntarily throw themselves in the arms of French sailors, whereas historically these first sexual encounters were very likely performed as diplomatic exchanges orchestrated by and under the supervision of the Tahitian male aristocracy.[46] Third, Bougainville describes "noble savages" living in harmony with a bountiful nature in a perpetual summer, when Tahitian food security historically required extensive labor from the manahune (the working class) and a strict observance of rahui (the Māʻohi fallow system).[47] Last but not least, Bougainville initiates a long tradition of imperial obliviousness, as he mentions the risk of epidemics but does not take any action to prevent their spread, instead accusing the British of bringing deadly diseases to the islands.[48]

As numerous scholars have shown, Bougainville was so imbued with Rousseauist theories of a prelapsarian utopia that he significantly altered his original logbook to further embellish his description of Tahiti.[49] His travelogue, *Voyage autour du monde* (*Voyage around the World*, 1771), was released two years earlier than the less idyllic travelogues of both Captain Wallis and Captain James Cook. And Bougainville's book was an instant best seller. It became the main reference for subsequent European philosophical speculations about "noble savages," from Denis Diderot's immensely popular *Supplément au voyage de Bougainville* (*Addendum to the Journey of Bougainville*, 1772) to John O'Keefe's hit play in London's Theater Royal, *Omai: A Voyage 'Round the World* (1785).

Scholars have abundantly documented these trends, and I will not dwell on this well-studied body of literature. I shall simply give a couple of examples of Isletist aesthetics, to highlight their continuity from the Enlightenment to the Atomic Age. Diderot's *Addendum to the Journey of Bougainville* is a particularly representative work of eighteenth-century Isletism. Largely responsible for the diffusion of the myth of the South Seas throughout Western Europe's upper classes, Diderot's *Addendum* is a philosophical dialogue questioning the laws of European society by comparing it with Bougainville's idealized island. Like Bougainville's journal, it features all the myths of Isletism. It describes Tahiti as a prelapsarian heaven, Tahitian woman as beautiful and promiscuous, and the whole population as unfortunately always already doomed to disappear in contact with Europeans.

What is striking in Diderot's text is the ways in which these myths are intertwined to co-constitute each other. In a famous scene, "L'Adieu du Vieillard" ("The Old Man's Farewell"), a Tahitian elder harangues Bougainville, accusing him of spreading deadly epidemics. The island was indeed historically ravaged at the time by lethal pandemics like the flu. However, rather than focusing on this rather unglamorous plague, Diderot foregrounds the impact of sexually transmittable diseases. French sailors are said to "contaminate . . . the unfortunate female companions of [their] pleasures" by their "deathly embrace."[50] This eroticization of Westerners' alleged fatal impact, suggesting that the only disease ever brought to the Pacific was syphilis, paradoxically glorifies white heterosexual masculinity. Indeed, the narrative interweaves elegies about Westerners' fatal impact with voyeuristic descriptions of the irrepressible lust they supposedly provoked in female islanders. Diderot's protagonists, despite regretting that the Westerners' deathly embrace "condemned women to demise," describe at length the "gorgeous female wooers" surrounding the French navigators, begging French men for intercourse while "kissing [their] knees."[51] Postcolonial scholars have described Diderot as the most radical critic of colonialism from the France of the Enlightenment.[52] Yet even this preeminent anti-colonial thinker is guilty of adopting and perpetuating Isletist ideological undercurrents.

As noted by Teresia Teaiwa, Tahiti soon turned into a metonymy for all of Polynesia, and Polynesia came to represent the entire Pacific. The cultural, historical, linguistic, and political diversity of Oceania, a region spreading over half of the globe, thus became reducible to the figure of the Polynesian dancing woman.[53] Despite its blatant historical and geographical inconsistencies, the Isletist myth of the Pacific Island paradise persisted throughout eighteenth-century literature, and the flower-crowned Polynesian woman continued to symbolize prelapsarian bliss, generous nature, and free love.

The myth of the South Seas suffered some alterations throughout the nineteenth century with the establishments of the first Protestant missions in the region, as British missionaries criticized Pacific peoples for their "loose morals."[54] Colonial administrators and businessmen also produced bitter administrative reports dismantling the myth of the paradise-like island in an attempt to justify their difficulties in transforming their Pacific colonies into profitable economic outposts.[55] Nevertheless, despite the negative mythologies of the administrators and missionaries, the myth of the South Seas endured among novelists, poets, and painters. Victor Hugo, Herman Melville, Pierre Loti, and Robert Louis Stevenson, all extremely popular among their contemporaries, were influential in perpetuating the idyllic reputation of Oceania.[56] Their works were particularly efficient in spreading the myth of the sexual availability of Pacific women throughout the nineteenth century. Other canonical writers and artists such as Paul Gauguin, Victor Segalen, Jack London, Somerset Maugham, Jean Giraudoux, Henri Matisse, and Georges Simenon relayed these stereotypes in the early twentieth century.[57] The myth of the doomed Arcadian tropical island was thus still a widespread ideology when World War II brought nuclear hell to the Pacific shores. These texts all share the same morbid erotica, eclipsing pervasive morbidity with the sexual availability of the vahine. Jack London thus eroticized Kānaka Maoli women in Hawaiian leprosarium, while Pierre Loti describes Tahitian women in his best-selling debut novel as "beautiful creatures ... very slowly disappearing in contact with the civilized races, [who] will probably be found to have disappeared in the next centuries."[58]

There is an obvious epistemological continuity between Diderot and Loti's morbid erotica, and in the French designer Louis Reard's decision to name his two-piece bathing suit after the Pikinni Atoll in which Americans tested their first hydrogen bombs. As Teresia Teaiwa denounced, "the sexist dynamic the bikini performs—objectification through excessive visibility—inverts the colonial dynamics that have occurred during nuclear testing in the Pacific, objectification by rendering invisible."[59] This is not to say that centuries of discourse on the Pacific Islands constitute a fixed and intangible discursive framework. Rather, it suggests that Isletism is informed by unifying undercurrents throughout different stages of Western expansionism.

Writing about Paradise under the Nuclear Sun

Three hundred nuclear bombs later, Isletism is alive and well. Isletist tropes persist to this day, in many of the contemporary works by writers traveling through or settling in the Pacific. Despite featuring a variety of literary styles and cultural referents, works by settlers and travelers tend to share several common ideological foundations. I will not dwell on this unsettling tendency among notoriously racist and right-wing writers, such as A. D. G. (Alain Fournier) or Jean Reverzy.[60] It is much more revealing to see that even the intellectuals who have participated in the struggle for racial justice and anti-imperialism in other contexts, such as Nobel Prize winners and nominees Pablo Neruda, J.-M. G. Le Clézio, and Aldous Huxley, blindly perpetuate Isletist tropes when writing about the Pacific.[61]

Consider, for example, Pablo Neruda's only full-length book on the Pacific, the collection of poetry *La Rosa separada* (*The Separate Rose*). Neruda published this book in 1972, after visiting Rapa Nui, which was annexed by Chile at the end of the previous century. Neruda is renowned for his leftist ideals, his opposition to imperial wars, and his support for social justice. However, while he left Chile as a victim of American imperialism, he landed on Rapa Nui as a colonizer. His book, regardless of its poetic qualities, propagates problematic myths about the Pacific Islands and Pacific peoples.

La Rosa separada consists of twenty-four poems, alternatively titled "Los Hombres" ("The Men") and "La Isla" ("The Island"). However, the poems titled "The Men" do not evoke the Rapanui (the Indigenous people of Easter Island). Rather, they give voice to the poet himself and his fellow tourists, whom he often criticizes for their lack of appreciation of Rapa Nui's beauty. Foreigners belong to the realm of masculinity, of culture. The Rapanui, in turn, are described in the poems titled "The Island," a feminine word in Spanish. They belong to the domain of femininity, of nature. This denotes from the outset Neruda's gendered dehumanization of Indigenous people. Furthermore, in most of the sections on "The Island," the Rapanui are blatantly absent. Neruda represents the island in a typical Isletist fashion, as an isolated islet, using precisely the vocabulary that nuclear colonizers had used throughout the previous decade to describe the neighboring atolls of Moruroa and Fangataufa as remote, empty, and unused.

Neruda calls the island "navel of death" ("*obligo de la muerta*") playing, perhaps, with the periphrasis that Rapa Nui people use to describe their land in Pascuan, Te Pito o te Henua (the Navel of the World). Seemingly convinced that Rapa Nui culture is extinct and the Rapanui people silent, the poet describes Rapa Nui as a "country without a voice" and "an oceanic emptiness."[62] This deliberate erasure of the Rapanui is even more evident in Neruda's lyrical descriptions of the famous moai sculptures erected on the island. He portrays them as "works carved by hands of air, gloves of sky."[63] These verses seem inspired by Western scientists' long-lasting conviction that the Rapanui could not possibly have been resourceful enough to erect these majestic statues—all the while failing to find which invisible hands could have been responsible for these works of art. In fact, Rapanui art and religious practices had evolved greatly in the previous two centuries. Throughout the seventeenth and eighteenth centuries, the island's religion gradually shifted from a "cult of the Ancestors," worshipped and represented by the gigantic statues, to the "cult of the Birdman," to communicate with the god Makemake.[64] Māori historian Madi Williams underscores that at the time of Europeans' intrusion in Rapa Nui, the island's main form of artistic production was not the carving of moai but the representation of Birdman images, which could be found in more than four thousand places across one thousand locations.[65] But foreigners were much more interested in ancient artforms from a seemingly distant past than in nineteenth-century Rapanui artistic and religious practices. Neruda's poems thus participate in the propagation of the Isletist leitmotiv of presenting the Pacific Islands as open-air museums where tourists can admire vestiges of the "past" while speculating about the conditions of disappearance of an "extinct" civilization. Such erasures of Rapa Nui culture are still common in the twenty-first century, for example in the best-selling book *Collapse* by geographer Jared M. Diamond, in which the Pulitzer Prize winner famously popularized Rapa Nui as an insular civilization gone "extinct" because of an ecocide.[66]

This is all the more paradoxical since Neruda was writing in the midst of Rapa Nui's cultural renaissance. Rapanui culture is vibrant and thriving, not only in the island, but also in the urban diasporic Rapanui communities that immigrated to Pape'ete (Tahiti) and Santiago de Chile. Back in 1964, Rapanui people had organized the largest protest march in their history, contesting the prohibition to leave their island, the interdiction to speak their native language, and their ineligibility to vote in Chilean elections. This led to a newfound pride in Rapanui identity, which translated in the creation of a vibrant artistic life. In the early 1970s, members of the Huke and Tuki family groups revived a number of traditional theatrical performances, inspired by a'amu tuai (the local cosmogony) and historical ceremonies (such as the Taŋata manu race, a swimming competition historically performed to designate the yearly leader of the island).[67] Far from being marginal practices, such performances gathered massive crowds, with three hundred of the fifteen hundred Rapanui living on the island becoming involved in the theater troupe Mata Tu'u Hotu iti after 1974.[68] Many of their performances took place on bays and mountains, using the whole island as an open stage. Neruda's book thus manages to erase Rapa Nui culture precisely at the time it was literally being performed in the open throughout the island.

Neruda's book is even more unsettling on the rare occasions it *does* mention Rapanui people. In his eighth poem ("La Isla"), the narrator alludes for the first time to the fact that tourists are not alone on the island:

Parece extraño ver vivir aquí, dentro
del círculo, contemplar las langostas
róseas, hostiles caer a los cajones
desde las manos de los pescadores,
. . . ver entre follajes . . .

la flor de une doncella sonriendo a sí misma,
al sol, al mediodía tintineante,
a la iglesia del padre Englert, allí enterrado,
sí, sonriendo, llena de esta dicha remota
como un pequeño cántaro que canta.[69]

It seems strange to find life here, inside
the circle, to contemplate the lobsters,
rosy, hostile, as they fall into crates
from the hands of the fishermen,
. . . to see between foliage . . .

the flower of a young maid smiling to herself,
to the sun, to the jingling high noon,
to the church of Father Englert, buried there,
yes, smiling, full of this remote happiness
like a chanting little jug of wine.

Here, Neruda adopts the tone of a biologist surprised to "find life" ("*ver vivir*") in what he has presented in the previous pages as an incongruously isolated island populated only by stone statues erected there "so the ocean alone could see them."[70] He reduces Rapa Nui culture to a mere biological fact (*el "vivir"*). This is an unfortunate word choice to make at a time when colonizing countries were justifying using Pacific peoples as human experiments by describing them as not fully human and setting different doses of "safe" maximum radiation exposure for Westerners and Islanders.[71]

Furthermore, the Rapanui are conflated with the exotic background, reduced to a metonymy ("the hands of the fishermen"), in a sentence whose active subject is not men but lobsters.[72] The first Pacific woman of the book, introduced theatrically in the last stanza by a run-on line, is an archetypal oversexualized "young maid smiling."[73] Like the fishermen, she is introduced through a metonymy—her flower—and she exists only through the voyeuristic gaze of the poet observing her without her knowing, through lush vegetation.

The only person on Rapa Nui who is given any depth and consistency in this poem is a German Capuchin missionary, Father Sebastián Englert. In fact, the only surname featured in the whole volume is that of Englert. He inspires Neruda with ludic puns (*"un pequeño cántaro que canta"* playfully associating jugs of wine and singing through homophony); and he is described as resting peacefully among smiling Islanders. This constitutes a stark reversal of the history of evangelization in Rapa Nui and of Englert's role in it. Mass conversions to Christianity took place between 1864 and 1868, a period during which 50 to 70 percent of the population is reported to have died of imported diseases.[74] The upheaval brought by this massive depopulation obviously played an important role in most Rapanui people's decision to convert to Christianity. Englert himself was far from a benevolent Christian. A settler in Rapa Nui from 1935 to his death in 1969, he participated in the oppression, confinement, and exploitation of the Rapanui, whom he describes in his writings as "children . . . incapable of controlling their emotions and instincts."[75] He forbade elders from transmitting reading knowledge of rongo rongo tablets to the youth. He forbade people from praying to Polynesian gods. And when young people went to study in Chile, Englert took to the newspaper to warn that the students were putting the island at risk of undergoing new epidemics.[76] In testimonies collected by anthropologist Hermann Fisher, an anonymous Rapanui witness recalls: "The truth is that Father Englert did not want students to be in contact with the outside world. Instead of educating the Rapa Nui people, he stultified us."[77] Presenting the missionary as a peaceful, beloved, paternalistic figure, as in Neruda's poem, eclipses the complex reality of a tragic historical moment and replaces it with the ever-lasting smile of the "Happy Native."

At the time of Neruda's visit to Rapa Nui, France had just begun its largest-ever series of atmospheric thermonuclear testing in Moruroa and Fangataufa. The explosions were taking place during the months of austral winter, when the winds mostly blow toward the eastern Pacific. The year prior to Neruda's voyage, in 1972, the radioactive clouds had been so lethal when reaching the coasts of South America that Peru, Ecuador, Colombia, Bolivia, and Chile threatened to end all diplomatic relationships with France if the tests were not immediately put to an end.[78] Rapa Nui, located directly windward of Moruroa, was exposed to unknown levels of radiation. All that can be said for sure is that this radiation exposure was necessarily far greater than what was recorded two thousand miles farther east in South America.[79] Neruda's erasure of Indigenous Pacific people at the time of their assault under nuclear imperialism, combined with his ambiguous status as a Chilean colonizer, makes this collection of poems a problematic thorn in his otherwise inspiring and empowering oeuvre.

The point of this close reading is not to suggest that Neruda *should* have used his Pacific travels as a platform to denounce the irradiation of Rapa Nui or the oversexualization of Pacific women. It shows, rather, that Isletist tropes are so pervasive that even upstanding advocates of racial justice and anti-imperialism are unlikely, during a brief visit to the Pacific, to develop the conceptual tools to see beyond the layers of ideological discourse that structure foreign perceptions of these islands.

The Isletist tropes evoked in Neruda's book are omnipresent in contemporary Isletist cultural production to this day. This massive corpus, spanning the publishing, artistic, cinematographic, and musical industries, cannot be analyzed in depth here. It suffices to mention that, in contemporary settler and traveler literature, many works continue to represent the Pacific Islands as frozen in time and as remnants of past centuries and to portray Pacific Islanders as primarily directed by emotions, instinct, irrationality, and superstitious beliefs.[80] There is a shockingly consistent tendency among foreign writers to depict Pacific men as dangerous rapists and violent assaulters.[81]

Pacific women are still oversexualized, perhaps even more than before the beginning of nuclear testing. After World War II, the Pacific Islands opened to the tourist economy. New market incentives led many settlers as well as many Oceanians to turn to the myth of the welcoming Native and to push aside earlier hegemonic representations of eroticized cannibalism that complicated the Isletist trope of Pacific women as sexually welcoming. The myth of the sexually available island girl circulates homogeneously in marginalized novels published by small presses as well as in internationally prized works by progressive writers, such as Aldous Huxley's *Island* and Mario Vargas Llosa's *El paraíso en la otra esquina* (*The Way to Paradise*).[82] This stereotype is particularly popular among male French writers, whose novels praise in unison the "extreme sexual availability of the vahine" in Tahiti.[83] Pacific women are explicitly portrayed as vestiges of the past, and twenty-first-century French novelists still write unironically that "island girls ... had kept from the bygone days this propensity to live in the moment and to make the most of a handsome man."[84]

Whether or not Pacific women have historically been more promiscuous than other women in other cultural and historical contexts is not relevant in light of these literary leitmotivs. As literary scholar Homi K. Bhabha famously pointed out, the process of stereotyping is not always problematic for being a false representation of historical or current events. It is problematic "because it is an arrested, fixated form of representation."[85] In literature, these tropes are expressed through the voices of omniscient narrators, protagonists, and secondary characters, and it is sometimes made explicit that this is not a view shared by the author. However, there is something disturbing about the systematic circulation of so many of these Isletist myths, in so many contemporary novels. I would contend that, by putting these myths in circulation in ambiguously polyphonic narratives without explicitly undermining them, most contemporary foreign literature fails to appropriately challenge these harmful stereotypes.

Conclusion: Isletism and Militourism

How can all these Isletist writers continue to fantasize about islands of easy love remote from the world's turmoil, when the Pacific is one of the most militarized and irradiated regions of the world? This surprising juxtaposition of touristic fantasies and military installations corresponds to what Teresia Teaiwa has called the "militouristic" exploitation of the Pacific. Militourism designates the process by which militarism and tourism can be intertwined to reinforce each other: "military or paramilitary force ensures the smooth running of the tourist industry, and the same tourist industry masks the military force behind it."[86] The most famous conflation of touristic and nuclear imagery is the French stylist Louis Réard's decision to call his sensational two-piece bathing suit after Pikinni Atoll. Describing it as an "anatomic bomb," the stylist speculated that the attire would have the effect of the H-bomb the Americans had just begun testing in the Marshallese atoll.[87]

Militourism informs Pacific life even in the islands that do not host nuclear testing facilities. Indeed, despite the fact that the Pacific Islands only account for a small fraction of the international tourist trade, they remain a primary reference for the petro-fueled fantasy of what vacation should resemble. As French historian Jean-Christophe Gay noted, the aesthetics and practices of international tourism were forged primarily with Hawai'i and Tahiti in mind. The sought-after combination of "sea, sex, and sun" was invented in Waikiki at the beginning of the twentieth century, as Duke Kahanamoku and Jack London popularized tanning and surfing, relayed by Hollywood and mass media. The figure of the *beach boy* in a so-called Hawaiian shirt (a garment invented in the 1930s by Asian businesses) soon replaced nineteenth-century conceptions of the beach as a therapeutic destination. In Europe, Club Med became one of the most popular companies offering replicas of a Polynesian vacation to the wider public. The wife of one of the founders of the club, Claudine Blitz, visited Tahiti and brought back the custom of clothing Club Med's tourists in sarongs, hosting them in Polynesian-style bungalows, and creating an Arcadian environment by making shell necklaces the currency of the club. While the Pacific Islands are the ideological backbone of contemporary tourism, the events that contributed to the islands' renewed popularity in industrialized countries are directly linked to their militarization: it was primarily World War II infrastructure that turned the islands into accessible tourists' heavens.[88] Few tourists are aware that the airstrips on which their planes land were constructed by or for the military.

Commodifying dancing, floral garments, and recreational water activities, twentieth-century Isletism portrays the Islander in direct continuity with eighteenth-century representations of the "noble savage." Pacific cultures are marketed to tourists as the spontaneous, instinctive expression of closeness to nature. However, this alleged proximity to prelapsarian times easily translates into Isletist assumptions about the outdatedness of Pacific cultures. Touristic enclaves thus feel justified in commodifying Pacific artifacts while simultaneously banning Pacific peoples from the premises. Tourists are flower-crowned in gated hotels from which locals are excluded, and foreigners buy postcards of South Seas beauties who are not Indigenous, since "the men who visit [the Pacific] want a woman they already possess in their head or in their libido."[89] Chantal Spitz calls this form of whitewashing "cultural cannibalism":

> by cannibalizing our culture our identity they deprive themselves of
> sharing with us what they are
> .... Nothing changed since Bougainville's visit[90]

In the era of militourism, Isletist tropes take the well-known Orientalist process of the simultaneous construction/erasure of a historically backward Other to its logical conclusion. Isletist cultural production erases Pacific Islanders, while using Pacific land, resources, and labor forces to further the military oppression of the islands. Economic, political, cultural, and military apparatuses sustain this ideology. These myths are produced by powerful actors, from Hollywood to publishing houses and art museums, ensuring the global dissemination of Isletist narratives. Countering the global scope of Isletist discourses, Pacific writers and artists offer a counterhegemonic narrative of Oceania—one based on transgenerational values, alternative geographies, and an ecologically conscious reinvention of collective identities. This other ideology, this alternative to Isletism, is the literature of Oceanitude.

OCEANITUDE

A Philosophy for the Anthropocene

As if the Pacific Ocean isn't the largest body
living today, beating the loudest heart,
the reason why land has a pulse in the first place.
—TERISA TINEI SIAGATONU, "Atlas"

[We are] the humanity of Oceanity
—LUC ÉNOKA CAMOUI AND WAIXEN WAYEWOL,
Pue Tiu, au cœur de la parole

the saltwarm of your
waters move
ancient in our blood
—NGAHUIA TE AWEKOTUKU, "Mururoa/Moruroa"

"Let us heed, let us read *oceanitude*: Henri Hiro, Chantal Spitz, Déwé Gorodé, Grace Molisa, and all the others showing us the way to value the living-together."[1] This is the conclusion of *Quand le cannibale ricane* (*When the Cannibal Sneers*), a novel by ni-Vanuatu author Paul Tavo published in 2015. In this book, Tavo coined a way to refer to a literary, political, and philosophical movement uniting decolonial writers, orators, and activists across Oceania. He called this movement Oceanitude.

Oceanitude offers a powerful alternative to other labels defining Oceania's decolonial cultural production. Calling it Pacific decolonial literature, for example, is doubly limiting. First, as discussed in the introduction, the term *literature* fails to encapsulate the wide diversity of oral, written, and digital creative discourses that Oceanians use to express themselves. Moreover, as Epeli Hauʻofa famously noted, the term *Pacific* itself presents several limitations. Defining the region as the Pacific allows for a disproportionate focus on Australia and Aotearoa / New Zealand, while the more specific expression *Pacific Islands* still too often denotes smallness and compartmentalization.[2] Hauʻofa prefers calling the region Oceania: "it sounds grand and somewhat romantic and may denote something so vast that it would compel [foreigners] to a drastic review of their perspectives and policies."[3] Tavo's neologism allows for a transfer of Hauʻofa insights in the field of artistic and literary production. Instead of reading Pacific decolonial literature, let us heed Oceanitude.

Tavo chose to name this movement Oceanitude rather than Oceanness or Oceanism for its obvious homophony with the Negritude movement developed across the Black Atlantic in the twentieth century.[4] This anchors Oceanitude in a long transnational history of decolonial struggle. Negritude philosophers defined a collective Black identity by highlighting Black people's fundamental contributions to world history, leading philosopher Souleymane Bachir Diagne to define the movement succinctly as "the self-affirmation of black peoples ... set out to revalorize people of African descent across the Atlantic."[5] The orators and writers that Tavo presents as the founders of Oceanitude, Henri Hiro and Chantal Spitz in Tahiti, Déwé Gorodé in Kanaky, and Grace Molisa in Vanuatu, contributed to a similar cultural revalorization of Oceania in the late twentieth century. However, Oceanitude's conceptions of collective identity are not based on race as was the case with Negritude. Rather, they are based on what Hiro, Spitz, Gorodé, and Molisa all have in common: a specific relationship to the ocean.

The notion of race derives from colonial constructions. While the philosophers of Negritude managed to reappropriate it and use it to foster decolonial solidarities, the construct of race has not been reappropriated in a similar way in the Pacific, for various reasons. First, as Maile Renee Arvin has extensively documented, colonizers have long speculated the existence of at least two races in Oceania, constructing Polynesians as quasi-whites descending from Aryans, and Melanesians and Aborigines as Black.[6] Many decolonial activists have challenged this colonial division of one ocean into two races, some Polynesians identifying as Black to distinguish themselves from white settlers.[7] Nevertheless, the notion of race has never been as effective as a concept to unify the

Pacific as it has been to unify the Black Atlantic. It is rather the concept of Indigeneity, which can function "as a natural claim to place," that has been most mobilized in Pacific decolonial movements.[8]

Unlike the concept of race, the notion of Indigeneity comes from customary Pacific epistemologies centering the importance of genealogy. Joyce Lindsay Pualani Warren explains the difference between the two modes of conceiving of collective identities as a conflict between two incompatible perspectives: "Oceanians recognize multiple, overlapping, and simultaneous claims, accommodating multiracial identity as a component of diverse, equally valid genealogical claims."[9] While the philosophers of Negritude emphasized race as a unifying concept, the founders of Oceanitude emphasized the ancestral lineage that links Pacific people to the Pacific Ocean as the core of Indigenous collective identities.

The English word *genealogy* does not encapsulate the nature of this Indigenous claim to place. As Kanaka ʻŌiwi scholars Nālani Wilson-Hokowhitu and Manulani Aluli Meyer explain, the English word prioritizes human relationships, whereas the Pacific words for genealogy (moʻokūʻauhau in Hawaiʻi, whakapapa in Aotearoa, paparaʻa tupuna in Māʻohi Nui, etc.) all indicate "the vastness of... familial relationships that extend well beyond the human realm to include islands, oceans, planets, and the universe."[10]

In many Pacific cosmogonies, humans and places share the same genealogy because everything came into being through procreation. While cosmogonic stories vary greatly from region to region across Oceania, most nonetheless posit that various feminine and masculine deities gave birth to the elements of creation. In Palau, the westernmost Pacific archipelago, all life sprang from Latmikaik, a giant clam that arose from the sea to give birth to all creatures that populate the land and the ocean.[11] Eight thousand miles away, in the easternmost island Rapa Nui, the land is customarily seen as a taina (sibling/relative) because humans arose from the procreation between the god Makemake and a calabash of water and earth.[12] Thus throughout Oceania, the notion of creation through the process of lineage remains a core principle of cosmogonic stories.

One consequence of this fundamental Pacific principle is that everything created on earth is related as kin and therefore has the same value, from the smallest single-cell organism to present-day humans. Contemporary scientific research has only recently caught up with the wisdom held in this ancestral knowledge about genealogical connections to all living beings. Molecular data analysis now challenges Darwinian understanding of life as a hierarchical evolution from simple to complex, showing that evolution itself is nondirectional, unpredictable, and poorly represented by the orderly metaphor of the tree of evolution.[13]

Oceanitude therefore differs from Negritude by proposing a different conception of collective identities. This philosophy does not center on race but rather on the lineage and the relationship uniting people and the places that sustain them. "We are simply from a place and thus have responsibility to steward and care for that place," writes Meyer.[14] That is what Oceanitude affirms as the philosophy of "valuing the living-together": living together means not only nurturing good relations with other humans across different islands and ethnicities but also nurturing loving relationships between humans and other-than-humans, be they animals, plants, or waters.[15]

Of course, this does not mean that all Indigenous people in Oceania adhere to these values. The Ocean Declaration of Maupiti makes clear that one should beware of abusive generalizations on this topic. An international call to protect the Pacific Ocean "for our ancestors and future generation," the declaration states that "for many Pacific communities . . . there are sacred and intrinsic links with [the] ocean. The Ocean is their identity . . . the ocean is a sacred, essential entity."[16] The text of this declaration was written by the Indigenous heads of states and political representatives of sixteen Pacific countries, all deeply concerned about environmental issues in the region. Yet these Indigenous leaders use third-person pronouns to describe the spiritual relationship that "some Pacific communities" share with the ocean, thereby refusing to bestow this worldview upon all Oceanians. This is very symbolic for a declaration redacted and signed in Māʻohi Nui, a country governed for decades by an Indigenous-led government that supported the nuking, mining, and selling of Māʻohi islands. Oceanitude is a decolonial ideology promoted by progressive people throughout history, not an atavism innate to anyone with Indigenous Oceanian ancestry.

Tavo's neologism remains largely unheeded in academic circles; yet the concept of Oceanitude has potent political ramifications. Its allusion to the other-than-human, to the ocean, connotes from the outset its environmental dimension. In these times of climate collapse, the philosophy of Oceanitude may speak to all people fighting alienation from other-than-humans. This does not mean that Oceanitude can or should be appropriated but simply that the wisdom shared by the founders of this movement can provide a moral compass—or a moral star path—on different ways of being in the world. This was recognized by the late Pacific studies scholar Teresia Teaiwa, who noted that the knowledge created in Pacific studies is not just important for Pacific people. She called for a rekindling of the dialogue between studies of the

Pacific and studies of humanity for the advancement of human knowledge.[17] As she saw it, Pacific thinkers "have something to teach the rest of the world as well."[18]

This chapter explores the genesis, development, and global relevance of Oceanitude. I begin by analyzing the foundational text of Oceanitude, Tavo's *When the Cannibal Sneers*, to show that Oceanitude foregrounds unity amid diverse Pacific epistemologies by positing attachment to landscape and seascapes as a fundamental Oceanian principle. I then explore the genealogy of Oceanitude itself. Analyzing texts by Negritude founders Aimé Césaire and Léopold Sédar Senghor, I show how Tavo's Oceanitude draws from theories developed by the philosophers of Negritude. Finally, I ask how the concepts underpinning the philosophy of Oceanitude illuminate a contemporary Pacific struggle: the fight against settler desecration on Mauna Kea. The political, philosophical, and artistic scope of Oceanitude suggests that this movement has the potential to reaffirm the importance of nurturing relationships between humans and other-than-humans on a global scale.

Genesis of Oceanitude: Oceanic Poetics by Paul Tavo

Paul Tavo was born in 1983 in Malakula, a large rural island in the north of Vanuatu, three years after Vanuatu obtained independence. The fifth of eight children, he began his schooling with Francophone missionaries in the town of Lamap before moving to the country's main island, Efate, to study with Anglophone teachers in the capital Port Vila. He completed a high school degree in English and obtained a scholarship to pursue his higher education in Kanaky before moving to Australia for a few months and France for a few years. He is fluent in Bislama, English, and French—the latter being the language of most of his published work.

Tavo is tied to various islands and languages of the Pacific, but his main commitment is to Oceania as a whole. When he returned to Vanuatu, he began writing poetry and performing public readings of his creative works. In 2011, he published his first collection of poems, *L'âme du kava* (*The Soul of the Kava*), and in 2015, he shared his debut novel, *Quand le cannibale ricane* (*When the Cannibal Sneers*).[19] The prologue explains,

> *Ce récit est une tentative personnelle de réhabiliter une histoire . . . : celle de l'insulaire. Cet insulaire océanien . . . qui a tour à tour été traité des pires injures: "cannibale," "race dégénérée," "foncièrement, génétiquement sale." . . . Non contents hier de discréditer sa culture, . . . aujourd'hui . . . ils empoisonnent l'océan (Fukushima)*

dans lequel il tire sa nourriture.... Le réchauffement climatique, la montée des eaux, menacent avant tout les îles de submersion.[20]

This narrative is a personal attempt to rehabilitate a history:... that of the Islander. The Oceanian Islander... who has been called successively by the worse insults: "cannibal," "degenerated race," "intrinsically, genetically filthy."... After having discredited his culture yesterday,... today... they poison the ocean (Fukushima) in which he finds his food.... Global warming, rising sea levels threaten above all to submerge the islands.

From the outset, Tavo asserts the relationship between Oceanians and the ocean. His prologue highlights that the colonizers' desecration of Pacific people paves the way for the desecration of the ocean, and vice versa. If Pacific people are described as "intrinsically, genetically filthy," then, he says, it becomes easy to conceive of the Pacific Ocean as "an excellent open-air dumping ground for industrial countries' toxic waste."[21] Similarly, he warns, if colonizers keep pouring carbon dioxide into Oceania, a flow of Pacific peoples displaced by climate collapse will "pour... upon the inhospitable coastlines of continents."[22] Tavo denounces nuclear contamination ("Fukushima") and carbon imperialism ("rising sea levels") as the main sources of ocean pollution. The sullied Islander invented by Isletist narratives, presenting Oceanians as "intrinsically, genetically filthy," is the embodiment of the environmental aggression suffered by the Pacific Ocean itself. In this sense, Oceania and Oceanians are *fusional*. This prologue sets the foundation for writing about the Indigenous mode of being in and relating to the world that Tavo will describe in the rest of his novel, exploring this link between Pacific peoples and the ocean as the foundation of Oceanitude.

This link between Oceanians and the Ocean is rooted in Indigenous epistemologies. In Vanuatu, personal essence and identity have historically often been seen as infused in the land.[23] In other words, the "environment" is not something that surrounds people but rather a place uniting people across generations and that living residents share with the memory of their ancestors and the future of their children. As eloquently put by Mildred Sope, famed ni-Vanuatu poet and decolonial activist who lost her land to seismic activity, losing one's island means losing one's identity, while a land that has lost its people becomes a "ghost-island."[24] In this perspective, defacing the ocean and its islands is inseparable from defacing its people too.

On a global scale, by contrast, the ocean is the favorite locus of waste disposal in carbon-addicted societies. Since the beginning of large-scale industrial pollution, water has been conceived of as a way to take the problem out of sight and out of mind. When Western countries faced the first significant waste management challenge with the democratization of sewage systems, the unprecedented volume of waste was dealt with by following a principle that has since become doctrine: dilution is the solution to pollution. Today, oceans are an open waste disposal for most continental detritus: and Oceania, the world's largest ocean, absorbs much of the world's waste. It takes in Fukushima's radioactive water, the so-called continent of plastic defecated by North America and Asia, and the bulk of the seven million metric tons of carbon released annually by carbon-addicted nations. And yet the environmental destruction that always accompanies Western-led industrialization is still often referred to as "waste*land*ing" (my emphasis).[25] Tavo's prologue puts the problem in perspective by reminding that it is not the land but the ocean that remains the primary victim of petrocapitalism's pollution. As CHamoru antinuclear activist Maria Pangelinan explains, there is something unique about water pollution: "At least on land you are able to monitor and prevent any disaster from happening, but when you dump in the ocean it's just irretrievable. You cannot monitor it. Even though you know that all the fish in the ocean are dying, it's too late. You cannot bring back what you have already put in."[26]

Tavo's novel explores this link between Oceanians and Oceania through a five-hundred-page epic saga. The book retraces the tribulations of a young fictional ni-Vanuatu migrant, William, who has left his rural island, Malakula, to find work in the corrupt industrialized capital of the country. The first part of the novel reads as a register of grievances, denouncing the injustices of colonialism, capitalism, and globalization. William appears as a lost soul, battling with alcoholism, poverty, and depression. He eventually decides to leave this alienating society and returns to his native island, to relearn ancestral values among his family members. Yet, just as he completes this redeeming return to his roots, his parents ask him to move back to the alienating city he has fled and to find wage labor that will help them pay for the family's needs.

It is interesting to note that the entire plot is set in Vanuatu. This spatial framework highlights both the outreach of globalization and the capital's sub-imperialism onto its other islands. Port Vila is associated with Western civilization, alienation, and drifting, while Malakula symbolizes Oceanitude, Melanesian values, and rootedness. The fact that the protagonist is asked by his loving family members to leave Malakula speaks to a common issue in Oceania's rural islands. With the expansion of capitalist modes of production, even self-sufficient societies end up developing cash needs: to pay taxes, to buy local goods that are used to barter, and to replace craft by industrial products.[27] No matter how sustainable a society's lifestyle may be, its people are eventually forced to enter the capitalist market, with only their labor force to sell. William's sacrifice is presented in tragic tones, as an inevitable fate. The family needs cash to pay his siblings' school tuition, fill up the oil lamp, buy machetes and manufactured clothing... and "he was the only one able to find a shitty job... to help them afford it."[28] Capitalism entraps even the people who pride themselves on living self-sufficiently from the gifts of the ocean.

The neologism of Oceanitude appears for the first time toward the end of the novel, after William has agreed to return to Port Vila. He is standing at sunset on the shore of Malakula, contemplating the sea that will soon take him away to the capitalist capital. He lives this voluntary exile as martyrdom. Yet he feels stronger, rooted: "The next day he would reintegrate the alienating life of the city, but he was now ready to go head-to-head with it."[29] Expressing this newfound determination in a lengthy poem, he explains finding strength in retrieving his people's "Melanesian values":

> *Moi et mon peuple*
> *On est debout...*
> *Dans le vent, sous l'orage*
> *Face à l'hideux tsunami*
> *Affrontant héroïquement*
> *La vague de la mondialisation....*
> *Notre océanitude une fois conquise...*
> *plus jamais ne sera soumise.*[30]

> Me and my people
> We are upright...
> In the wind, under the storm,
> In front of the hideous tsunami
> Heroically facing
> The wave of globalization....
> Our oceanitude now conquered...
> will never again be subdued.

As the novel first introduces the concept of Oceanitude, it is framed as a foil to globalization. In addition to spreading pollution, globalization also spreads uniform commodities, uniform modes of consumption, and uniform lifestyles. Western culture has set the terms for global culture, and the world is threatened by this gangrenous "mass civilization."[31] Tavo's choice of words to describe this phenomenon is highly symbolic. Globalization is metaphorically identified with maritime referents: it is a "wave," a "tsunami," a "storm" threatening to drown the Oceanian way of life, just as rising sea levels threaten to drown the narrator's shores. By choosing to represent globalization as a rising ocean, a king tide, the narrator highlights the links between globalization and carbon imperialism. Tavo's poetic choices thus frame Oceanitude not only as an identity but also as a political, economic, and environmental movement. Grounding his resistance to globalization in cultural particularism, the poet implicitly frames his resistance to climate collapse in Oceanians' traditional affinity with the ocean. "We are not drowning—we are fighting," chant the Pacific Climate Warriors. "We are upright, heroically facing the wave of globalization," echoes the poet of Oceanitude.

The fact that the novel switches narrative styles when first introducing the concept of Oceanitude is very telling. To denounce globalization, the narrator switches from conventional prose to chant-like metrics reminiscent of Vanuatu's oral traditions, thus giving more weight to his affirmation of the strength and vitality of his ancestors' culture. One may wonder, however, why he chose to write this passage exclusively in French. It may be linked to the fact that Vanuatu is one of the most linguistically diverse places on earth, with over a hundred languages spoken throughout the eighty islands of the archipelago. In Malakula alone, Tavo's fifty-eight-mile-long home island, no fewer than thirty-six Indigenous languages are spoken daily in addition to Bislama, English, and French.[32] Yet Vanuatu is not compartmentalized in isolated linguistical areas. Rather, the country is united by a juxtaposition of distinct yet mutually understandable languages, creating "pathways of intelligibility" to counterbalance the archipelago's extraordinary linguistic diversity.[33] Choosing to write in French, one of the three languages of Vanuatu present throughout the country, Tavo continues to travel those traditional pathways of intelligibility that unite the many islands of the archipelago. French has ceased to be the language of the colonizer to become a language of the living together.

While rooted in local ni-Vanuatu values, Tavo's book tackles global issues. The poet insists that the planet is increasingly connected—and increasingly unequal. In this context, it is more urgent than ever to underscore the interdependency of humans and their environment. The protagonist-turned-poet thus claims:

Puis en homme-océan,
En peuple-océan,
Nous ouvrirons notre cœur-océan

Déversant notre amour
(Sur les rivages hostiles des continents,
Sur ces rives inhospitalières bien gardées,
Armées jusqu'aux dents)
Embrassant l'humanité
De cette étreinte fougueuse, océanique.[34]

As ocean-men,
As ocean-people,
We will open our ocean-heart
Pouring our love
(Upon the inhospitable coastline of continents,
Upon well-kept hostile shores,
Armed to the teeth)
Embracing humanity
With this vigorous, oceanic clutch.

Pacific people are often portrayed, in Western discourses, as helpless casualties of the global climate collapse, to be rescued by well-intentioned white saviors. This poem completely shifts perspectives. The narrator presents Pacific migration toward thermo-industrial centers as an unstoppable invasion. The parentheses framing "inhospitable coastlines" and "hostile shores" in the poem form a rather weak fortification against the tides of Oceanitude conquerors.

Furthermore, this invasion is depicted as an opportunity to *rescue* Euro-Americans from their own alienation. Europe and North America are isolated behind their walls, alienated from humans and other-than-humans alike. (Even before the emergence of COVID-19, Americans spent on average 90 percent of their time indoors, leaving enclosed buildings primarily to go grocery shopping or commute to work; and their children spent less time outside than incarcerated Americans.)[35] This structural alienation from the world of the living constitutes a dramatic psychic disconnection characteristic of carbon-addicted societies, a total "extinction of experience."[36] By contrast, the "ocean people" pouring on continents in the poem appear as the saviors of Euro-Americans. These "ocean-men" can be construed as fighting Westerners' extinction of experience, as Tavo describes them "embracing humanity" in a "vigorous, oceanic clutch." Oceanitude thus replaces alienation from the world with its opposite: *fusion* with the world. Where Euro-Americans build walls against the ocean, the philosophy of Oceanitude advocates for living with the ocean. The poem portrays the global spread of transgenerational Oceanian values as a redeeming invasion that will reshape humanity, concluding:

Nous dirons à cet homme apeuré: . . . .
Empoigne cette main tendue
Homme aliéné, névrosé
Puis relève-toi et suis-nous.[37]

We will tell this frightened man: . . . .
Grab hold of this extended hand
Alienated, neurotic man
Then pick yourself up and follow us.

Advocating for such a fusional relationship with the ocean is a pan-Pacific aspiration. Creative writers and orators from the whole Pacific often express the same worldview in their art, as in Craig Santos Perez and Terisa Tinei Siagatonu's poetry: "The source of every breath," the ocean is a living organism, "the largest body / living today, beating the loudest heart, / the reason why land has a pulse in the first place."[38]

While the ocean is a living being, living beings are also part of the ocean, united by genealogical links and millennia of a mutually beneficial relationship. This fundamental value has been powerfully reasserted in contemporary times, as many Oceanian writers, artists, and philosophers have theorized their deep connection to the ocean. Epeli Hau'ofa famously claimed that "the sea is our pathway to each other and to the world, the sea is our endless saga, the sea is our most powerful metaphor, the ocean is in us."[39] In one of her most famous quotes, Teresia Teaiwa similarly said: "We sweat and cry salt water, so we know that the ocean is really in our blood."[40] In the francophone Pacific, Stéphanie Ariirau Richard-Vivi, who publishes as Ariirau, identifies the ocean with Oceanians' tears for nuclearized atolls: "An expense of lachrymal drops overflew from the surface of our islands and our atolls. If you thought it was the ocean, you were wrong."[41] Echoing her from Niue, John Puhiatau Pule claims: "My heart is full of saltwater."[42] Countless other contemporary Pacific poets have linked Oceanians and Oceania, depicting Pacific people as "fish-men," "people of the sea," "ocean people," or the "humanity of Oceanity."[43]

Therefore, when the narrator of *Cannibal* describes Pacific people as "ocean-men" with an "ocean-heart," the ocean is no longer a metaphor. A metaphor, from the Greek *meta* (over) and *pherin* (to carry), creates theoretical links between distinct objects. By contrast, Oceanians and the Pacific Ocean are more than symbols or even signifiers of each other in the literature of Oceanitude. Tavo, Hau'ofa, Teaiwa, and the countless Pacific poets to link Oceania and Oceanians all suggest that the ocean and its people are not metaphorically but rather consubstantially, genealogically, and historically related. "Such comparisons go beyond the rhetorical conceits of metaphor or personification; our authors are articulating an intimacy" between people and their land, concludes Jamaica Heolimeleikalani Osorio.[44] The Pacific poets who come from the ocean and care for the ocean define their identity not through symbolically associating with the ocean, but rather by embracing the long-lasting relationship between them.

Differentiating between the ocean as metaphor and the ocean as a relationship/identity has tangible political implications. In a different Indigenous context, Hupa scholar of Native American studies Cutcha Risling Baldy denounces that the knowledge contained in Indigenous stories is often treated by settlers as "a universalized metaphor," erasing the various ways in which these referents tie specific Indigenous people to a specific land (or ocean).[45] When Tavo describes Pacific people as "ocean-men" with an "ocean-heart," he does not put forward a metaphor but rather an entire knowledge system originating from Oceania.

At the close of *When the Cannibal Sneers*, the narrator presents Oceanitude as the philosophy of the future. The protagonist has battled throughout the entire novel to eventually define this identity/relationship. At the end of this struggle, he appears to have found a new balance, asserting that "our Oceanitude, now conquered . . . will never again be subdued." Far from promoting enclosed identities and narrow parochialism, Oceanitude is a philosophy of the "living-together" (*"le vivre-ensemble"*) in times of climate collapse on a global scale. Tavo's poem emphasizes that carbon colonizers and globalization survivors must learn to live together, forgoing walls, arms, and hostile shores. It also emphasizes that humans must (re)learn to live with, rather than against, other-than-humans, in a holistic relationship with the other beings and places of creation. The philosophy of Oceanitude thus challenges what Candace Fujikane has called "liberalism's governance of difference," or capitalism's claims to be able to distinguish life from nonlife.[46] Here, the ocean is brought back where it belongs in Indigenous epistemologies, in the realm of the living, the nurturing, and the loving.

Genealogy of Oceanitude:
From the Black Atlantic to the Pacific Ocean

To understand the genealogy of the philosophy of Oceanitude, we must go back to the roots of Negritude. Negritude is a movement launched by poets, philosophers, and politicians Aimé Césaire in Martinique, Léopold Sédar Senghor in Senegal, and Léon Gontrand Damas in French-occupied Guyana. They had political, literary, and philosophical goals: fighting for their colonized countries' sovereignty, creating distinctly Black arts counterbalancing the Western canon, and challenging the Western-led glorification of Cartesian thinking. Negritude was one of the most influential philosophical, literary, artistic, and political movements of the twentieth century. Its thinkers were immensely significant in revalorizing Black cultures, reuniting Africa and its diaspora across the Atlantic Ocean, and dismantling colonialism. One of Negritude's most notable legacies, and the one that interests me here, is its critique of analytical, mechanical, Cartesian modes of inquiry as an impoverished mode of relating to the world.

According to Léopold Sédar Senghor, the French Revolution marks the triumph of Cartesian reasoning. Beheading the king, a source of divine authority, posits reason and logic as the exclusive source of all certain knowledge. Negritude constitutes a counterrevolution, a call to arms to the end of the exclusive and destructive valorization of blind positivism. Throughout the twentieth century, from the universities of Dakar to the cafés of Harlem, anti-colonial thinkers attacked the insufficiencies of Cartesianism by referring to Senghor, Césaire, and Damas's philosophy. Cartesian reasoning, according to Negritude thinkers, is a form of knowledge that, in order to understand a given object, distances it from oneself and dissects it. Science in particular, the idealized form of language in Cartesian thinking, is a language that reduces a being to its working parts and analyzes them as inanimate objects.

Take, for example, the Cartesian analysis of movement. Technoscientific reasoning analyzes movement as a series of segments going from point A to point B. As French philosopher Henri Bergson describes it, Cartesian reasoning "only understands immobility. When it wants to represent movement, it rebuilds it with juxtaposed stillness."[47] This geometric, mathematical approach misses what is essential to movement: mobility. Scientific reasoning, analyzing exclusively inert matter, produces weak facsimiles of the world's vitality. "We are at ease only in the discontinuous, the immobile, the dead. Intelligence is characterized by a natural incomprehension of life," bemoans Bergson.[48] The Euro-American's most valued form of reasoning—Cartesian, analytical, scientific thinking—petrifies the world by calculating it (from the Latin *calculus*, or pebble), that is, turning it to inanimate matter. Césaire described such Cartesian thought as a "progressive devalorization of the world, which very naturally leads to the appearance of an inhuman universe."[49] A scientific approach to the world reduces it to lifeless atoms and fails to capture its life. By contrast, Negritude wants to manifest knowledge of the world's *vitality*.[50] The philosophers of Negritude rejected the discontinuous, the immobile, the dead, and set out to understand the world according to its vital forces, its rhythm, its movement.

The philosophy of Negritude had identified three diverging directions of life development. According to these thinkers, the original sin of the Euro-American industrial civilization "was to see in vegetal life, instinctive life, and rational life three successive degrees in a single tendency that is developing (Aristotle); whereas these are three diverging directions of an activity that split as it grew."[51] Knowledge, they argued, should encompass all three dimensions. Yet the dominant Euro-American discourse, which has set the terms for global values, has elevated science (rational life) above all other modes of understanding the world.

While the West does not have a monopoly on science, it does seem to have made headway on making it a religion. Cartesian obsession with science, notes Césaire, means "substituting an abbreviated version of the world to the dialectical tonality that the world is, which may be convenient, but constitutes an impoverishment, a pale copy of the world."[52] The cortege of devastations that characterizes the nineteenth and twentieth centuries abundantly proved the limitations of this type of reasoning. It led the poets of Negritude to inverse the hegemonic scale of values and take pride, with Césaire, in being described as follows:

> ceux qui n'ont inventé ni la poudre ni la boussole
> ceux qui n'ont jamais su dompter la vapeur ni l'électricité
> ....
> mais ... s'abandonnent, saisis, à l'essence de toute chose[53]

> those who have invented neither powder nor the compass
> those who have tamed neither gas nor electricity
> ....
> but ... abandon themselves, possessed, to the essence of all things

While immensely influential in the mid-twentieth century, Negritude has often been criticized since as an essentialist movement. It has been accused in particular of perpetuating colonial tropes, by equating Europe to Reason and Africa to Emotion.[54] However, as philosopher Souleymane Bachir Diagne demonstrated, this is a reductive understanding of the movement.[55] Negritude writers did not believe in an essentialized Black mentality. "Isn't reason the same in all men?" asked Senghor.[56] Negritude thinkers adopted an essentialist language at times, but their work emphasizes that Cartesian thinking, while universal, has expressed itself violently in European expansionism. By contrast, empathic thinking, while also universal, may be found in eloquent and vivid form in African art. Negritude is not, as French philosopher Jean-Paul Sartre famously argued, an "anti-racist racism." It is rather a revolution in how to think about arts, philosophy, and politics, and a much-needed criticism of the Western-led global worship of science.

Senghor calls the Cartesian form of scientific reasoning "reason-eye" ("*raison-œil*") and opposes it to what he termed "reason-embrace" ("*raison-étreinte*"). If René Descartes marks the triumph of the reason-eye, Negritude marks the ascent of reason-embrace. Yet the Negritude movement only brought back incomplete unity to the Cartesian dissection of the world. The Cartesians had identified three modes of knowledge production through a problematic, hierarchical classification, dividing knowledge into the vegetal, the instinctive, and the rational. The poets of Negritude, criticizing Cartesians' overemphasis on "reason," set out to revalorize the "instinctive" way of life. But Negritude did not go far enough in deconstructing Cartesian categories. One century later, Oceanitude would offer a new holistic epistemology, fully realizing the emancipatory potential of the Negritude movement.

Oceanitude turns to the third term of the equation: the "vegetal" way of life, defined as the ability to "borrow directly from the air, water, and soil the elements necessary to maintaining life."[57] Pacific activists are fighting against environmental collapse by underscoring the co-constitution and codependency of humans and the other-than-humans. Oceanian climate movements emphasize that human life is also a form of "vegetal life," inasmuch as it depends on the places that sustain it to survive. Tavo puts it eloquently in his novel, using the semantic field of vegetal life to illustrate his point. He argues that Western culture and globalization make people "as uprooted as a grass tuft vegetating on sand."[58] He defines the Oceanian mode of relating to the world as follows:

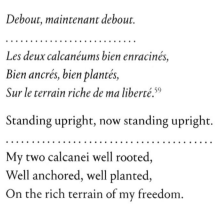

Debout, maintenant debout.

. . . .

Les deux calcanéums bien enracinés,
Bien ancrés, bien plantés,
Sur le terrain riche de ma liberté.[59]

Standing upright, now standing upright.

. . . .

My two calcanei well rooted,
Well anchored, well planted,
On the rich terrain of my freedom.

TABLE 2.1. The Three Modes of Relating to the World

Cartesian terminology	Reasoning life	Instinctive life	Vegetal life
Senghor's terminology	Reason-eye	Reason-embrace	"Reason-fusion"
Tavo's terminology	Delirious reason	Negritude	Oceanitude

Source: Table by the author.

Tavo's novel insists on the interdependence of Oceanian people and Oceania's islands, using a vegetal semantic field to suggest the interdependence, the *fusion* of the two. I propose to call this mode of relating to the world *reason-fusion* (see table 2.1).

While the "reason-embrace" promoted by the Negritude thinkers did challenge the Cartesian dualism between mind and matter, it did not shatter it thoroughly. Senghor sought to rehabilitate "reason-embrace" to "rebuild the unity between Man and the World; linking the body and the soul, man with his kind, rocks and God, . . . the real to the surreal—by making Man not the center, but the hinge . . . of the world."[60] The very word choices used by Senghor intimate the incompleteness of his revolutionary thinking. "Embracing" means putting one's arms around something, getting closer to it while still experiencing a sense of distinct individuality. Reason-embrace still keeps the other-than-humans at arm's length. Reason-fusion, by contrast, acknowledges that the human cannot even exist without the other-than-humans. It underscores that, as Marshallese poet and climate activist Kathy Jetñil-Kijiner chants:

we
are nothing
without our islands.[61]

Oceanitude thus constitutes the last of the three revolutions that redefined the human since the beginning of the scientific revolution. With Cartesianism, (some hu)man(s) became master and possessor of nature and simultaneously became alienated from the world. Negritude sought to bring the human back a little bit closer to the world. Today, the thinkers of Oceanitude are staging another revolution. The human is no longer seen as the hinge of the world but rather one of many components of the world, part and parcel with the world, and directly suffering from any harm done to the world. When Tavo claims that Oceanians are "ocean-men" with an "ocean-heart," he abolishes the distinction between the human and the other-than-human and restores pre-Cartesian unity to the cosmos.

Retracing the genealogy of Oceanitude, we can see that it tackles global questions and answers them through an oceanic perspective. Nurturing an intimate relationship with the landscapes and seascapes that sustain human life is a universal act, but it may be found in a particularly enduring and vivid form in Oceania. The philosophy of Oceanitude is thus both localized and universal. It creates continuity between Cartesianism, Negritude, and Oceanitude, emphasizing the continuousness and complementarity rather than the ruptures between these different modes of thinking. As Kanaka Maoli philosopher 'Umi Perkins explains, this is also characteristic of Pacific Indigenous epistemologies, whose genealogies tend to focus on the continuity of lineages, whereas Western Foucauldian epistemologies tend to emphasize ruptures.[62] Oceanitude is the eloquent Pacific instantiation of a universal quest for wholeness.

The hermeneutic tools drawn from Negritude and Oceanitude—reason-eye, reason-embrace, and reason-fusion—are particularly helpful to analyze environmental movements in times of climate collapse. The fight on Mauna Kea lead by Kānaka Maoli activists is one of the many sites of Indigenous struggles underpinned by the philosophy of Oceanitude. Turning now to the inspiring actions taken by the Kia'i (the protectors of the mountain), the next section analyzes the scope of Oceanitude's reason-embrace as a political project.

Embodiments of Oceanitude: Pacific Politics on Mauna Kea

In 2009, a team of international scientists selected Mauna Kea (Big Island, Hawai'i) as a site to build the world's largest visible-light telescope. The project was spearheaded by the Gordon and Betty Moore Foundation, an organization created by the multibillionaire founder of the Intel corporation. After a five-year around-the-world campaign to find an "ideal" site for its project, the foundation promised hundreds of millions of dollars to build the Thirty Meter Telescope (TMT) on Mauna Kea. The telescope would be the most enormous structure to be built on the mountain, where thirteen other telescopes have already been built (some of them used to develop military technology).[63] Estimated to cost US$2.4 billion, the TMT follows the capitalist logic of seeking infinite growth, requiring ever more "land, . . . money and capital in order to manufacture scientific 'progress.'"[64] This latest, most expensive, and most destructive industrial project would bring environmental devastation to the mountain on a previously unknown scale.

Mauna Kea, or Mauna a Wākea, is a sacred place in Kānaka Maoli epistemology. Mauna Kea is related to Kānaka Maoli people through a specific moʻokūʻauhau (genealogy, family continuity). In the Kumulipo, the Kānaka creation chant that tells the story of how the islands came to be, Mauna Kea is the first child of Wākea, the sky father, and of Papahānaumoku, the Earth mother. Wākea and Papahānaumoku also gave birth to the first Kanaka man, Kane, and the first Kanaka woman. The mountain is thus a genealogical relative of Hawaiian people. The mountain is also a piko (navel) of the universe and a dwelling place of several akua (deities).[65] Historically, religious and political elites saw Mauna Kea as highly restricted sacred spaces for healing, worship, and burials.[66] The mountain is thus also the dwelling place of the kupuna (ancestors) who have passed and are embodied in the mountainscape.[67] This familial, genealogical relationship to Mauna features prominently in Indigenous activists' opposition to the TMT: "That is the home of our Wao Akua, our deities, that is our genealogical link. [Astronomers] can go somewhere else. We are not going anywhere else. And that is the plea of Native people around the world," argues Pua Case, Kanaka activist defending the mountain since 2010.[68] Honoring this moʻokūʻauhau means perpetuating this nurturing relationship between Mauna and its siblings, the Kānaka Maoli.

Opposition to the TMT started with six families entering contested case hearings against the telescope and rapidly grew to a mass movement. Protectors who gathered on Mauna in 2014 and 2015 successfully blocked construction work and filed new court appeals. In the summer of 2019, their resistance gained international visibility when police arrested thirty-three people—most of them Hawaiian elders—as they blocked a road to prevent construction crews from reaching the TMT construction site. The images of the peaceful elders Walter Ritte and Pualani Kanakaole Kanahele being thrown to the ground by armed men quickly became viral, and within a few days, the crowds protecting the volcano went from a few dozen people to several thousands. Despite growing opposition in Hawaiʻi and abroad, the state's Democratic governor, David Ige, initially signed an emergency order granting police more power to clear the way for construction equipment. The state spent a fortune—$11 million— in paying private security to fight the Kiaʻi. This should not be construed as the government's steadfast investment in a scientific project but rather as its clear understanding of the issues at stake, warns Osorio: "This is certainly the biggest threat we pose to the State of Hawaiʻi: we live in abundance in the face of a society that is drowning in scarcity."[69] The Kiaʻi challenge the foundation of petrocapitalist logic and embody the viability of alternative modes of relating to the world. At the time of this writing, construction has been temporary halted, and the Kiaʻi continue to organize to transform this temporary respite into a definitive victory.

The warning that injustice anywhere is a threat to justice everywhere rings particularly true on Mauna Kea because the environmental impact of the TMT would literally trickle down the mountain to contaminate the entire ocean. The telescope would severely impact the island's watershed and water aquifers.[70] This was immediately underscored by cultural practitioners in the movement, who understand water in an Indigenous Pacific perspective as the force that connects all of Oceania. Watersheds, like moʻokūʻauhau (genealogies), give unity to the world. They are the link between mountains and plains, islands and oceans, ʻāina and moana. Protecting the watershed is protecting the integrity and the unity of the entire region. Mauna Kea activists have made clear that their fight for the mountain is a fight for restored unity of the whole archipelago. As Case summarized, "because Mauna Kea is the highest mountain in the world from seafloor, and [because of] ... the integrity and the essence of water in our spirituality, ... we must not allow eighteen stories to be built on the northern plateau of our mountain."[71] The Kiaʻi thus challenge the Isletist dichotomy between islands and oceans and contest the idea that destruction can be contained to specific sites. The chant and hashtag "We are Mauna Kea" echoes the now proverbial declaration made last century by Epeli Hauʻofa, "We are the Ocean," uniting Kānaka Maoli with all the other Pacific people fighting for the protection of water in the spirit of Oceanitude.

Saying #WeAreMaunaKea and "We are the Ocean" suggests alternative ways of relating to places that sustain life. As Kanaka scholar-activist Haunani-Kay Trask notes, "Native Hawaiians have a special relationship to our one hānau or birthsands." Care for one's place, or mālama ʻāina, stems from "two thousand years of practicing a careful husbandry of the land and regarding it as a mother."[72] Saying #WeAreMaunaKea or "We are the Ocean" illustrates an understanding of space through genealogies and relationships, which, while universal, is particularly prominent and vibrant in Pacific discourse.

Thinking about space genealogically allows for a different understanding of one's relationship to the world, reminding us that humans depend on land for literal survival, that humans cannot be separated from the rest of the world, and that humanity must relate to other-than-humans by acknowledging interdependency. The fight on Mauna is also a universal fight against Cartesian modes of thinking. Pacific activists have thus described the issue on Mauna Kea as different ways of *looking* at the world. Tulsi Gabbard, a Samoan American congresswoman, eloquently denounced the issue by pointing out how "it's hypocritical that many TMT proponents speak of their own spiritual quest for knowledge and wisdom, while simultaneously closing their eyes to the spiritual inspiration and significance that Mauna Kea offers, not only to Native Hawaiians, but to humanity at large."[73] The telescope is shortsighted.

The struggle on Mauna Kea can therefore be analyzed as a contemporary instantiation of the competing modes of knowledge that are Cartesianism, Negritude, and Oceanitude. One way to relate to the world is to stare, like astronomists, into space-time thirteen billion years back, to characterize and analyze planets orbiting around distant stars. This is what Aristotle calls "rational-life"; Senghor "reason-eye"; and Tavo "delirious reason."[74] That is the path chosen by the investors of the TMT. Another mode of relating to the world, by contrast, acknowledges the material conditions subtending the production of scientific knowledge. The TMT is the demolition of a sacred mountaintop, the hauling of hundreds of tons of cement atop the volcano, the building of eighteen stories of concrete, the constant thrumming of cars and construction engines, the excretion of sewage and waste directly into the islands' watersheds, and the desecration of sacred lands. This form of knowledge sees beyond the advertisement for pristine technology to view the TMT in its complete materiality. That mode of knowledge is the one adopted by Mauna Kea protectors. It is Tavo's Oceanitude, it is reason-fusion, a mode of reasoning that does not create separations between plants, animals, rocks, and peoples of the land, whose lives are ecologically, historically, and culturally interwoven.

Unsurprisingly, the fight on Mauna Kea has been harshly criticized by proponents of the status quo who claim both the emptiness of the land and the backwardness of the people protecting it. Indeed, both the Mauna and its protectors are routinely described in Isletist terms. The Mauna, explains Indigenous studies scholar Hiʻilei Hobart, has long been portrayed by settlers as an empty space, a terra nullius, like the ocean around it. In the nineteenth century, travelogues described it entirely in the negative, as a place "without humans, spirituality, nation, or even atmosphere."[75] Contemporary astrophysicists mobilize the same rhetoric when describing the Mauna. A dormant volcanic site filled with life, Mauna is portrayed as an "extinct volcano," the dead metaphors suggesting that the mountain, like its people, is also a relic of a once vibrant past. Mauna Kea protectors are similarly portrayed by their detractors in Isletist terms, bracketed in precolonial times. As denounced by protector Bryan Kamaoli Kuwada, "any time Hawaiians—or any other native people, for that matter—come out in force to push for more respect for our culture and language or to protect our places from this kind of destruction, we are dismissed as relics of the past, unable to hack it in the modern world with our antiquated traditions and practices."[76] This discourse is eerily similar to those used by nuclear powers to nuke the Pacific.

The opposition between reason-eye and reason-fusion thus cannot be reduced to an opposition between "traditional" beliefs and "modern" science. As noted by Pua Case:

> We are not anti-science. . . . We are against the building of anything eighteen stories over our watershed, water aquifers, on our sacred mountain. . . . Let's work together to make sure that in the quest of science and knowledge, we are not destroying Native peoples' land basis, life ways and water sources in the process, as if it didn't matter, as if they have a right to it, as if we, as Native people, are supposed to, in the name of science, economy, corporations, and business, supposed to just lay down and allow that to happen.[77]

The fight on Mauna Kea is part of an ongoing struggle to highlight and critically examine the material reality of science's advancement. Where Cartesian thinking has elevated scientific knowledge to a sacred religion to which everything should be sacrificed, Mauna Kea protectors highlight the importance of other sacred beliefs. The fight of the Kia'i participates in the global conversation about the role of science and helps promote visions alternative to reason-eye. Kanaka 'Ōiwi protector Lanakila Mangauil summarizes the scope of this struggle in no uncertain terms: "We are starting to look at the world in a different way. . . . What the generation before has called progress, I call suicide."[78]

Reason-eye is ironically incapable of seeing what surrounds it. It inadvertently warmed the planet and engineered the sixth mass extinction without even realizing it. French philosopher Bruno Latour famously pondered its shortcomings: "How to speak of 'efficiency' to discuss technical systems that did not integrate into their plans the capacity to last for more than a few decades? How to call 'rationalist' a civilizational ideal guilty of such a remarkable forecast error that it forbids parents from leaving an inhabitable world to their children?"[79] In this context, it is not surprising that many in the scientific community appeal to reason-fusion to put an end to the TMT. No fewer than 750 astronomers and astrophysicists around the world signed an open letter calling on the scientific community "to recognize the broader historical context of this conflict, and to denounce the criminalization of the protectors on Mauna Kea."[80] This is not to say that these scientists, astronomers, and physicists do not believe in science. What these scientists and philosophers do oppose, however, is the belief that reason-eye is the *only* mode of relating to the world and that all other considerations should be subordinated to the quest for endlessly growing scientific knowledge.

The fight on Mauna Kea does not only call for an alternative mode of relating to the world; it also offers an alternative language rooted in Indigenous values to mobilize the principles of Oceanitude. Identifying as ʻaipōhaku or rock eaters, Mauna Kea protectors challenge the Cartesian boundaries between the organic and the inorganic. "The term ʻaipōhaku is not used lightly," notes Pacific studies scholar Kahikina de Silva. "The eating of stones is not smooth and easy. . . . Those who do, whose mouths eat rock, consequently speak with the solidity and mana of the pōhaku they have absorbed."[81] Mauna Kea protectors are inspired here by "Kaulana Nā Pua," a song written in 1893 by Eleanor Kekoaohiwaikalani Wright to protest the American theft of the islands. One passage goes:

Ua lawa mākou i ka pōhaku
I ka ʻai kamahaʻo o ka ʻāina

We are satisfied with the rocks
The wonderful food of the ʻāina

Today, young activists turn to this song to find wisdom and strength, argues ethnic studies scholar Aanchal Saraf. An anonymous activist interviewed by Saraf explained: "We'd rather eat rocks. So all those pōhakus (stones) in the road? They say 'fuck your money, we eat rocks, you go home.'"[82]

Wright's song's lyrics have become an ʻōlelo noʻeau, literally a wise saying, usually translated in English as "proverb." Many literary studies scholars consider proverbs to be a form of Pacific literature: often expressed in chant-like forms, they are an important way in which Pacific people have expressed their creativity.[83] ʻŌlelo noʻeau in Hawaiʻi, Jabonkonnan in Aelōñ in Ṃajeḷ, and whakataukī in Aotearoa are thus codified literary forms that are meant to inspire, guide, and instruct in difficult times.[84] The language of the ʻōlelo noʻeau traverses generations to erase the boundary between humans and stones.

Protectors on Mauna Kea insist on the sacred nature of their battle and call on other supporters to remain in kapu aloha. An attitude, a philosophy, and a spiritual space, kapu aloha calls for action while privileging kindness, love, and empathy.[85] Like genealogies and waterways, kapu aloha is a powerful uniting force. "Aloha is not about love, it's about loving," explains philosopher Manulani Aluli Meyer. "It is the frequency in which all connect. . . . Our beloved lands/ocean/waterways *have always loved us*. The love we hold for land thus inspires and extends compassion for others as practiced in the Kapu Aloha."[86]

Therefore, when the believers in reason-eye sent police in riot gear, Mauna Kea protectors responded with nonviolence, solidarity, and chants reminding the long lineage of love of their land. In this way, the struggle on Mauna Kea offers a model for environmental movements worldwide: "If movements are to survive and to be effective," notes Kanaka 'Ōiwi cultural practitioner Luana Palapala Busby-Neff, "they must affirm something instead of protest what should not be done."[87]

By chanting "We are the ocean" and tweeting #WeAreMaunaKea, protectors curtail Cartesian hubris and advocate for a loving relationship with other-than-humans. Privileging the plural pronoun "We" over the singular "I," these calls differ starkly from other contemporary rallying cries in the West, such as #IAmCharlie and #MeToo, which still foreground individualism even as they purport to promote the formation of collective identities. This call for valuing the living together resonates loudly and globally today from the top of Mauna Kea. Oceanitude's politics, poetics, and spirituality are thus shared with a world starved for healing, beauty, and meaning.

Conclusion: Reason-Fusion in the Literature of Oceanitude

I do not want to imply here that Oceanitude is a dogma with solutions to the climate crisis, capitalism overgrowth, and the extinction of experience. The material conditions for environmental chaos and the collapse of the mainstream form of the collective organization of life are already in place. The publication of Tavo's novel will not change this. However, as the current world (dis)order collapses, the philosophy of Oceanitude defined in Tavo's book gestures to what the next world could look like. It echoes customary Indigenous knowledge expressed in creative discourse over generations, and its finds its embodiment in contemporary decolonial struggles throughout Oceania.

It is also worth pointing out that the philosophy of Oceanitude has not been formally theorized before.[88] The lack of translation and diffusion of Pacific literature in French is a major obstacle as well as the prohibitive pricing (at about US$50 for many novels) of many of these works printed in limited numbers. Tavo himself, as I have shown, only uses the word twice: first in a poem by his protagonist; then in the afterword of his novel, seemingly speaking in his own name. I attempted to highlight the main tenants of Oceanitude by interpreting the narrative plot, the poetic tropes, and the references to transgenerational Indigenous values deployed in the text in which the word was invented. I submitted those interpretations to Tavo, who responded that he approved of such a reading. This, however, only calls for further discussion of his seminal concept. I am hopeful that other scholars and activists will feel inspired by Tavo's pan-Pacific text and will use it as one of the many inspiring Pacific philosophical texts to analyze other environmental struggles. After all, the word *Negritude* also first appeared in a then-obscure poem, the *Cahier d'un retour au pays natal* (*Notebook of a Return to My Native Land*), published in 1939 by a then-unknown Martinican writer by the name of Aimé Césaire. And the Negritude movement has transformed the world by providing a philosophical framework of reference for the decolonization of the Black Atlantic. Tavo's Oceanitude might prove to be an impactful concept to address the main challenges of this century.

In the following chapters, we will follow Tavo's injunction to "heed and read" some of the creative writers, orators, and singers of Oceanitude. Each chapter tackles a specific issue presented as an imminent threat in climate science: the threat of mass extinction of biodiversity, the threat of increased deaths and diseases, and the threat of mass migration. Each of these threats has already been experienced by Pacific peoples during the era of nuclear imperialism. Nuclear victims have seen marine life, once the basis of their cultures, turn poisonous and disappear overnight. They have faced increased cancers, sterility, and reproductive issues in the wake of nuclear fallout. And Marshallese, i-Kiribati, and Māʻohi people have had their homes vaporized, erased from the map, and/or made poisonous for hundreds of thousands of years, forcing them into a life of migration. Creative works and poetic performances addressing these issues further incriminate reason-eye. But more importantly, this corpus offers unique insights on how to live on in the face of environmental chaos. It shows how to relate to the world of the living, even as this world is radically changing. By exploring the Pacific's nuclear past, the literature of Oceanitude shows new ways of envisioning the future.

3

ATOMIC ANIMALS

The Hidden Face of the Sixth Mass Extinction

To be a fisher . . . is not to pillage the oceans' depths to fill fridges or export canned food.
It is first and foremost knowing the fish and their habitat. We do not say: "I am going fishing."
We say: "I am going to fish some iihi (red mullet) in this haone (reef rift) at the time of the
oharaa avaè (rising moon)." These precisions are of the utmost importance.
 —HENRI HIRO, quoted in Jean-Marc Tera'ituatini Pambrun,
Henri Hiro, héros polynésien: biographie

Nuked fish and now we have to eat canned tuna to be sure it is nuke-free. Fish are our
lifeblood. We are islands surrounded by sea—and here we are reduced to eating canned fish.
—CATHIE DUNSFORD, *Manawa Toa*

Floating face down
In water that is more muck than crystal—
. . . .
Washed up on some commercialised tropical reef,
Tainted by radiation and foreign words.
—MOMOE MALIETOA VON REICH, "Floating Face Down"

The sixth mass extinction has begun. Scientists warn of a grim future: silent
springs, oceans with more plastic than fish, rain forests replaced with soy fields.
Yet as CHamoru poet Craig Santos Perez suggests in his poem "Th S xth M ss
Ext nct n," life can go on in a world decimated of life:

Th S xth M ss Ext nct n
An m ls surro nded our anc st rs. An m ls wer th ir fo d, cl th s, adv rs
ries, c mp nions, jok s, and th ir g ds … In th s age of m ss ext nct n and
th ind str al zat on of l fe, it is h rd to touch th sk n of th s l ng and de p
c mp n onsh p.[1]

Just as the reader may laboriously decipher the text of the poem and still grasp
the meaning of the original palimpsest, contemporary generations can go on
living in an impoverished world in which two-thirds of wildlife is missing.[2]

Humanity's relationship to marine life manifests this paradox. Since the
beginning of the industrial era, 90 percent of the biomass of large pelagic fish
has disappeared.[3] Oceans have been all but emptied of life. Yet conservation
biologists observe that in communities of fishers, this has seamlessly become
the new normal. Few industrial fishers even realize that their high-tech vessels
only bring back 6 percent of what sailors were able to catch a century ago after
spending the same amount of time at sea.[4] More than half of the ocean's letters are missing, yet humanity still manages to make meaning of the remaining
text, often without being aware that we are only deciphering an impoverished
version of the original palimpsest.

Conservationist efforts have proven woefully ineffective at reversing this
trend, and living organisms continue to suffer and die at a wrongfully rapid pace.
Today, as a cofounder of Greenpeace deplores, there are "more protected areas
but less species; more carbon taxes but greater green gas emission; more green
products but less green spaces."[5] Worse, mass extinctions now occur in chain re-
actions, as the disappearance of a given form of life often deprives other species in
their ecosystem of crucial means of survival.[6] Even within species groups that are
not considered endangered, individual animals and plants still die in hitherto un-
seen numbers. Given the slow rate at which carbon warms the atmosphere and
its very slow decrease over time, scientists have warned that many more other-
than-humans will be lost before the end of the century.[7] Industrial capitalism has
spawned more death than any other human mode of social organization.

In this context, mainstream environmentalists' frequent focus on wilder-
ness preservation seems tragically belated. It fails to address the main questions facing humanity. The issue is no longer simply to find solutions or quick
fixes to the death waves rippling through our planet. The window to ensure
that life's diversity would remain sensibly similar to what it was before industrialization has already passed. Humanity now faces the challenge of mourning
the other-than-humans that petro-fueled industrialization has killed or already
condemned to certain death.

It can be helpful to turn to art to process the feelings of loss and despair triggered by this mass murder of the living. Yet the vast majority of literary works and scholarly critique often fall short of confronting head-on this unparalleled loss. Most of the award-winning literary works addressing mass extinction have taken the form of speculative fiction. From N. K. Jemisin to Ursula Le Guin and Alain Damasio, most contemporary writers in carbon-addicted countries grapple with the massive withdrawal of life by exploring futuristic developments—either dystopian or positopian—to the current impoverishment of the world of the living, which paradoxically tends to minimize the scope of the suffering that already took place. Academic scholarship, on the other hand, tends to focus on preservation over mourning. The definitive reference work in the field, the award-winning monograph by Ursula K. Heise titled *Imagining Extinction: The Cultural Meanings of Endangered Species*, foregrounds heartfelt calls for protection of endangered species and argues that critical scholarship can help preserve biodiversity.[8] While calls to action are of course crucially important, they fail to help process the already shattering loss of two-thirds of the world's wildlife. These works keep their gaze focused on the daunting future. Pacific literature, by contrast, looks for answers in the past.

Indigenous peoples have long had their ecosystems radically reshaped by anthropogenic action. As Potawatomi philosopher Kyle Powys Whyte highlights, "for many Indigenous peoples, the Anthropocene is not experienced as threatening in precisely the same sense because [settler colonialism] forced many of our societies to let go of so many relationships with plants, animals and ecosystems at a wrongfully rapid pace."[9] Many communities have already experienced tragic alienation from plants and other-than-human animals whose existence was central to life in a multispecies society.[10]

In Oceania, this alienation from other-than-humans can be dated back to the era of great migrations, when Pacific navigators hunted some endemic species like the moa to extinction. But attacks on multispecies societies scaled up when Westerners chanced upon Pacific shores, bringing with them invasive viruses, weeds, herds, and extractivist capitalist logics that would assault Indigenous biota.[11] They continued with renewed deadliness during the era of nuclear imperialism, as nuclear bombs violently separated Indigenous people from the coral reefs, fish, birds, plants, and entire islands with which they had developed cultural and spiritual relations over millennia.

For this reason, Pacific narratives have rarely taken the form of speculative fiction.[12] Oceanian stories of the collapse of multispecies societies are postapocalyptic. They mourn extinct multispecies relationships and describe post-traumatic forms of resilience. These stories do not provoke fear or anxiety but upend more productive feelings in their audience, spurring them to action through stirring anger, admiration, or determination. These nuclear postapocalyptic stories shed a new light on the stages of grief awaiting the overindustrialized world. Indigenous peoples are sometimes treated as the last people living in Holocene conditions.[13] The truth, however, is that Indigenous communities were the first to be thrust into the Anthropocene and to develop the tools and language to process this era's lethality.

This chapter explores three postapocalyptic nuclear stories and analyzes how they shed light on the current mass extinction crisis. The first one, "Eden" (1990), is a text by Māʻohi writer Raʻi Chaze. In this short story, Chaze explores how multispecies societies in Māʻohi Nui have been shattered by nuclear imperialism when fish, once the basis of the Māʻohi diet, became toxic overnight. Rather than focusing on wildlife preservation, she presents the mass extinction of fish as both psychologically disturbing and as carrying a moral imperative to act radically—in its etymological sense, as tackling the root of the problem and frontally challenging nuclear imperialism. The second example I turn to is the famous bestseller by Māori writer Witi Ihimaera, *The Whale Rider* (1981). In this novel, Ihimaera puts a (cetacean) face on the abstract concept of population collapse, making vivid how much individual animal pain hides behind abstract statistics about extinction. Drawing on traditional Māori aesthetics such as the koru—a spiral motif in Māori tattoo and oral narrative—Ihimaera asserts the continuity of ancestral relationships between humans and other-than-humans, even in times of nuclear apocalypse. Finally, I turn to the poetry of CHamoru poet Craig Santos Perez to explore how poetry can serve as lisåyo (CHamoru prayer for the dead) to process contemporary alienation from and celebrate the lives of lost other-than-humans. Read together, these three Pacific stories provide complementary narratives of mourning and fighting contemporary estrangement from life.

Mourning Multispecies Societies in Raʻi Chaze's Radioactive Paradise

Raʻi Chaze, also known as Michou Chaze, Rai Chaze, and Rai a Mai, was born in Papeʻete in 1950 to a Paumotu mother and a French father. She grew up in the underprivileged suburbs of the capital, where immigrants from the Tuamotu archipelago had migrated en masse when France started testing its nuclear bombs in the country. When I interviewed her, she underscored that, although she lived a thousand miles away from Moruroa and Fangataufa, the beginning of the nuclear program was a traumatic experience for her: "I witnessed the complete transformation of my society with the arrival of the CEP.

I saw my neighborhood turned upside down. I lived in the Fataua valley; it was a peaceful neighborhood, just with my grandmother's house and ours, and in less than three years it became a slum."[14] After completing her high school degree, Chaze moved to the United States and married an American. "My life was wonderful. We lived in our car; we transformed it so that everything we owned fitted in it. We lived in the university's parking lot and we would go to the beach on the weekends." After eleven years traveling, studying, and working as a photographer, Chaze became homesick and returned to her fenua in the 1980s. There, she met the famous Mā'ohi poet and antinuclear activist Henri Hiro and became his close friend. She joined the first antinuclear protests at his side. She subsequently worked for the Mā'ohi pro-independence party, the Tāvini Huira'atira. This experience, however, discouraged her from getting more involved in politics: "I really longed for independence, and when Oscar Temaru was elected in 2004, I was greatly relieved. I thought it was the end of a system, the beginning of a new era. But then I worked for the government. . . . It was worse than George Orwell's *Animal Farm*."

Chaze began writing when Hiro became sick. He was diagnosed with terminal cancer at only forty years old. His untimely death haunts her first work: "The bomb was a death machine, and we had already seen many people die. . . . Back then, we did not even know what leukemia meant. When I began writing my first book, I was exorcising all this grief." Her debut work was a collection of short stories that came out in 1990 under the bilingual title *Vai: La Rivière au ciel sans nuages* [*Water: The River under the Cloudless Sky*]. It was the first work of fiction published in French by a Mā'ohi writer, and it frontally denounced nuclear imperialism in the language of the colonizer. Publishing this work required great courage, as it was a time when France was still detonating nuclear bombs in Moruroa and Fangataufa, when Mā'ohi Nui was under the semidictatorial control of pronuclear Tahitian president Gaston Flosse: "In my book, I changed the names, and I transformed the stories, because I was afraid of them. You know, people like Henri and I were dragged through the mud." *Vai*, however, is far from an obscurely coded manuscript: "I did not want my book to be too abstract. I wanted everyone to be able to read me." *Vai* remains untranslated in English and has not been reedited since 2013 in French. This is unfortunate, since this short volume reads as a searing political pamphlet written in powerful poetic prose.

Vai explores at length what Henri Hiro has called Mā'ohi peoples' "harmonious relationship with nature."[15] Scholars have long debated whether claiming that Indigenous people live in harmony with nature perpetuates the colonial myth of the "noble savages," but as Mā'ohi Pacific studies scholar Vehia Jennifer Wheeler points out, there is a difference between romanticizing Indigenous peoples' relationship to the environment and acknowledging that there are many ways to live in the world and with the world.[16] Living in harmony with nature, as Tonga-Fijian anthropologist Epeli Hau'ofa defines it, is the act of perpetuating "balance and continuity in the ecological relationship" through "traditional technologies [that] link natural cycles and cycles of human activity."[17] This harmonious relation did not mean that Pacific people lived "in permanent osmosis with their birds, their plants, their fish, but rather that they lived in cultural and spiritual relationship with them," seconds French anthropologist Bruno Saura.[18] It is this cultural and spiritual relationship that was shattered by nuclear imperialism.

In the short story "Eden," Chaze retraces the last hours of a fisherman on an irradiated Pacific atoll. He dies from having eaten contaminated fish. In this piece, Chaze explores how an enduring, total ecological relationship between humans and fish was affected by the bomb. Her demonstration hinges upon a play with biblical symbolism. "Eden," from the title, plays with the myth of the paradise-like Pacific Island. The protagonist is described as "un pêcheur," an ironic syllepsis since in French, a *pêcheur* written with a circumflex accent means a fisherman, but it is also the homophone of a *pécheur*, with an acute accent, which means a sinner. The scene thus begins:

> *Je connais quelqu'un qui, pour un petit poisson, s'est frotté au cocotier;*
> *Il est mort.*
> *Dans l'île de la nuit, où le feu ronge le corail, il n'a pas pu résister au petit poisson*
> *défendu de l'Eden corallien.*[19]

> I know someone who, for a little fish, rubbed himself against the
>   coconut tree;
> He is dead.
> In the island of the night, where the fire gnaws on the coral, he was not
>   able to resist the little forbidden fish of the coral Eden.

The tree of knowledge is here replaced with a coconut tree, and the fisherman/sinner commits Adam's sin of tasting forbidden food. This tropical paradise, however, is openly dystopian, as immediately indicated by the monosyllabic sentence "He is dead."

Ra'i Chaze makes it clear that this paradise has been irradiated. She describes it as an island "where the fire gnaws on the coral," a choice of words evoking atomic heat. And in her radioactive paradise, eating forbidden food has even more dire consequences than in the original Garden of Eden:

Pauvre pêcheur, la tête lui tourne.

Il a froid. Il a chaud.

Les lèvres qui ont embrassé ont mal. Il veut les gratter. Elles démangent. Il les
gratte. Il se gratte aussi les bras, les jambes et le dos. Les ongles usés ne peuvent
plus gratter. Gratter pour soulager. Gratter toute la nuit.

Au lever du jour, il n'en peut plus, il est contre un cocotier. Il se frotte et se gratte
dans tous les sens contre le tronc de l'arbre qui ne peut l'abriter des rayons du
soleil qui lui donnent froid.

Pauvre pêcheur, se gratte jusqu'à ce que la nuit ait pitié de lui et l'emporte hors
d'Eden.[20]

Poor fisherman, he is dizzy.

He is cold. He is hot.

The lips that kissed are in pain. He wants to scratch them. They itch.
He scratches them. He also scratches arms, legs, back. The worn-out
nails cannot scratch anymore. Scratch to relieve. Scratch all night.

At sunrise, he cannot stand it any longer, he is against a coconut tree. He
rubs himself and scratches himself all over the trunk of the tree that
cannot protect him against the beams of the sun that make him cold.

Poor fisherman, scratches himself until the night takes pity on him and
takes him out of Eden.

Oxymora structure this text. The fisherman is simultaneously "cold" and "hot,"
and "the beams of the sun" "make him cold." His environment is further described counterintuitively, mixing water and fire: "The fire will get at you, little
fish! . . . The fire that makes waves and tsunamis."[21] Everything is turned upside
down, as salvation paradoxically consists of being expelled from paradise. This
conflation of oxymora alludes to the oxymoronic nature of nuclear imperialism. Indeed, the fisherman dies for having eaten the animal that has been the
basis of his life and his culture, turning his reality upside down.

Fish are particularly susceptible to radioactive contamination due to the ongoing concentration of radioisotopes such as iron-55 in the marine food chain.[22]
Many Mā'ohi artists have denounced the contamination of fish in their work,
playing with the near homophony in French between *poisson* (fish) and *poison*
(poison) and underscoring the similarities in the outlines of aquatic fauna and
nuclear missiles (see figure 3.1). But Chaze eludes discussing the specifics of fish
irradiation in her story. Reflecting the subversive nature of nuclear imperialism, the narrative merges the problem of radioactive contamination with an issue occurring in the wake of nuclear testing: the epidemics of ciguatera.

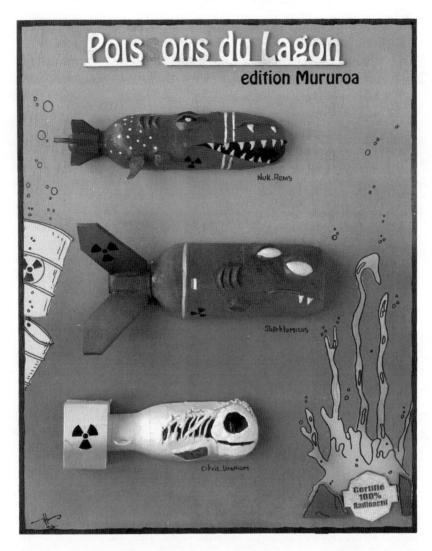

FIGURE 3.1. THS!, *Atomic Fish*, circa 2016.

Ciguatera, also known as *la gratte* (the scratch), is an ailment caused by the development of an alga that poisons fish. In Mā'ohi Nui, not only were many fish killed by nuclear detonations and poisoned by radioactive fallout. There has also been an upsurge of ciguatera after the beginning of the tests, and the quantity of fish carrying the disease in the country is only matched in Aelōñ in Ṃajeḷ (the Marshall Islands). As Swedish antinuclear activist Bengt Danielsson highlights, "ciguatera had become a serious problem in French Polynesia only after the nuclear tests had begun. . . . The annual number of reported cases—between 700 and 800—was higher than in all the remaining islands south of the equator taken together."[23] Even more revealing is the geographical distribution of the disease within Polynesia, where ciguatera develops "mostly in islands where the French army deposited garbage and cleaned its warships."[24] Before the tests, ciguatera was present in the islands but was only affecting a few species of fish and had never been lethal.[25] The inhabitants of Mangareva Mā (Gambier archipelago) testifying in Mililani Ganivet and Marie-Hélène Villierme's podcast *Nu/Clear Stories* also insist that ciguatera used to be confined to a few locations well known by the population but that, after the tests, the fish became contaminated everywhere in their archipelago.[26]

Although there have been upsurges of ciguatera in the archipelagoes where Western nations tested their bombs, the link between radioactivity and ciguatera has not been scientifically demonstrated.[27] Ciguatera is therefore rarely under the spotlight as a primary plight of the nuclear tests. It has, however, impacted the daily lives of communities that rely heavily on fishing and accelerated the spread of waged economy as former fishing people became more and more dependent on imported food. Not only did it poison numerous fishers and their families; it also forced many rural Mā'ohi people to migrate to Tahiti's capital since their major food source had been drained.[28] As Mā'ohi essayist Lucas Paeamara recalls in his autobiography, the entire archipelago of Mangereva contracted the disease in 1969. According to him, Mangareva's economic switch from fishing to pearl farming and dependency on imported food can be directly traced back to the ciguatera epidemics.[29] Chaze's story therefore politicizes a topic that has been deemed apolitical by mainstream media and politicians.

In "Eden," the godly interdiction to eat the forbidden fruit reflects CEP officials' injunction not to eat fish in contaminated atolls. Most of the Mā'ohi workers employed in Moruroa, however, report having breached this prohibition, making it a matter of cultural pride: "We are human beings, we are Mā'ohi, we have to eat fish," anonymously reports a contaminated worker.[30] Civilians in contaminated islands could not stand the contamination of their fish either: "We are Polynesian people; we cannot eat chicken after chicken. After a while, you return to the sea."[31] Mā'ohi activists have looked back on this widespread contamination of fish and interpreted it as a moral issue: as summarized in the first independent study of CEP workers commissioned by the Mā'ohi Protestant Church, it was agreed that "turning the most important part of the Mā'ohi diet into poison (either through radioactive contamination or indirectly through ciguatera) has always been regarded by many workers as the ultimate offense."[32] By drawing from the tropes of the Gospel, Ra'i Chaze emphasizes the moral dimension of this issue. She describes a radioactive paradise with all the elements of the Garden of Eden, implying that the detonation of the bomb is akin to an original sin.

The only element missing in Chaze's radioactive Garden of Eden is Eve. According to Chaze, the myth of the beautiful, carefree, and sexually available Tahitian woman has been very harmful for Polynesian women: "The myth of the vahine is dramatic. We have a bazillion beauty pageants on the island. They have just started a Miss Teenager beauty pageant! Unfortunately, for many young girls growing up here, it becomes an ideal, a purpose.... Despite us, despite herself, the Tahitian woman wants to resemble the image described by writers of exotic literature."[33]

The mythical vahine, however, is not completely absent from "Eden." She is simply reduced to a metonymy. Indeed, the fisherman dies for having eaten contaminated food described through a compelling running metaphor:

> *Les bénitiers des îles de la nuit sont différents. Lorsque tu écartes les lèvres, il y a tout au fond un petit point rose. Derrière les lèvres, tout est rose.*
>
> ....
>
> *Ta langue glissera sur le petit point rose pour mieux goûter au bénitier. Tu en redemanderas et tu en redemanderas.*
>
> ....
>
> *Le pêcheur regarde le pahua s'épanouir et doucement s'ouvrir devant lui.... Et, de ses mains nues et gourmandes, il écarte les lèvres, les dévore et ne s'arrête plus.*[34]

> The clams of the islands of the night are different. When you push the lips apart, there is a little pink dot at the very bottom. Behind the lips, everything is pink.
>
> ....
>
> Your tongue will move smoothly on the little pink dot to taste it better. You will ask for more and you will ask for more.
>
> ....
>
> The fisherman looks at the pahua [tridacna] blossoming and slowly opening in front of him.... And, with his naked and eager hand, he pushes the lips and endlessly devours them.

Here, the myth of the sexually available Pacific woman is brought to its dystopian paroxysm: the vahine has been reduced to a radioactive vagina. Ultimately, the sun does not rise to disclose the man in a woman's embrace as in every Isletist novel but rather shines on an irradiated corpse that has scratched itself to death. Far from sustaining life, seashells and female genitalia have both become "a soaked contamination" (*"une contamination imbibée"*).[35] In "Eden," harmonious relationships between humans and other-than-humans are replaced by radioactive pornography.

The final scene of the story focuses on the manu ura (red bird) that has overseen the death of the fisherman. It almost reads as hallucinatory:

> *Manu ura*
> *Arrête un instant de voler. . . . Ton collier de pierres est trop lourd. Il fond au*
>   *soleil, dans le feu, il coule.*
> *Faites fondre vos pierres au soleil.*
> *Arrête un instant de voler. Et pense.*
> *La joie s'en va en faisant la pirouette.*
> *La démence est là.*[36]

> Manu ura.
> Suspend your flight. . . . Your rock necklace is too heavy. It melts in the
>   sun, in the fire, it sinks.
> Melt your stones under the sun.
> Suspend your flight. And think.
> Joy leaves, pirouetting.
> Insanity is here.

This scene is open to many interpretations. It seems to toy with a couple of Isletist tropes: the leis, the birds flying in the sunset. In the Pacific, foreigners have long been welcomed with a flower necklace. Leis have become a prominent symbol of the much-marketed Polynesian hospitality in the local tourist industry. However, this custom has taken on a different meaning under nuclear imperialism, when visitors bring nuclear bombs with them. In this context, it seems meaningful that Chaze's leis are not made of flowers but of stones—heavily symbolizing the weight of nuclear imperialism. The sun that melts stones can be interpreted as the radioactive sun of a nuclear bomb. When the narrator exclaims: "Melt *your* stones under the sun" (my emphasis), it can be read as an address to French readers: drop your bomb above your *own* land; you are not welcome here. Chaze echoes here, in a highly poetic language, one of the main slogans of the antinuclear movement in the Pacific: "if it's safe, test it in Paris, dump it in Tokyo, store it in Washington—but keep my Pacific nuclear-free." Melt your own stones under the nuclear sun.

Chaze bemoans Māʻohi's alienation from biodiversity because fish, once the basis of Tahitian culture, have become poisonous. But fish is more than a

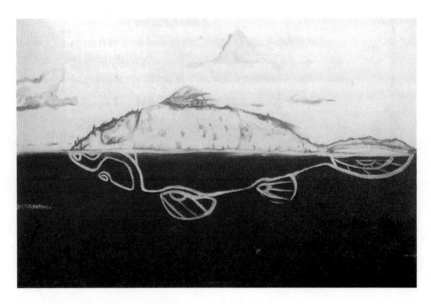

FIGURE 3.2. Vaianu Hunter, *Tahiti*, 2012.

source of food in Māʼohi culture. According to oral history, Tahiti itself is a fish. As John M. Orsmond and Teuira Henry recall in *Ancient Tahiti*, Orohena, the narrow ridge that culminates above Tahiti Nui, is the fish's dorsal fin, and Tahiti Iti, the peninsula, is its head. Tahiti the fish broke off from Havaiʼi, separating the original island into Raʼiātea and Tahaʼa. But the fish was unstable, and men wanted to cut its sinews to stabilize it. Tafaʼi-upoʼo-tu sought Te-pa-huru-nui-ma-te-vai-tau, a sacred axe that belonged to Tinorua, god of the Ocean. He then succeeded to cut Tahiti's tendons where all the island's warriors had failed. There is now an isthmus, Taravao, where his axe fell. The district of Taiarapu, the-dirty-sea, was thus named for the murkiness that followed Tafaʼi's blow.[37] This oral history continues to inform contemporary artists' vision of Tahiti, as demonstrated by Māʼohi painter Vaianu Hunter's rendition of the island as the emerged parts of a giant fish in his 2012 painting *Tahiti* (see figure 3.2).

In an essay published in 2000, "Pasts to Remember," Epeli Hauʻofa highlighted that destroying Oceanians' environment (and the other-than-humans who inhabit it) constitutes a sacrilegious act "of the same order of enormity as the complete destruction of all of a nation's libraries, archives, museums, monuments, historic buildings, and all its books and other such documents."[38] In Oceania, landscapes and seascapes are not only a traditional source of livelihood but also the source of a people's identity. Oceanian oral history is inscribed in specific sites, whether on land or at sea. Looking at the landscape, seascape, and the other-than-humans who inhabit it is reading Oceania's history and keeping the past alive. Landscapes, seascapes, and all the creatures of Moana Nui a Hiva, the Mā'ohi name of the Pacific Ocean, thus have cultural meaning well beyond their equivalent in many other societies. By writing a story about the collapse of a balanced relationship between humans and fish, Chaze goes beyond bemoaning the loss of a source of food. She underscores nuclear imperialism's impact on Mā'ohi identity. Yet her description of this new estrangement from biodiversity does not read as a eulogy. It is an attack on Western colonizers, a pamphlet telling the French to go back home and to keep the Pacific nuclear free.

Chaze's story carries lessons for times of climate collapse. The problem with mass extinction, like other environmental issues, is often reduced in mainstream narratives to a problem about lack of information.[39] Most nonprofit campaigns to "save wildlife" and preserve biodiversity are organized around the information deficit model, assuming that if only people knew, they would act differently: they would boycott palm oil, become vegetarians, pressure politicians to ban pesticides, et cetera. Well-intentioned nongovernmental organizations (NGOs) thus mobilize the imagery of sad pandas, starving polar bears, and other charismatic megafauna to palliate this alleged lack of information. But the problem is not that people don't know about the issue. In our age of mass communication and unprecedented connectedness, biodiversity collapse deniers are a tiny minority, even in the bastion of denialism that is the United States. The problem is that people deny what they know. This is a phenomenon that South African sociologist Stanley Cohen has identified as implicatory denial: according to him, "what is minimized is not information, but the psychological, political or moral implications that conventionally follow."[40] Issues such as biodiversity collapse can be recognized "but are not seen as psychologically disturbing or as carrying a moral imperative to act."[41]

Stories such as Chaze's help shift the dialogue from an issue about information to an issue of collective implicatory denial. "Eden" presents the collapse of multispecies society as both psychologically disturbing and carrying a moral imperative to act. It is psychologically disturbing because by the end of the story, the narrator has become insane. They have abandoned the flowery language of the incipit, and speak in monosyllabic, uncoordinated sentences ("Joy leaves, pirouetting"[42]). It is carrying out a moral imperative to act because it implies that the French must go home and that nuclear imperialism must end ("Melt your stone under the sun"[43]). "Eden" thus changes the emotional tone of discussions surrounding biodiversity collapse. Chaze substitutes small fish and clam for charismatic megafauna and replaces pity with outright anger. This is precisely the emotional shift needed to face mass extinction.

The murder of two-thirds of wildlife is not simply sad. It is madness. In Ra'i Chaze's words: "Insanity is here." This folly is poorly represented by the panda emblazoned on the World Wildlife Fund's logo. It is much better conveyed by the contaminated fisherman in "Eden," who has suffered so much in his destroyed environment that he ends up welcoming his own death. How to process this knowledge and these emotions, how to mobilize against this madness: that is the question that I now turn to.

Processing Mass Extinction with Witi Ihimaera

Witi Ihimaera, like Ra'i Chaze, is a trailblazer in Oceanian literature. Born in Tūranga-nui-a-Kiwa (Gisborne) and college educated in Te Whanganui-a-Tara (Wellington), he is accredited as the first Māori novelist. His biography and accomplishments are well known—novelist, poet, diplomat, literary scholar, and emeritus professor—and his contributions to Aotearoa's cultural landscape have been rewarded by several prizes. He also received the New Zealand Order of Merit for services to literature.

The Whale Rider, his fifth novel, was published in 1987. It instantly became a best seller and was later adapted as an award-winning motion picture. The narrator of the novel, Rawiri, tells the story of his iwi (tribe) in Whangara, focusing on two main characters: a little girl, Kahu; and her grandfather, Koro Apirana. Koro is the leader of the iwi. His main worry in life is to identify his successor. Obsessed by his desire to find the next leader amid the young boys in the village, Koro does not realize that his own granddaughter is gifted. Just like the founder of the tribe and the first whale rider, Kahutia te Rangi, after whom she was named, the young Kahu can communicate with whales.

The novel takes an unexpected turn when a great herd of whale shores on Wainui beach, not far from Whangara. The scene is tragic: "The whales kept dying. As each death occurred, [people] would weep and clasp one another. . . . All the time the animals were uttering cries of distress or alarm, like lost children."[44] By evening, the two hundred whales, spread along three kilometers of coastline, have all suffocated to death. But the worst is yet to come. The following night, the most ancient whale of the herd, the original bull once ridden by Kahutia te Rangi, comes crashing on the beach of Whangara. This epic scene can only be conveyed by being quoted at length:

Leviathan. Climbing through the depths. Crashing through the skin of the sea. . . . Together, we had all watched the whale with the sacred sign plunging through the sea towards us. The attending herd had fallen back, sending long undulating calls to the unheeding bull whale, which had propelled itself forcefully onto the beach. We had felt the tremor of its landing. As we watched, fearfully, we saw the bull whale heaving itself by muscle contraction even further up the sand. Then, sighing, it had rolled onto its right side and prepared itself for death.[45]

Many readers will be familiar with the major motion picture directed by Niki Caro, *Whale Rider* (2002), awarded with numerous international prizes upon its release. Caro, however, deleted all references to nuclear testing in her interpretation of Ihimaera's book. She chose to focus on issues of more importance to her as a Pākehā (white) woman, primarily foregrounding Ihimaera's denunciation of Māori sexism. This is, however, an impoverished interpretation of Ihimaera's novel, which has deep roots in Oceanian antinuclearism. Indeed, the herd of whales shores on the beach in Aotearoa because of nuclear imperialism in Moruroa. At the beginning of the novel, an omniscient narrator reveals that, while the animals were still in the Tuamotu archipelago, they crossed a nuclear bomb detonated in the Tuamotu. "A flash of bright light had scalded the sea, and giant tidal soundwaves had exerted so much pressure that internal ear canals had bled."[46] Seeing some of his kin dying and "afraid of the genetic effects of the undersea radiation on the remaining herd," the bull whale hurried his herd to escape. "For the first time in all the years of his leadership, the ancient whale deviated from his usual primeval route."[47]

In an interview, Ihimaera said that the idea for writing *The Whale Rider* came to him during a stay in New York City. His daughters' complaints about girls' helplessness in movies and the reports that a whale had been spotted in the Hudson gave the spark to his imagination.[48] Yet despite being conceived abroad, *The Whale Rider* is deeply anchored in Oceania and resonates particularly with the Pacific antinuclear movement. Oceanians began protesting nuclear tests as early as the 1950s, when Mā'ohi leader Pouvanaa a Oopa began an antinuclear petition in the Tuamotu archipelago heading the Stockholm Peace Appeal.[49] Ri-Majel activists launched their own petitions against American nuclear testing in the Marshall Islands after the 1954 Bravo test, and Samoa similarly turned to the United Nations Trusteeship Council to protest British nuclear tests.[50] In 1970, the Pacific antinuclear movement amplified when an international coalition of Indigenous activists formed the committee Against Tests on Moruroa (ATOM). Realizing that their vision included much more than an end to the tests on Moruroa, these activists from the Pacific Theological College, the University of the South Pacific, and the Fiji Young Women's Christian Association, backed by the Pacific Conference of Churches, subsequently renamed their movement the Nuclear Free and Independent Pacific (NFIP). After their first conference in Fiji in 1975, NFIP activists held numerous other international conferences and gatherings across the Pacific. Their relentless efforts at collective diplomacy culminated in 1985 with the Rarotonga Treaty for a South Pacific Nuclear-Free Zone, supplemented by declarations by the governments of Vanuatu, Palau, and Aotearoa / New Zealand that their lands and waters would be nuclear weapons free.

For the peoples of Aotearoa, 1985 marked a turning point. That year, just sixteen months before Ihimaera published *The Whale Rider*, French spies attacked the *Rainbow Warrior*, a Greenpeace antinuclear ship anchored in the harbor in Tāmaki (Auckland). The crew of the *Rainbow Warrior* was preparing to head to Moruroa to protest France's nuclear testing, after having helped relocate ri-Roñḷap (Rongelapese people) from their contaminated atoll. The two French spies, dispatched by the Direction Générale de la Sécurité Extérieure (DGSE; the French equivalent of the CIA), were instructed to sink the ship when the crew was ashore, but a photographer, Fernando Pereira, had stayed on board and was killed during the bombing. This occurrence of state-sponsored terrorism gave new visibility to antinuclear organizations, providing the Nuclear Free and Independent Pacific movement with an unprecedented international platform.

Ihimaera's novel draws on this intergenerational Pacific resistance to nuclear imperialism. As scholars such as Epeli Hau'ofa, Nic Maclellan, and Talei Luscia Mangioni have pointed out, the struggle for a nuclear-free and independent Oceania was co-constitutive of the (re)emergence of a collective sense of regional identity.[51] By linking Moruroa, whales, and Māori iwis, Ihimaera relocates Pacific antinuclearism in its original decolonial framework.

Nuclear tests' devastating impact aboveground is well known and documented by veterans and workers from the test sites. After atmospheric tests, islands were covered with rotten shells and dead fish.[52] Anare Bakale, Fijian engineer stationed in Kiribati, recalls that when fallout reached the vegetation, plants "withered as if they had been watered with boiling water. Nothing was left. Everything from the stem to the leaves disappeared."[53] As Fijian veteran Paul Ah Poy explains, "the poor seabirds flew into what was left of the trees or the side of buildings, as most were blind."[54] British military officials further report that some birds would have "their feathers burnt off, to the extent that they could not fly."[55] But the impact of French so-called underground military tests is far less documented and much harder to describe. Some military reports indicate that underwater explosions destroyed marine life: "For the majority of the fish killed, it is found that the viscera is expelled through the natural orifices of the animal (oral and anal prolapse) and that the eyes bulge out."[56] But for the most part, the impacts of underwater explosions remain underdocumented.

France is the only country in the world that tested nuclear bombs in the basaltic base of coral reefs. France switched to testing underground in Moruroa and Fangataufa in 1975, following international outcry against its atmospheric tests. Given that the French military had already conducted several underground tests in Algeria before resorting back to atmospheric tests in Tahiti, historians have speculated whether France's military had initially deemed the atolls' basalt base unfit for underground testing.[57] Evidently, the fragile structure of Moruroa and Fangataufa could not contain the destructive power of thermonuclear bombs. Yet for three decades, the French government maintained that underground tests had not led to radioactive leakage and that radioactivity remained trapped in the rock. Independent studies conducted after the end of the tests report that tritium in Moruroa's lagoon is ten times higher than in the open ocean, as a result of leakage from cavities created by the bombs. Scientists also noted that the reef is fractured in a dozen locations and that the fissures could lead to further radioactive leaks.[58] Paris eventually recognized that not all underground tests had been safe, although the government only acknowledged 26 "uncontained" tests out of the 140 explosions that took place between 1975 and 1996. By contrast, veterans report having witnessed gas coming up and having to remove contaminated material after every single underground test.[59] As summarized by Māʻohi politician Francis Ariioehau Sanford, "even if France now monitors the situation, what can we do if the atoll cracks and spills more radioactivity in the ocean? . . . The financial compensations received by the territory will not change anything and will not bring back to life my family members who died of leukemia."[60]

Ihimaera tackles the recounting of this submerged tragedy by drawing from traditional Pacific storytelling. The omniscient narrator recounts the event by adopting the perspective of the ancient whale:

Suddenly a flash of bright light had scalded the sea. . . . He had led them away in front of the lethal tide that he knew would come. On that pellmell, headlong, and mindless escape, he had noticed more cracks on the ocean floor, hairline fractures indicating serious damage below the crust of the earth. . . . Suddenly, the sea trench seemed to pulsate and crackle with a lightswarm of luminescence. Sparkling like a galaxy was a net of radioactive death. . . . The herd thundered through the sea.[61]

The tests do not appear to be underground so much as underwater, blurring the boundaries between earth, water, air, and fire. The bomb seems to annihilate simultaneously the ocean and the land: "scalding the sea" and "cracking . . . the crust of the earth." The thundering herd, "hovering in the goldened sea like regal airships," seems aerial; while water, "crackl[ing] with a lightswarm of luminescence" and "sparkling like a galaxy," recalls combusting stars.[62] As Hauʻofa famously noted, in Pacific oral traditions, the universe "comprised not only land surfaces but the surrounding ocean as far as [Oceanians] could traverse and exploit it, the underworld with its fire-controlling and earth-shaking denizens, and the heavens above with their hierarchies of powerful gods and named stars and constellations that people could count on to guide their ways across the seas."[63] In other words, Pacific storytelling has historically been prone to merging the four elements, creating an immense three-dimensional universe expanding far beyond the shores of the islands.

The French government maintained that the rock in which the bombs were exploded was sealed off from the seas and the skies. Earth, water, air, and fire were supposed to be strictly compartmentalized. By narrating the explosion of an underground nuclear bomb with maritime and celestial metaphors, Ihimaera implicitly challenges the lies of French officials. Simultaneously, he reasserts that Pacific environments cannot be hermetically compartmentalized between land and sea. The nuclear bombs of Moruroa seeped into the Pacific Ocean, and their impact ripples from Antarctica, where the whales took refuge, to Aotearoa, where they eventually shore themselves.

The final scenes of the book shed new light on contemporary mass extinctions. I will outline the denouement briefly to emphasize its philosophical implications. On the first night of the tragedy, two hundred whales shore themselves and agonize to death on Wainui beach, in front of national news reporters and scores of helpless volunteers. On the following night, the herd of the ancient bull whale shores in Whangara. Kahutia Te Rangi's descendants are the only witnesses to the scene. The twenty-seven male members of the iwi set out to pull the ancient whale back to the sea, under the leadership of Koro Apirana. According to the patriarch, the whales want to die because men have severed the relationship that united the world's creatures:

Once, . . . beasts and Gods lived in close communion with one another. . . . But then, man assumed a cloak of arrogance and set himself up above the Gods. . . . In the passing of Time he divided the world into that half he could believe in and that half he could not believe in. The real and the unreal. The natural and the supernatural. The present and the past. The scientific and the fantastic. He put a barrier between both worlds and everything on his side was called rational and everything on the other side was called irrational.[64]

Koru's critique takes on a particular meaning in the era of nuclear imperialism. As French philosopher Jean Rostand points out, nuclear bombs destroyed this aforementioned division between the rational and the irrational. With the first atomic explosion, science, the alleged bastion of rationality, gave birth to the most irrational nightmare conceivable. For the first time, "it was not a simple technical application that pure scientists could pretend to ignore and whose consequences they were not required to bear: the newest and most subtle physics were at play, the noblest scientific minds had, lucidly, voluntarily, and nominatively been involved in the crime."[65]

In light of this failure of the new hierarchization of values, Koro Apirana thus asserts the sacredness of their task: "The whale is a sign," he warns. "If it lives, we live. . . . Not only its salvation but ours is waiting out there."[66] When the whale eschews their efforts to push it back to the sea, Koro pronounces their own eulogy: "Our ancestor wants to die. . . . There is no place for it here in this world. The people who commanded it are no longer here. When it dies, we die. I die."[67]

Yet despite his dire prophecy, Koro is already proven wrong by the subtle symbolism at play in the scene. The whale facing the iwi stands out not only for its size but also because it has "a swirling tattoo imprinted on the forehead."[68] In the Pacific, explains Samoan writer Albert Wendt, tattoos are not just beautiful decorations; they connect their wearer to "everything else that is the people, the aiga, the village, the community, the environment, the atua, the cosmos" to indicate tattoo wearers' place in the world in terms of relationships.[69] In Aotearoa specifically, tattoos on the forehead indicate the rank of the wearer, while the spiral motif, or koru, represents the cyclical and genealogical nature of time—its circular shape evoking perpetual movement but its inward coil emphasizing the importance of the point of origin.[70] This koru on the forehead of the whale thus presents it as the embodiment of genealogical continuity between the Māori and their ancestors. As Kanaka literary scholar 'Umi Perkins argues, the presence of this motif of the koru in many Pacific works suggests that "despite the ravages of colonization/occupation, Indigenous peoples have maintained a consistent worldview," since this image shows the connection between past, present, and future.[71] This tattoo is the literal embodiment of the limitations of linear time as described by Koro Apirana—the time that puts barriers between the present and the past, the scientific and the fantastic, the natural and the supernatural. Even as the situation seems hopeless, the spiral of the koru thus reads as a powerful symbol of hope.

But spiral time is not the same as cyclical time. American literary scholar Elizabeth DeLoughrey notes in her analysis of temporalities in Māori literature that, while cyclical time repeats itself unchangingly, spiral time "signifies *repetition with a difference*."[72] In this case, change must come because Koro Apirana himself is not the one who can communicate with the whale. It is his granddaughter, Kahu, who carries the gift. Yet she is banned from engaging with the whale, as she was from receiving a traditional chief's education, because of her gender. She carries the same name as the first whale rider, Kahutia te Rangi; but history repeats itself with a difference: the Kahu swimming toward the whale is no longer a man "shining with splendour" like the mythic hero but just a "little head bobbing up and down in the waves, . . . in [a] white dress and white ribboned pigtails."[73] Without anyone noticing, Kahu had entered the water and introduced herself to the bull whale: "Ko Kahutia Te Rangi ahau."[74] Like her ancestor, she orders it to swim back to the sea. While everyone watches in awe, she rides the sacred whale, followed by his herd, into the depths of the ocean. Her encounter with the whale does not symbolize a return to the past but rather signals the vitality of Māori values rooted in the past and adapted to the present.

Three days later, Kahu is found unconscious, floating in a nest of kelp. She wakes up in the arms of a loving and repenting Koro Apirana, recognizing the error of his way for neglecting her because of her gender and praising her as the next leader of the tribe. While her grandmother comically bickers with him, threatening to divorce him for the thousandth time, Kahu hears the whales singing in the distance: "let everyone live, and let the partnership between land and sea, whales and all humankind, also remain."[75] This happy ending to the tale of the whale rider does not mean that Koro's worries were unfounded. The iwi is linked to whales since the first whale rider was given the powers to communicate with them. The people of Whangara are connected to whales through the whakapapa (Māori system of genealogy), which links peoples to gods, heroes, and other-than-humans. This connection is acknowledged by the omniscient narrator, underscoring that Kahutia Te Rangi, "the golden rider," was "long part of [the whale's] whakapapa and legend."[76] This whakapapa unfolds like a koru, each part connecting to the next all the way to the center of the spiral.

Like whales today, Māori people have long been described by foreigners as on the brink of extinction. This widely spread belief is even inscribed in Aotearoa's landscape, in the form of the Maungakiekie obelisk, a morbid monument to the still-living Indigenous peoples of Aotearoa, towering over the country's capital. While many Māori people died during colonial wars and imported epidemics, the Tangata Whenua survived and endured the onslaughts of settler colonialism. Read in light of this heroic history, the whales' future rings with new implications. Māori people's survival of settler colonialism and the whales' survival of nuclear imperialism reads as a sign of hope, today, in times of carbon imperialism. Historical estimates of the Māori apocalyptical encounter with colonizers suggest that the population went from hundreds of thousands to just forty-two thousand by the end of the nineteenth century. Yet Māori culture was passed down by generations of survivors and is today a thriving force guiding all of Aotearoa.[77] In Ihimaera's epilogue, two hundred whales suffocate to death, yet the future of the herd is ensured by the surviving sixty members of the ancient bull's companions. Even in the face of upcoming population collapse and mass disappearance of sea life, a few whales remain, enough to keep the songs alive, "broadcasting their orchestral affirmation to the universe."[78] Ihimaera's happy ending reads as a happy beginning.

Th S xth M ss Ext nct n in Craig Santos Perez's Poetry

These stories of past societal collapse inform the way contemporary mass extinction is portrayed in contemporary Pacific literature. No one proves this better than Craig Santos Perez, whose poetry introduces this chapter. Craig Santos Perez was born in Mongmong-Toto-Maite, Guåhan (Guam), an island occupied by the American military since World War II. Perez moved with his family to California when he was a teenager. As he writes in his collection of poetry titled *From Unincorporated Territory [Guma']*, they were following the trajectory of many fellow Guamanians: "1980: 30,000 Chamorros live off-island *removed from*. 1990: 50,000 Chamorros live off-island *removed from*. 2000: 60,000 Chamorros live off-island *removed from*. 2010: more of [us] live off-island than on-island."[79] He studied comparative ethnic studies at the University of California, Berkeley, and is now a leading scholar in Pacific studies, teaching at the University of Hawai'i at Mānoa. He has published several books of poetry awarded with numerous literary prizes, written an award-winning monograph on CHamoru literature, and reshaped the publishing world in Oceania by editing several Pacific literature anthologies. He is also a dedicated advisor of younger scholars, and his mentoring is shaping the future of Pacific studies. In 2010, the Guam Legislature passed a resolution recognizing and commending him "as an accomplished poet who has been a phenomenal ambassador for our island, eloquently conveying through his words, the beauty and love that is the Chamorro culture."[80]

Craig Santos Perez's poetry treats marine-life extinction as inevitable. In doing so, he is in line with the contemporary scientific consensus, which predicts that 99 percent of coral reefs will disappear by the end of the century and that the pelagic fish population will collapse.[81] He is also inspired and perhaps hardened by the long history of alienation from other-than-humans undergone by CHamoru people under American militarism. He therefore approaches the topic of mass extinction as a parody of white people's fears of apocalypse. Consider, for example, his poem "One fish, Two fish, Plastics, Dead fish," subtitled "recycling Dr. Seuss." Here are the last stanzas of the poem, emblematic of Perez's spin on the famous nursery rhyme:

O me! O my! What schools
Of bloated fish float by!

Here are fish that used to spawn, but now the water is too warm

Some are predators and some are prey,
Who will survive? I can't say.

. . . .

Two fish, One fish, Filet-o-Fish, No fish.[82]

Perez's poetics of "recycling" convey a philosophical message. Recycling is the process of rebuilding useful items from discarded trash. In his book, Perez manages to re-create poetry out of old bits of twentieth-century verse. It is precisely this capacity to re-create harmony out of ruins that characterizes the postapocalypse aesthetic. Drawing from Pacific peoples' experiences under nuclear imperialism, he describes current fish population collapse in a childish tone. Ironically remarking "how climate change is finally making white people uncomfortable," Perez pokes fun here at white panic at the apparent novelty of mass extinction.[83] Western culture is, in fact, in its infancy; it has not learned to mourn the other-than-humans that are dying at its own hands.

But Dr. Seuss is not the only poetic form that Perez is "recycling" in this poem. One can also discern, in between the lines, an echo of the CHamoru prayer for the dead, the lisåyo.[84] After a death in Guåhan, the deceased's loved ones gather for novenas—two series of prayers lasting nine days each.[85] The novenas are organized around meals and recitations of the rosary for the dead—lisåyo in CHamoru.[86] The first rosary, lisåyon linahyan (group rosary), consists of public prayers, while the second, lisåyon guma' (home rosary), is reserved for private prayers by close friends and family members. While the lisåyo is suffused with imported Spanish themes and forms, anthropologists have shown how the practice continues to draw from traditional CHamoru orature such as kåntan chamorrita, a form of singing in which performers dialogue and respond to each other, usually through improvised lyrics.[87]

In his poem "One fish, Two fish, Plastics, Dead fish," Perez offers a traditional CHamoru mourning ritual to the marine life destroyed by nuclear imperialism and carbon imperialism. The first nine verses evoke dangers threatening marine life globally: overfishing ("some fish are sold for sashimi"), farm fishing ("Farmed fish, . . . frankensfish"), and the collapse of the fish population:

From the Pacific to the Atlantic,
from the Indian to the Arctic,
from here to there,
dead zones are everywhere![88]

This is a lisåyon linahyan, a public prayer delivered in a parodic tone for all the oceans affected. The next nine verses, however, explore issues that are closer to home, in the radioactive waters of the Pacific. Focusing on the cancers that affect marine life, the poem goes on:

This one has a little radiation.
This one has a little mercury.

. . . .

Say! Look at its tumors! One, two, three . . .
How many tumors do *you* see?

This is a lisåyon guma', a private prayer for the marine life lost to the violence of nuclear imperialism that has affected Oceania more than any other ocean. More than a "recycling" of Dr. Seuss, Perez's poetry thus suggests that despite "growing up . . . read[ing] books by American authors" in a nuclearized colony, the traditional CHamoru attachment to other-than-human life forms still survives and is paid homage to through "recycled" traditional CHamoru aesthetics.[89]

Like many other Pacific people, CHamoru people have already experienced alienation from marine wildlife because of nuclear imperialism and ongoing military occupation. US military strength has been shifting in recent decades to nonsovereign spaces because of increasing resistance in sovereign sites like the Philippines and Okinawa.[90] Guahån has thus been chosen by the American military as an important site in the United States' Pacific Pivot strategy.

The proposed military buildup in Guahån would make the island population grow from fourteen thousand to forty thousand within a decade.[91] Craig Santos Perez's poetry regularly returns to the double bind of mass emigration of Guamanians to the United States and the mass immigration of American military to Guam. Interestingly, Perez has chosen to use CHamoru people's alienation from native wildlife as a symbol of a growing alienation from their home. In the series of poems titled "*ginen* the Micronesian kingfisher *[i sihek]*," Perez explores at length the plight of the eponymous native bird, threatened by the bird-eating snakes introduced by foreigners:

> [our] nightmare : no
> birdsong—
> the jungle was riven emptied
> of *[i sihek]* bright blue green turquoise red gold
> feathers—everywhere : brown
> tree snakes avian
> silence—
>
> the snakes entered
> without words when [we] saw them it was too late—
> they were at [our] doors sliding along
> the passages of *[i sihek]*
> empire—[92]

Perez's bracketing of CHamoru words has long fascinated literary critics, who have interpreted these typographic choices as a way to suggest a conflictual relationship between colonial and Indigenous languages by isolating or imprisoning Chamorro words and highlighting them as separate from the English text.[93] In this context, Perez's bracketing of the CHamoru name for the Micronesian kingfisher, *sihek*, visually evokes a bird's cage. This typography reflects American colonizers' approach to biodiversity preservation efforts. As Perez explains at the end of his collection, "the Guam Bird Rescue Project (initiated in 1984) captured 29 Micronesian kingfishers and transferred them to US zoos for captive breeding. The current population descends from these birds. The last wild birds were seen on Guahan in 1988."[94] In his poem, the fate of the birds is tied to that of the CHamoru people:

> the zookeepers came—
> called it *species survival plan*—captured *[i sihek]* and transferred
> the last
> twenty-nine micronesian kingfishers

to zoos for captive breeding *[1988]*—they repeated *[i sihek]*
and repeated :

"if it weren't for us
your birds   *[i sihek]*
would be gone
forever"

what does not change / [95]

Western environmentalists parrot here the most appalling settler colonial discourses. Indeed, America's official rhetoric is that CHamoru people were saved
from Japanese occupation by the US Army. The liberators/colonizers also believed
that if it weren't for them, CHamoru people would be worse off under Japanese
rule. They put CHamoru people in a new cage, an unincorporated territory, which
reflects the legislator's perception of "its inhabitants as neither capable of self-
government nor civilized enough for U.S citizenship."[96] Western environmentalists inadvertently reproduce this settler narrative, perpetuating an ideological
stance that American literary scholar Aimee Banhg has called "settler environmentalism."[97] The conservationists' efforts in Guam literally ended up setting
nature apart, taking the Micronesian kingfishers thousands of miles away from
Micronesia. To put it in the words of Canadian ecocritic Cheryl Lousley: "the
environmentalist preoccupation with resolving...society's apparent alienation
from nature (for which the solution is reconnection to nature) contributes to the
obfuscation of our environmental predicament. It sets 'nature' apart as a static,
unchanging entity at a time when neoliberal economics support even greater in-
tensification and a more extensive reach in the transformation of living beings and
the physical world, all the way from genomes to planetary climate."[98] In this context, the bracketing of the bird's native name *[i sihek]* throughout the poem reads
not only as a volatile relationship between Indigenous and colonial languages but
also as a desperate cry for help. Perez's throbbing repetition of their Indigenous
name between brackets gives onomastic resonance to this new alienation.

Further quoting press release articles from American zoos and turning them
into poetic prose, Perez continues:

the saint louis zoo has hatched 41 chicks since 1985. recent
modifications to bird house habitats have now made it
possible to house *[i sihek]* a pair of these rare birds for visitors

what does not change / is the will

to see[99]

Again, Perez subtly links native birds and CHamoru people: like zoo's visitors, tourists flock to Guåhån, eager to bask in the myth of the Paradise Island and the myth of the Welcoming Native artificially created by the tourist industrial complex.

Perez eventually clarifies explicitly the link between bird depopulation and CHamoru migration by inserting references to the zoo's cages in his descriptions of the CHamoru diaspora. Zookeepers describe the ideal enclosure for a breeding pair of kingfishers as a cage of "ten feet by eight feet with a height of ten feet containment—this cage . . . can be either solid material wire mesh or glass."[100] This description becomes a leitmotiv as the poet retraces his own deculturation at the hands of the American education system:

> I attended a university in California with scholarships, loans *a cage can be either solid material wire mesh or*, work-study, and my parents' help.
>
> . . . .
>
> even though I speak English like an American, even though I am a US citizen *this cage can be either solid material wire mesh or.*[101]

This recurring leitmotiv highlights mass extinction and forced migration not as a recent development but as a cyclical apocalypse, returning to Guåhån in regular patterns since the sixteenth century. Thus, the brown snakes that killed the sihek after arriving on US navy ships are not only a metaphor for but also a continuation of militarism. The cyclical nature of the problem is embodied by the poem's structure, as the different parts of *"ginen* the Micronesian kingfisher *[i sihek]"* are strewn several pages apart in a regular pattern throughout the volume.

Perez's poetry tends to include both endangered native species and endangered Indigenous languages. In an interview about his 2020 book *Habitat Threshold*, he explained that his desire to revitalize the CHamoru language parallels his desire to restore habitats threated by colonialism.[102] In this perspective, the title of this series of poems reads as a denunciation of Western conservation movements, be they zoologic or linguistic. *"Ginen* the Micronesian kingfisher *[i sihek]"* translates as "Since the Micronesian kingfisher." This temporal framing, followed by the Indigenous name of the bird within brackets, suggests that the bird's problems began with Western naturalists' taxonomy endeavors, which compartmentalize zoologic and linguistic diversity into neatly defined Western categories. As soon as the sihek was renamed the Micronesian kingfisher, the bird was put in a cage and the CHamoru language became endangered.

By contrast, Perez's poetry follows an opposite tendency. Rather than neatly translating and referencing CHamoru language in glossaries and paraphrases, the CHamoru words keep erupting across the page, refusing to be contained to footnotes and indexes. Perez's attitude toward language diversity is thus at the antipodes of the zookeepers and American scientists' agenda described in his poem. Rather than labeling, translating, and compartmentalizing Indigeneity in order to "preserve" it, Perez strategically sows Indigenous words throughout the book, telling another story through their appearance and reappearance spatially and sonically on the page. Indeed, the CHamoru bracketed words [i sihek] in his poetry tend to resurface after alliterations in "s," evoking the hissing of brown snakes that drove the bird to near extinction:

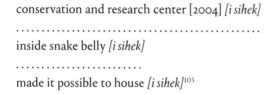

conservation and research center [2004] *[i sihek]*

....

inside snake belly *[i sihek]*

....

made it possible to house *[i sihek]*[103]

In other words, the CHamoru language is presented not as a relic of the past to be preserved through artificial means but rather as a vital force that survived the settler/reptilian invasion (the screen mesh and the snake belly) and continues to share its musicality with the world at the end of each alliterative verse. Perez's choice to include the definite article "i" before the name of the bird *[i sihek]* is also very telling. It makes the three syllables of the bracketed CHamoru words *[i sihek]* rhythmically echo the song of the sihek, which comes forth in a series of three high-pitch whistles. Perez's creative use of Indigenous words is a sonic testament to the resilience and vitality of the CHamoru language and the sihek alike, even after the destructive shock of militarism and settler environmentalism. The very structure of the poem thus intimates what Indigenous-inspired conservation efforts could look like. Away from mesh cages and taxonomic indexes, life can flourish.

Indigenous art is too often misconstrued as elegies of past lifestyles to preserve rather than as artistic practices for a better future. Perez's poetry questions the dominant narrative about climate change to anchor it in longer histories of colonization, and to provincialize whiteness in the climate movement. What Perez offers, in other words, is a new framework for mass extinction narratives. His stories about sihek surviving in zoos and fish surviving in radioactive waters are postapocalyptic stories, not science-fiction speculations, in which wildlife is harmed but still here. Rather than wildlife conservation, Perez's poetry focuses on resilience and the power of regeneration.

Conclusion: In Defense of Mourning and Beyond

Pacific literature puts alienation from other-than-humans to the forefront of its narratives because this violent dismantling of multispecies societies has been Pacific peoples' lived reality for centuries. As Potawatomi philosopher Kyle Powys Whyte aptly underscores, climate change is but the latest stage of "colonialism as a form of human expansion that continues to inflict anthropogenic environmental change on Indigenous peoples."[104] Yet all the stories analyzed here do more than mourning the other-than-humans lost to the nuclear apocalypse. Ra'i Chaze turns her eulogy to Tahitian fish into an angry pamphlet against ongoing French colonialism. Witi Ihimaera moves from the tragic narrative of a nuclear-triggered massive whale die-off to the joyful retelling of the vitality and adaptability of Māori multispecies relationships. And Craig Santos Perez's writing functions as a refuge to give extinct animals the traditional mourning ritual they deserve while keeping the melody of their songs vibrant and alive in Indigenous poetry. These three writers/performers have all grieved for loss, but they have also found the strength to move beyond mourning and continue sharing the stories of mutual relationships between people and the sea that have sustained both for millennia. This literature guides its audience through the stages of grief: pain and anger with Chaze, reconstruction and working through with Ihimaera, acceptance with Perez.

Sharing stories of regeneration and renewal after the apocalypse is crucial to begin challenging the violence of nuclear imperialism and carbon imperialism. "We are deluged by information regarding our destruction of the world and hear almost nothing about how to nurture it. It is no surprise then that environmental becomes synonymous with dire predictions and powerless feelings," warns Potawatomi biologist Robin Wall Kimmerer. "The participatory role of people in the well-being of the land has been lost, our reciprocal relations reduced to a KEEP OUT sign."[105] Focusing on the last stages of grief, anger, reconstruction, and acceptance may inspire both writers/orators and their readers/ listeners to "once again enter into positive, creative relationship with the more-than-human world."[106] Stories are one of the most essential and most readily available ways to (re)connect to the land and (re)nurture the relationships between humans and the rest of the living.

4

~

THE H-BOMB AND HUMOR

The Arts of Laughing at Death and Diseases

Colonization keeps laughing.
Global warming is grinning
at all your grief.
—TERISA TINEI SIAGATONU, "Atlas"

I don't mind admitting I'm scared . . .
it's times like this you need a sense of humour.
—ALBERT WENDT, *Black Rainbow*

This capacity for laughter, for grabbing moments of joy in the midst of suffering,
is one of the most attractive things about our islands.
—EPELI HAU'OFA, interviewed by Subramani, "A Promise of Renewal"

The coronavirus epidemic was a brutal reminder for the overdeveloped world
that climate collapse is inseparable from deadly diseases. Since the great industrial acceleration after World War II, new viruses and microbes have appeared
or reappeared all over the globe.[1] Climate collapse and carbon-fueled capitalism are bound to create more and more epidemics as habitat loss, deforestation, and a changing climate bring wild animals and disease carriers in closer
contact with humans.[2] Beyond epidemics, global human health is threatened
by a number of new predicaments. Pesticides, GMOs, microplastics, endocrine

disruptors, toxic spills, chemical leaks, and nuclear accidents dramatically increase cancer rates. Air pollution, water contamination, and the degradation of food quality are leading to the recrudescence of scores of diseases, some of which were thought to have been eradicated. Last but not least, psychological distress of the exploited classes under late capitalism provokes an increase in drug overdoses, alcohol poisoning, and suicides. Life expectancy in overindustrialized countries has begun to decline, while quality of life in the Global South is not increasing.

Despite new scientific treatments, these diseases are likely to have increasingly dire consequences. A growing number of infections are becoming harder to medicate as the drugs used to treat them become less effective, leading the World Health Organization to declare that "antibiotic resistance is one of the biggest threats to global health, food security, and development today."[3] Deforestation and displacement of Indigenous communities is leading to the irreparable loss of both medicinal plants and other-than-human animals as well as eradicating the knowledge of how to include them in the global pharmacopeia.[4] Furthermore, in the increasingly intricate, hyperspecialized, and interconnected economic system, epidemics can spread globally in a very short amount of time, while the death or confinement of a small percentage of the workforce due to epidemics can stall vital sectors of the economy and endanger large swaths of the population.[5] Epidemics can lead to famines, bankruptcy, and a number of non-virus-induced deaths. In short, the world is at risk of experiencing wider spread, longer, and deadlier diseases in the next century.

Oceanians have long known what it is like to live in a world that has become poisonous. In Aelōñ in Ṃajeḷ (the Marshall Islands), Kiribati, and Māʻohi Nui (French-occupied Polynesia), many people have developed nuclear cancers such as leukemia, thyroid tumors, brain tumors, skin diseases, eye cataracts, and chronic cardiovascular and respiratory diseases.[6] Not only are the rates of thyroid cancer and acute myeloid leukemia the highest in the world in Pacific nuclear colonies; these cancers also occur in people at unexpectedly young ages.[7] Nuclear health issues are transgenerational, as people exposed to radioactive fallout have had sterility issues and molar pregnancies and have given birth to children with cancers and congenital disabilities, and to stillborn babies.[8] And nuclear-induced health issues go beyond radiation-induced diseases. As Australian physician Tilman A. Ruff underscores, health hazards also include chemical contaminations linked to the broader nuclear infrastructure, ciguatera epidemics, and "the social impact of disempowerment; victimization; abuse of basic human rights; disruption of traditional communities, ways of life and means of sustenance; displacement; justified concern about unpredictable long term health impact extending to future generations; and concern about transmitting genetic mutations to one's children, [which] can all have profound and long-term direct and indirect physical and mental health consequences."[9]

Nuclear testing continues to impact Pacific people's health to this day. Nuclear programs have produced radioactive waste that will contaminate ocean life for hundreds of thousands of years. The rate of birth defects is unlikely to decrease in the near future.[10] Additionally, climate change will intensify the consequences of radioactive pollution. As sea levels rise, nuclear waste stored in low-lying atolls will begin to spread even more quickly into the environment. The concrete shafts in Moruroa and the Runit Dome on Pikinni (Bikini) Island will erode long before the plutonium they cover reaches its half-life.[11] France's series of underground tests in the basaltic core of Moruroa and Fangataufa have led to a uniquely dangerous situation by creating the conditions for a reef collapse, which would spread highly radioactive material in the ocean. It is difficult to obtain reliable data on the situation since all information on the (in)stability of the atolls comes from the French government, but we do know that the first geomechanical movements on the atolls were registered as early as the mid-1970s. Furthermore, we know that between 2015 and 2018, the French Department of Defense spent more than 100 million euros to build Telsite 2, a set of installations on Moruroa "monitoring the risk of reef collapse."[12] Tureia, an island located just seventy miles away from Moruroa, is most vulnerable to the tidal wave that would be created by such a reef collapse, although the spread of plutonium into the ocean would affect all life in a much larger radius. The French government, while aware of this hazard and closely monitoring seismic activity in the atoll, has no plans to reinforce the reef. While the Department of Defense asserts that this risk of collapse is less and less likely, it is difficult to understand why France would spend more than 100 million euros to monitor a structurally stable atoll.[13] Nuclear imperialism did not end with the last test. Its effects will continue to be felt for millennia.

Yet Oceanian writer-activists and artists have organized around radiation-induced health issues to imagine a different world, and they often turn to humor to address the health impact of nuclear imperialism. "The antinuclear movement has a chronic humor deficiency," warn the founders of the International Campaign to Abolish Nuclear Weapons (ICAN).[14] This is not entirely surprising: as American scholar-activist Ray Acheson remarks, it is "absolutely unfunny" that nuclearized nations are killing everything and everyone else with militarism.[15] But sheer horror in the face of this deadliness is only one possible coping mechanism. The Pacific antinuclear corpus presents many other alternatives, including the possibility of laughing in the face of nuclear collapse.

In this chapter, I turn to the works of Hawaiian, Māʻohi, and Māori artists Bobby Holcomb, André Marere, Cronos, THS!, Alexandre Moeava Ata, and Albert Wendt. In their creative pieces, death and diseases are explored through the prism of parody, irony, and caricature. I argue that these writers and artists creatively mobilize the trope of nuclear morbidity, not only to critique imperialism but also to deride their oppressors and to process the pain of environmental collapse through dark humor. These works go beyond a justified critique of oppression; they also suggest new strategies to make communities relate to each other through humor in times of death and diseases. Drawing from traditional modes of comical storytelling such as Ariʻoi comical theater in Tahiti and fale aitu comedy sketches in Samoa, these paintings and texts open an alternative space for dialogue around the trauma of imperialism and imagine alternative solidarities in times of climate collapse.

Nukes and Nudes: Ariʻoi Humor in Atomic Art

Antinuclear artists' prime target of satire is the Isletist myth of the sexually available South Seas woman. For example, the posters designed for the Nuclear Free and Independent Pacific (NFIP) often mobilize the image of the irradiated Pacific woman, playing with the Isletist cliché of the South Seas beauty to attack nuclear imperialism. The use of parody and caricature is particularly prevalent in Tahitian visual art, uniting painters from the early days of the antinuclear movement and contemporary graffiti artists.

It all started with the iconic work of Bobby Holcomb. A multimedia artist of Black, Portuguese, and Kanaka ʻŌiwi origins, Bobby Holcomb, who goes by Bobby, migrated from Hawaiʻi to Tahiti in 1976. Rising to fame for his talents as a singer and his role in the Māʻohi cultural revitalization movement, Bobby was also a visual artist who experimented with a variety of mediums. His paintings focus on extolling Māʻohi traditions and glorifying the precolonial Tahitian pantheon, but he also produced at least three arresting antinuclear drawings. The first one, an untitled pencil drawing, represents a crew of Māʻohi people on a canoe paddling over a nuclear cloud, the reversal of sky and water ominously suggesting the scope of nuclear contamination. The second one, a colorful painting titled *Taureʻareʻa maʻohi, taureʻareʻa api*, features a young Māʻohi man sporting consumerist items with a nuclear cloud in the background, denouncing the financialization of the Tahitian economy in the wake of the CEP. And

TE TUPAPA'AU ATOMI

NUCLEAR FREE PACIFIC

NOBODY WANTS AN ATOMIC PARADISE

FIGURE 4.1. Bobby Holcomb, *Te Tupapa'au Atomi*, circa 1980s.

the last one, *Te Tupapa'au Atomi*, would become the face of the Pacific antinuclear movement (see figure 4.1).

In this last drawing, Holcomb uses the trope of the sexually available vahine (Tahitian women) to turn it into a nightmare. The artwork focuses on the disembodied portrait of a vahine modeled after a friend, the Tahitian antinuclear activist Denise Valentin.[16] Bobby entrusted this drawing to her when she left Tahiti to attend a Nuclear Free and Independent Pacific conference. There, the drawing was selected to become the cover of *Greenpeace* magazine and was printed as part of several posters pinned in Tahiti's various antinuclear associations' offices.[17]

In this piece, completed in the 1980s, Bobby subverts Isletist tropes to evoke nuclear morbidity. The woman's face on the right is mirrored by a symmetrical skull on the left, and the tipanie flower on one of her ears is mirrored by another shaped like an atom. While the flesh-and-blood part of her face appears stern and avoids the gaze of the observer, the skull half stares directly into the viewer's eye, its skeletal smile extending over the whole bony face. The fact that the poster is written primarily in English suggests that it is intended for a foreign audience. Centering on an exoticized woman, the poster uses the trope of the typical Tahitian postcard, which, as American anthropologist Miriam Kahn has documented, commonly features scantily clad Tahitian women with long black hair and tropical flowers.[18] Yet here, nuclear colonizers are the butt of the joke. Paradise is radioactive. Where foreigners expected to find sexually available exotic women ready to fall in their arms, they are now faced with a skeleton's laughter. The mythical vahine escapes their gaze, glancing to the side. Only the radioactive corpse looks at them straight in the eyes, welcoming them with a smile, hence the caption of the drawing: "nobody wants an atomic paradise"—not even the foreigners responsible for the nightmare of militourism.

Portraying a vahine as a smiling skull is clearly intended as a parody of French institutional discourse at the time. The myth of the sexually available vahine was one of the reasons why France decided to set its nuclear testing center in Māʻohi Nui. A former military official recalls that Tahiti was favored over the Kerguelen Islands in the South of the Indian Ocean because the latter would be less "seducing" to the French military.[19] The military brochures issued by the CEP insisted heavily on the attractiveness of the vahine to motivate its new conscripts, multiplying pictures of lascivious Tahitian women on tropical beaches without featuring a single Tahitian man in its pages.[20] When seven thousand male members of the French military disembarked on the streets of Papeʻete, a small colonial town of twenty-one thousand people, they all wanted to meet the mythical South Seas beauties who had been lauded to them.

This soon led to tensions with Tahitian men, and nightly brawls became a fixture of Papeʻete's nightlife. While Tahitians complained that there were too many military personnel in the streets, the French authorities saw the problem differently. For them, there were not enough women in the streets! French governor Aimé Grimald thus decided to revoke the antiprostitution laws in place on the island since 1946 and to open brothels in the port of Papeʻete. The bordellos were to be housed in special ships offshore and reserved exclusively for the military.[21] This project was halted by the unprecedented mobilization of Tahitian high schoolers, who took to the press and the radio to declare: "We do not accept that our sisters or our future wives supply this flesh trade."[22] While the floating brothel project never saw the light of day, the French military continued to rely on militourism and the myth of the sexually available vahine to lure French recruits and eclipse its military destruction. In this context, Bobby's poster reads as a parody of the CEP's glossy promotional brochures. The CEP promised sexually available women to everyone, but this art piece reminds that nuclear imperialism only brings death and diseases.

The title of Holcomb's poster, *Te Tupapa'au Atomi (sic)*, loosely translates as "The Atomic Specter." In Mā'ohi cosmogonic stories, the tupapa'u are the wandering spirits of the dead who manifest themselves at night. They can be benevolent or malevolent and are generally feared. Belief in tupapa'u was dismissed as superstition by European missionaries, but they remained prominent in Mā'ohi spirituality. With the arrival of the CEP and its westernization of Tahitian culture, however, tupapa'u were further derided by colonizers, and some Tahitians repudiated the belief. This evolution was recorded in 1979 in a famous antinuclear poem by Charles Teriiteanuanua Manu-Tahi:

Ua haere mai te ratere e ua hohora ia oe.
To oe moana e to oe tahatai, ua î i te ino.
I roto i te mau motu, ua vavahihia te mau marae.
Tae noàtu i te mau tupapau ua mahau anaè.[23]

The stranger came and robbed you.
Your lagoon and ocean are polluted.
On the islands, the marae are destroyed.
Even the tupapa'u have fled away.

Bobby's painting echoes Manu-Tahi's poem, but instead of adopting the latter's tragic tone, he opts for a different tonality. While Manu-Tahi addresses Mā'ohi readers to deplore that nuclear pollution had driven the tupapa'u away, Bobby tells his public that the tupapa'u have not disappeared. They may have been hiding for a while, but they were brought back to life by nuclear fallout. They now haunt what Westerners had constructed as a flawless paradise. Representing Mā'ohi nuclear victims as laughing tupapa'u is therefore an act of subversive empowerment. It is a form of political satire that targets official French discourse and perverts it into a grotesque and morbid farce.

Much has been written about the subversive power of parody and satire. However, using antinuclear satire in French-occupied Polynesia has a unique political scope given the history of humor in the region. Bobby's antinuclear visual art brought back to life a secular Tahitian tradition: the art of political satire practiced from the sixteenth to the nineteenth century by the religious society known as the Ari'oi. Simultaneously religious figures, dancers, and comedians, the Ari'oi were a highly regarded group of artists that rose to prominence in the sixteenth century. For the next two hundred years, the Ari'oi traveled the archipelagoes of eastern Polynesia every year. They were welcomed by ari'i (kings) and were feasted to the point that many islands faced food shortages for weeks after the Ari'oi's canoes departed. During their visit, they would dance, sing, eat, honor the gods—and poke fun at the political figures whose land they visited. As Mā'ohi literary scholar Goenda Turiano-Reea highlights, political satire used to be an institutionalized practice, conducted at regular intervals throughout eastern Polynesia by the voyaging Ari'oi: "Using comedy, political and social satire, parody, and pantomimes, they made people laugh in ceremonial rituals codified by religious practices."[24] This institutionalized humor served as a cathartic opportunity to challenge powerful ari'i and helped maintain cultural order through codified outbursts of comical disorder.

The Ari'oi horrified the first European settlers by their sexual practices and by their tradition of infanticide. The Ari'oi society was banned, and missionaries did not record the elaborate art of political satire in which the Ari'oi excelled. As a result, notes Turiano-Reea, "Tahitian people only inherited in writing what Europeans considered serious."[25] Banned from the public sphere, political satire retreated to the private sphere and survived primarily in popular Tahitian songs performed at family feasts. The ensuing lack of institutionalized humor, concludes Turiano-Reea, "is the characteristic of a muzzled society that lost its critical outlook when it lost its freedoms."[26]

Responding to nuclear imperialism with public humor revives the tradition of political satire inherited from the Ari'oi. It shows that in the 1980s, Mā'ohi society had entered a new artistic period, one in which public art could once again serve to challenge powers in place and restore order through satirical disorder. This revival of traditional comic artforms, however, was riskier in Bobby's times than in the sixteenth century. While the Ari'oi had free license to lampoon the ari'i and tahu'a (kings and priests), France, on the other hand, closely surveilled antinuclear activists and did not hesitate to exile vocal antinuclear opponents.[27] As an American citizen, Bobby Holcomb was particularly worried about having his visa denied by French authorities. For this reason, he refrained from signing any of his antinuclear paintings. As his friends Bruno Saura and Dorothy Levy report, on some occasions Holcomb would sign his political artwork with the pseudonym Teuru, in reference to the breadfruit (te 'uru), a symbol of life and vitality in Mā'ohi Nui.[28]

With this famous poster, Holcomb set an artistic trend that continues to this day. For the past four decades, Mā'ohi artists have parodied the Isletist

Pacific postcard to denounce that nuclear imperialism only brings death and diseases to Pacific people. Consider, for example, the painting titled *After Gauguin* by antinuclear activist André Marere, created in 1986. This piece parodies a famous 1899 painting by Paul Gauguin titled *Two Tahitian Women* (see figure 4.2). The French painting represents two anonymous Marquesan women from Hiva Oa, evoking what Gauguin called the Tahitian Eve: "very subtle, very knowing in her naïveté," and "capable of walking around naked without shame."[29] Offering a platter of fruits and flowers, the two figures stand statuesquely still, offering their stripped bodies to the male gaze of the painter. Given that what many Westerners know of French-occupied Polynesia comes exclusively from Gauguin's paintings, the canvas remains harmful to this day. Such depictions "establish us in an immutable immobile identity reduce us to silence to absence leave us without voice without consistency . . . A soundless people," denounces Chantal T. Spitz.[30]

André Marere parodied Gauguin's iconic painting by replacing the "Tahitian Eve" with a Māʻohi woman wearing a gas mask and carrying not fruits but a radioactive bomb on a platter (see figure 4.3). She remains overly sexualized, but her denuded breasts now stand out somewhat incongruously on each side of the nuclear mushroom. Her gaze, hidden behind the shield of her gas mask, now evades the concupiscent viewer. The second woman, on her end, no longer holds flowers but is instead grasping bank notes. This is a subtle denunciation of the nuclear money that France gave the Tahitian government in an unofficial exchange for its nuclear testing program—a gesture frequently decried by Māʻohi antinuclear activists as the prostitution of the islands.

By foregrounding bare breasts, phallic-looking mushroom clouds, and references to prostitution, Marere's work inscribes itself in continuity with the Ariʻoi theater's frequent focus on sexual banter and inuendo. Indeed, the very few written records of Ariʻoi theater that were preserved all mention that Ariʻoi comedy heavily references breasts and genitals. Consider, for example, the performance titled *Maititi Haere Mai*, performed in 1774 in Raʻiātea in front of Captain Cook's crew and reconstructed through available early records by literary scholar Diana Looser.[31] This Ariʻoi performance features star-crossed lovers having sex without the vahine's father's approval, a comical birth scene performed by a man pretending to be in labor "with a great many wrigglings and twistings of the body," and a clowning scene in which the actor runs after the newborn child "squeezing his breasts between his fingers and dabbing them across the youngsters Chaps."[32] This focus on sexualized humor in ritual clowning is not innocuous. As Pacific studies scholar Vilsoni Hereniko underscores, it evokes the importance of reproduction by simulating it: it is "not just recreation, it [is] re-creation."[33] Marere's

FIGURE 4.2. Paul Gauguin, *Two Tahitian Women*, 1899.

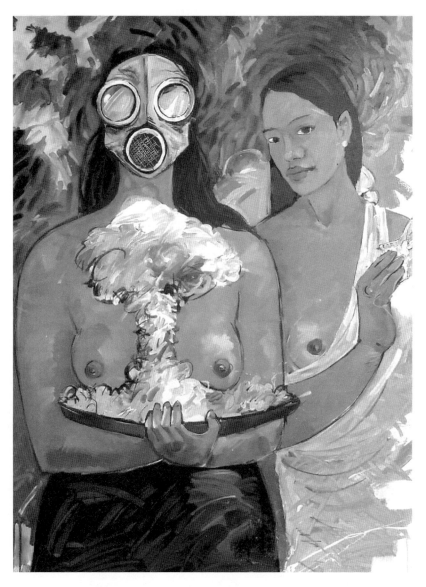

FIGURE 4.3. André Marere, *After Gauguin*, 1986.

piece is not just a caricature of Gauguin; it is a creative moment reaffirming the regenerative power of traditional Pacific humor.

Marere's painting is so powerful that it was chosen in 2016 by the nuclear survivors association Moruroa e Tātou as the illustration for the commemoration of the fiftieth anniversary of the beginning of French nuclear tests. The painting became ubiquitous and could be seen on posters on the walls of Pape'ete and all over social media. However, Marere initially refused to sign his painting at a time when antinuclear activism was still severely surveilled and censored. He only recently added his signature at the bottom of the canvas. The painting is now on display, with the name of its creator, at the headquarters of the antinuclear and pro-independence radio station Radio Tefana.[34]

While rooted in the precolonial traditions of the Ari'oi, contemporary public satire has adapted its techniques to fit new definitions of public art. In an increasingly financialized society, artists are often required to sell their work to make a living, at prices that make their work unaffordable for the working class and the unemployed. Such artworks, navigating from private galleries to personal collections, may not qualify as public, accessible, and readily available art. However, I would argue that the newest generation of antinuclear painters, by rooting their inspiration in street art, still try to remain true to the Ari'oi tradition of public satire.

Consider, for example, works by the up-and-coming Mā'ohi painter Cronos. Originally a graffiti artist (he was one of the five Tahitians selected in 2014 to participate in Tahiti's first graffiti festival, Ono'u), Cronos turned to antinuclear painting to commemorate the fiftieth anniversary of Moruroa's desecration. The inspiration for his parody was the famous photographs of Adolphe Sylvain, best known for his pre-CEP black-and-white photographs of Tahitian model Jeanine Tehani Vidal (see figure 4.4).[35] Sylvain's pictures of a barebreasted and sarong-girded island beauty posing on tropical beaches became iconic throughout the island and beyond. Sold as postcards and calendars, featured on ashtrays and lighters, they contributed greatly to spread the myth of the sexually available vahine.

Tackling this iconic image, Cronos flips it on its head in a 2016 painting titled *French Apocalypse Now*. The painting reproduces an inversely symmetrical image of the vahine's famous silhouette, in stencil style (see figure 4.5). In the background is a looming nuclear cloud rising against an enormous rising red sun. The parody becomes flagrant as Cronos includes a small red "censored" box above the woman's nipples, while the red of the nuclear detonation spreads freely across the canvas. This is once again in keeping with Ari'oi theater traditional themes, with its focus on sexualized body parts.[36] Yet here, the

FIGURE 4.4. Adolphe Sylvain, *Jeanine Tehani Vidal*, circa 1950s.

comic reads more as a satire. Clearly, the French do not have their priorities straight regarding what should be banned, between nukes and nudes.

While this painting is a small canvas, the stencil aesthetic reminds viewers of Cronos's debut as a graffiti artist. This anchors this piece firmly as a form of public art, albeit displayed on the walls of a private gallery and purchased by a private aesthete. In other words, despite the financial constraints facing contemporary artists, the use of street art aesthetic can continue the Ari'oi's tradition of public satire under late capitalism.

The last example of nuclear parody I want to turn to is a piece by Cronos's colleague and frequent associate, the Mā'ohi graphic artist THS! This piece, titled *Moruroa Resort 2*, was also created in 2016 for the commemoration of the fiftieth year of nuclear imperialism in Mā'ohi Nui. While it departs from Bobby, Marere, and Cronos's disruptive play with the trope of the sexually available Tahitian woman, it stands out by bringing parody to the next level and turning it into a caricature.

FIGURE 4.5. Cronos, *French Apocalypse Now* (detail), 2016.

Moruroa Resort 2 is a collage on wood planks, imitating a promotional poster for a musical band (see figure 4.6). Yet here, the musical performers are French presidents Charles de Gaulle (on the right), who initiated France's nuclear testing program, and Jacques Chirac (on the left), who made the decision to resume nuclear tests in 1995 after a temporary interruption under the previous government. Sporting flower shirts, hats of coconut frond, ukulele, and guitar, the two presidents are described as "an explosive duo" (un duo explosif)—the ominous double meaning of the adjective emphasized by the two mushroom clouds looming over this promotional caption and possibly evoking the two nuclear atolls of Moruroa and Fangataufa. THS! multiplies ironic references and plays on words in his piece to suggest the omnipresence of nuclear morbidity behind the postcard: the music notes coming from Chirac's ukulele are shaped like radioactive symbols, while the caption "EN CONCERT" (performing) has its *O* replaced by the anarchist circled *A*, suggesting the alternative reading "EN CANCER" (cancerous). To denounce death and diseases, THS! chose not tragic tones but a play on words.

Again, this art form is anchored in traditional Ari'oi aesthetics. Vilsoni Hereniko notes that Ari'oi performers commonly "lampooned those in positions of authority," while Diana Looser underscores that the Ari'oi's comic sketches

FIGURE 4.6. THS!,
Moruroa Resort 2
(detail), 2016.

used "clowning techniques to critique [people in power]."[37] By ridiculing two of the most powerful and murderous French presidents, THS! reconnects with the secular Tahitian tradition of using art to challenge the structural order of society.

Finding inspiration for contemporary satire in traditional comedic genres anchors current political activism in a transgenerational history of resistance. These artworks by Holcomb, Marere, Cronos, and THS! all denounce the problematic imbrication of militourism, women's objectification, and nuclearism. Yet they do so in a playful mode, using parody, caricature, and dark humor. This is not to say that Pacific artists are "resilient" in the face of radiation-induced deaths and diseases but rather to highlight that these Polynesian painters have reclaimed the right to represent their people's suffering in their own way. Whether empowering or despairing, this laughter is decidedly political.

First as Tragedy, Then as Farce: Death and Diseases in Alexandre Ata's Fiction
Why use comedy to revisit the darkest hours of nuclear imperialism? One may
venture several explanations. First, humor may be a strategy of resistance —
showing that Mā'ohi people have not only survived but also thrived through
several threats of annihilation. Inversely, humor may be a by-product of apocalypse exhaustion. After fighting epidemiological, nuclear, and now climate
tragedies, one may become desensitized to their horrors. The use of political
parody in Tahitian art may be read as a bitter accusation of colonizers: political
action being too often foreclosed to Mā'ohi people, sneering at tragedy is the
last recourse left to its victims. Lastly, humor may be a way for artists to urge
Oceanians to reappropriate the nuclear narrative. So much of Oceanian antinuclear art takes the form of an open denunciation of nuclear powers' crimes
against humanity. So many writers and artists have simply tried to share their
story with foreigners, to let the world know what had happened on these Pacific Islands. But sometimes, artists want to make art for their own people.
Such seems to be the case of the late Mā'ohi novelist Alexandre Moeava Ata.

Writing about radiation-induced diseases in a light-hearted fashion, Ata
puts death and diseases in historical perspective to highlight Oceanians'
transgenerational resilience since the era of mass-imported epidemics. In this
section, I propose to read Ata's novel *Tautai* as a humorous denunciation of discourses that have predicted the disappearance of Pacific peoples for more than
five centuries. Replacing Indigenous stories in the long history of the last millennium, Ata takes his contemporary readers out of the catastrophism of contemporary climate discourse on death and diseases to highlight instead Mā'ohi
people's transgenerational resilience.

Tautai ou le ruisseau de Bali (*Tautai or Bali's Stream*, 2011) opens with the announcement of the death of the eponymous heroine, Tautai, whose body has
been found in a river in Bali. Tautai is represented in a classical Isletist fashion:
she is by the sea, surrounded by flowers, bare-breasted, and girded with a sa-
rong. Yet this South Seas trope is immediately shattered as the narrator notes
that it is her cadaver floating on the water and that it had rapidly decayed: "de-
composition, vultures, and scavengers had neatly done their job."[38] After this
morbid opening, an analepsis brings the reader back to Tautai's childhood in
Tahiti, narrates her journey in the United States, and concludes with her return to French-occupied Polynesia in the wake of the nuclear tests. The morbid incipit informs all subsequent developments. Throughout the novel, the
ultimate death of the heroine hangs over all her actions — just as the threat of
slow death from radiation hangs over all Oceanians.

In sharp contrast with the sordid and morbid incipit, the first chapters immerse the reader in a joyous, epicurean atmosphere, narrating Tautai's coming of age in Tahiti. She grows up as construction for the center for nuclear tests is underway, but the narrative does not yet evoke the nuclear dangers about to be unleashed on the island. Rather, it focuses on the atmosphere of insouciance that followed Tahiti's new millions in nuclear subsidies. Throughout this first part of the novel, the narrator multiplies descriptions of the debauchery of the islands' elite, preoccupied primarily with "sex, lucre, and lust."[39] Tautai herself is an epicurean pleasure seeker whose life goal consists of pursuing sexual fulfillment. Her childhood and teenage years are described primarily through her discovery of her sexuality with numerous and mostly anonymous partners.

These first chapters are an ironic rewriting of the myth of New Cythera, satirizing Isletist descriptions of Tahitians as innocent people obeying "nature's pure instinct."[40] Here, Ata presents an island where pleasure seeking is interwoven with economic and political ambition. Tautai's promiscuity does not only satisfy her lust but also finances her longing to be part of the cosmopolitan upper class. Seducing Western lovers, Tautai becomes upwardly mobile and can afford to leave her Tahitian valley for the idealized United States. Her promiscuousness was a "passport of voluptuousness" that "crossed the oceans."[41] The passive vahine trope is thus subverted by a character who plays into Isletist sexual stereotypes precisely to win her way off the island.

In the second part of the novel, Tautai settles in Los Angeles and becomes a porn actress. There, she falls in love for the first time, with a gay Californian surfer named Andrew. The section, titled "Wandering" ("En Errance"), relates the years she spends living with Andrew and her attempts to deal with his sexual indifference to her. Ata further derides the myth of the sexually available vahine, as its heteronormative foundations are exposed. Tautai spends a decade hovering around Andrew, topless and erotically girded in motley sarongs, performing the epitome of a South Sea stereotype while Andrew's gaze "lingers on anatomies different from hers."[42]

The novel takes on a different tone in the third part, after France announces that a new series of nuclear tests will be conducted in Moruroa. In this last section, the myth of the South Seas is criticized, not by being parodied but by brutally showing its contradictions in times of nuclear imperialism. After having learned about the reprisal of nuclear testing, Tautai decides to return to Tahiti, only to find her island irreversibly transformed by the CEP. Just as Tautai's body was described as rapidly decomposed in the incipit, Tahiti is portrayed as precipitously decaying in the last chapter of the novel. Quite strikingly, the narrator employs the vocabulary of death and disease to paint the island's transformation. He describes Tahiti as "a mutating society."[43] He equates consumerism with "a pulsating succession of palpitations."[44] The government's boondoggle is compared with "diabetes," while the rapid urbanization gives birth to "leprosies of tarmac."[45] Tautai and Tahiti mirror each other, as the consequences of nuclear fallout bring death and diseases to both the heroine and her island.

Despite the dramatic evolution of the novel, however, Ata's story stands out as a surprisingly playful narrative. He approaches nuclear trauma with humor, double entendre, and parody. In particular, he plays at length with the ironic rewriting of French writer Victor Segalen's famous debut novel, *Les Immémoriaux* (1907), translated into English under the title *A Lapse of Memory*. Taking a closer look at this story in palimpsest, I suggest that irony, parody, and playful distortion allow Ata to assert Mā'ohi strength in the face of environmental apocalypse.

Segalen's book narrates the sociocultural changes brought to Tahiti by the arrival of Monseigneur Nott and a handful of other proselytes of the London Missionary Society (LMS) in 1797. Segalen's narrative starts by describing an island of orgiastic love and carefree Islanders cast as "the masters of pleasure" ("*les maîtres du jouir*"). But in the aftermath of the LMS's arrival, the socioeconomic dynamics of the island are challenged. The novel's protagonist, Terii, is forced to leave Tahiti while the island is on the brink of civil war. He comes back after twenty years at sea, only to discover a depopulated, amorphous, and lugubrious Christianized island, in which the former masters of pleasure are condemned to forced labor and tortured by the new missionary order.[46] *A Lapse in Memory* is a canonical rendering of the myth of fatal impact, inasmuch as it presents the settling of a handful of missionaries as a cataclysm leading to the immediate collapse of the island's sociopolitical structures, putting an end to a joyful civilization of orgasmic pleasure with sexually licentious women. Ata, however, uses Segalen's text ironically, rewriting Segalen's tragedy as a Mā'ohi farce.

Ata's novel is structured like Segalen's book, in three movements. Their protagonists grow up before a crisis, spend a decade away from the island, and come back after Tahiti has been thoroughly transformed. Ata also uses Segalen's descriptions to portray nuclear imperialism. He compares the myth of the French clean bomb to a new religion, preached by "missionaries in charge of infiltrating a drowsy civil society," who "spread the good word."[47] He makes his intent to use Segalen as a palimpsest very clear when he resorts to a substantivized verb, "*les hommes au nouveau parler*" (the new-speak people), to refer to those new missionaries—a neologism coined by Segalen himself to refer to Msgr. Nott and his crew of proselytes. All these references to Segalen's novel highlight a playful and ironic attitude toward the idea that Tahitian society will collapse. After all, Segalen had predicted Tahitians' imminent disappearance a hundred years ago.

This ironic palimpsest also nuances the postapocalyptic descriptions of nuclearized Tahiti. The narrator describes the capital, Pape'ete, as a devastated landscape: "The Orovini's Mormon temple is no more . . . , Tekau Pomare's venerable abode, ravaged, exhales a pitiful pathetic cry: *Help!*"[48] This postapocalyptic scene focuses on the destroyed symbols of Christianity (the Mormon temple) and of the first Tahitian monarchy (the house of Princess Tekau Pomare, daughter of Queen Pomare V). This is another jab at Segalen: in *A Lapse of Memory*, Christianity and the Pomare dynasty are the spearhead of havoc and destruction.[49] Yet under nuclear imperialism, these relics of the epoch that Segalen presents as the darkest page in Tahitian history become symbols of bygone peaceful times. Ata thus manages to provincialize the eighteenth-century myth of fatal impact while simultaneously highlighting the rhetorical continuity of colonial discourses. His ironic rewriting of Segalen helps put nuclear violence in historical perspective.

Social scientists have highlighted this "great silence, maybe even general disinterest in these first encounters" on the part of Pacific activists and storytellers, who seldom fictionalize encounters with the first Westerners.[50] In literature, "the writing of first contact history has been very much a European preoccupation."[51] This is a meaningful silence specific to Pacific literature.[52] "Disaster writing" is common among other oppressed groups who have organized their resistance to imperialism around commemorations of massive massacres, particularly in Caribbean and Aboriginal literature.[53] The rarity of anti-colonial historical novels about the Pacific genocide may be seen as a political decision to challenge ongoing annihilation racism. Many decolonial activists have emphasized their discomfort with fatal impact narratives and the assumptions about the disappearance of Pacific cultures that come with this history.[54] Reading Ata's novel in this perspective highlights the subversive potential of ironically using fatal impact literature in the era of nuclear imperialism. Building on Segalen's tragedy, Ata provincializes Western aggression and sarcastically deconstructs the myth of fatal impact.

Ata's engagement with Segalen's novel goes beyond semantic similarities. The arrival of Msgr. Nott and his sixteen fellow missionaries can be compared to the arrival of the CEP and its thousands of soldiers inasmuch as both events mark the beginning of a radical transformation of the islands' socioeconomic dynamics. Under Ata's pen, however, the comparison becomes sarcastic: if the first missionaries brought Christianity, a religion now embraced by the over-whelming majority of Māʻohi citizens, the new missionaries' manna takes on a much more questionable form. The narrator writes that "the military air-port would also finally offer an entirely beneficial fallout: a touristic one. Truly, these were funny times!"[55] Rather than directly denouncing the dangers posed by fallout, Ata choses to use a play on words, as the word *retombées* could re-fer in French to either economic benefits ("*les retombées économiques*") or nu-clear fallout ("*les retombées nucléaires*"). The new religion's morbidity is ironically revealed when its missionaries themselves start turning into unconventional martyrs, such as this anonymous doctor claiming that the nuclear test could be a godsend as it could trigger a genetic upheaval regenerating the species.[56] The French doctor's lies are belied by his own radiation-induced death: "A new missionary of a paradisiac future, the doctor was struck down by leukemia."[57] The irony of the situation is underscored by the narrator's sour laugh—these were "funny times" indeed!

The novel then proceeds to depict the 1995 antinuclear riots as a comical farce, featuring antinuclear characters laughing out loud at their own uprising:

> CNN *diffusait en live quelques bûchers enflammés à son intention par quelques maraudeurs, aux forfaits desquels on assistait,* hilares, *sur l'écran de télévision (les malfaiteurs improvisaient des essayages* burlesques *d'effets avant d'emporter leur butin...). Sur les hauteurs qui surplombaient l'aéroport, des apprentis incendiaires confectionnaient des cocktails molotov dont pas un n'explosa.*[58]

> CNN was live streaming a few stakes, set ablaze for the TV channel by a few marauders. People witnessed such infamy on a TV screen, *laughing merrily*—the miscreants were improvising *a burlesque show*, trying on stolen clothes before carrying away their booty. In the mountains above the airport, wanna-be arsonists were making Molotov cocktails, none of which exploded. [my emphasis]

Painting burlesque antinuclear protestors and peeved arsonists, Ata turns the events of 1995 into a gaudy carnival, encouraging his readers, if not to join the TV spectators in their hilarity, at least to smile at the creative chaos created by the antinuclear protestors.

Ata's novel highlights that Māʻohi people have been living through dystopia for centuries. By using irony, parodying palimpsests, and caricaturing Isletist tropes, he further implies that Tahitians have nevertheless managed to sur-vive and laugh in this apocalyptic setting. Insisting on the circularity of apocalyptic episodes, Ata's novel suggests that Mā'ohi people, having survived mass epidemics and nuclear apocalypse, are ready to withstand whichever threat climate change brings their way. One needs to be familiar with Tahitian stories and histories to get the joke, to appreciate the palimpsests, the parodies, the play on words, and the double entendres that structure the last part of the novel. Ata appears to be writing for—and chuckling with—a local audience. This is Mā'ohi empowerment.

Farcical Fale Aitu:
Subversive Humor in Albert Wendt's Postapocalypse World

This satirical laughter can be seen as a pan-Pacific trope. Indeed, Epeli Hau'ofa once noted that "laughing at problems, especially at seemingly intractable ones, is a feature of many Pacific cultures.... We laugh and we cry and we often do them simultaneously."[59] Antinuclear humor can thus be found from the art galleries of Pape'ete to the printing presses of Aotearoa that published the work of Albert Wendt. Originally from Samoa, Wendt spent much of his life in Aotearoa, where he became one of the best-known Pacific writers and a founding father of Pacific literary studies. His novel *Black Rainbow* stands out among his many works of fiction as a very direct denunciation of nuclear imperialism in the Pacific. The novel is tellingly named after a series of paintings by Māori artist Ralph Hotere, who created a series of litographs titled *Black Rainbow* to denounce French nuclear tests in Moruroa and Fangataufa. In this section, I turn to *Black Rainbow* to analyze Wendt's use of humor to depict the impact of nuclear imperialism in the Pacific. "I had lots of fun with it," Wendt chimed in when interviewed by Vilsoni Hereniko. "It's a very serious novel, but it's also not that serious. Depends on how you define serious."[60]

Black Rainbow takes place in a fictional post–World War III New Zealand, but the narrator does not dwell at all on the violence of this total nuclear war. Instead, he immerses his readers in a conspicuous overlit postapocalyptic dystopia underscoring the longue durée of nuclear violence. In his dystopia, an omniscient Tribunal, explicitly shaped after the Orwellian Thought Police, controls every citizen and "reordinarinises" those who fail to comply with its norm, filling them with predefined personalities. The Tribunal came to existence after the world underwent "three World Wars, nuclear pollution, and AIDS epidemics," and it provides its citizens with compulsory comfort and peace.[61] The Tribunal outlawed crime, war, and most importantly, as various characters repeat like a mantra, "the Tribunal and our President have defeated death." Thanks to advances in science, people can age but they cannot die. Even when people suffer accidental death, the Tribunal reincarnates them. "No one ever dies permanently."[62] The protagonist, nameless throughout most of the novel, discovers over the course of his quest that this "peaceful" world was established at the expense of Indigenous Pacific people, who now call themselves Tangata Moni. When he meets the handful of Indigenous outlaws who have refused the compromised comfort promised by the Tribunal, he discovers that he is himself Polynesian—although his "reordinarination" has "left [him] brown on the outside and filled [him] full of white, other-worlder bullshit."[63]

Literary scholars such as Paul Sharrad, Elizabeth M. DeLoughrey, Teresa Shewry, Julia A. Boyd, and Rebecca H. Hogue have saliently shown how Albert Wendt's *Black Rainbow* subtly denounces nuclear testing in the Pacific.[64] In the following pages, I aim to complement these insightful readings of the novel by focusing on the surprising use of humor in Wendt's representations of nuclear apocalypse. I argue that *Black Rainbow* uses irony to ask crucial questions about the nature of death, disease, and Indigenous health in times of environmental collapse. What is the relationship between science, medicine, and nuclear technology? How does the quest for omnipotent science affect Indigenous people? Can survivors laugh about it all?

Black Rainbow opens in the suburbs of Auckland, where the protagonist, then unnamed, lives with his wife, Margaret. They jog, they cook, they watch TV. Yet there is something uncanny about their suburban life, as the protagonist's wife's chatter takes on surprisingly morbid undertones. "Our neighbourhood's full of old people's homes and hospitals," she notes. "And flats and apartments for them.... A lot of houses up for sale too. A whole generation who can no longer care for themselves selling up and going into the homes."[65] As she goes on gossiping about their neighbors, the reader realizes that all of them are seriously ill. The neighbor to their right: "paralyzed in the left leg." The one to their left: "he's going to be put in a nursing home by his only child." Behind them: "bedridden. Been like that for five years."[66] Worse, their own son's health was "precarious most of the time, suffering from diseases that were supposed to have been eradicated."[67]

This hints from the outset at a main paradox of the novel. On the one hand, Science has vanquished Death. On the other hand, most characters seem to be suffering from mysterious illnesses and are repeatedly attempting suicide. The President himself, his goons, and many of his citizens crave death, begging the protagonist to assassinate them whenever they cross his path.[68] The hero graciously obliges them, "freeing" them from life.[69] In this dystopia, the worse consequence of scientific progress is the obligation to live forever.

Further deepening the protagonist's obsession with death, his main love interest, the bodybuilder, seems to fascinate him for her ability to deliver this much sought-after eternal oblivion. "More myth than woman," she shares many characteristics with the Māori goddess Hinenuitepō.[70] She fled her home after surviving incest, and when a trickster attempted to rape her, she "crushed [him] between her thighs."[71] The protagonist is hypnotized by her monstrously strong body, which reminds him of Hinenuitepō's ability to bestow death upon even seemingly immortal demigods like Maui. "Maui had been crushed to death between Hine-nui-te-Po's thighs when he'd challenged her," he recalls. "I couldn't push out the picture of her enormous thighs squeezing, grinding around his head, his eyes bulging as he choked and his head started cracking inwards."[72] In a world in which death has become forbidden, being killed by the goddess's thighs becomes endowed with orgasmic—and comic—relief: "As I reached the car John had waiting for me, Maui's ballooning eyes popped like bubblegum."[73] Eventually, the hero himself seeks a similar liberation in his own demise. Arrested for his "murders" of oblivion-seeking characters, he is given the option to be reincarnated by the Tribunal. It's an offer he declines: "I chose permanent death."[74]

The Tribunal's obsession with eternal life and the characters' obsession with finding solace in death resonates with the problematic that emerged in the wake of nuclear technology. At the turn of the twentieth century, when French scientist Marie Curie discovered that radioactivity could destroy cancerous cells, radioactivity became seen as a miraculous cure and was applied to everything. Radioactive water cures were prescribed to treat all sorts of ailments, from gout to loose teeth, diabetes, and constipation.[75] The deathless radioactive utopia portrayed in Black Rainbow echoes the first atomic scientists' wildest dreams.

After World War II, while the dangers of radioactivity were becoming known, atomic technology fueled another, even grander delusion. With the atomic bomb, thermo-industrial civilization became closer than ever to realizing the goal of Enlightenment thinkers: to become master and possessor of nature. The mastery of the atom marked a new age for scientific prowess: from World War II resurrection technology to contemporary species revivalism, assertions that science could soon provide perpetual life became abundant. Yet this Enlightenment ideal has dystopian connotations. Literary critic Elizabeth DeLoughrey thus remarks that "nuclearization leads not to a planet determined by darkness, a lack of light, but total light."[76] In Black Rainbow, Wendt does not narrate the nuclear explosions of World War III but rather situates his readers in a postapocalypse world suffused with nuclear light—a "fully enlight-ened earth radiat[ing] disaster triumphant."[77]

To understand the characters' obsession with death, one must analyze the Polynesian cosmogonic references weaved throughout the novel. In Wendt's dystopia, all history, including Māori creation stories, has been banned. Yet the narrator encounters it serendipitously when listening to an audio cassette of Māori orator Hone Tuwhare's poetry. The poem "We, who live in darkness" de-scribes this famous original creation of light.[78] The world was originally noth-ingness. Out of this nothingness emerged the long night te Pō, which then gave way to Papatūānuku (the earth mother) and Ranginui (the sky father), locked in an eternal embrace. Out of their union were born numerous children, who became the first atua (gods) populating the world. Yet Papatūānuku and Rang-inui were so closely intertwined that no light could reach their children en-trapped between them. Cramped in the darkness, the children conspired to separate their parents, finally allowing light (te Ao) to flow to the world. The separation of Papatūānuku and Ranginui brought balance to the world, which now alternates between night and day, te Pō and te Ao.

The Polynesian night, the Pō, is thus a fecund space, the state out of which the universe emerges. In the words of Mā'ohi anthropologist Jean-Marc Tera'it-uatini Pambrun, "the Pō is the primordial locus of inspiration and creation. It's a magical space which gives man his deepest thoughts. It's in darkness that beings dream and that everything gets created."[79] The gods and their children need both Ao and Pō, day and night, the natural and the supernatural, ratio-nality and creativity, the profane and the sacred, life and death.

This balance disappeared, withered away by the nuclear sun.

In *Black Rainbow*, everything glows under the light of the President's eternal smile. Zones of shadows are carefully eradicated, hunted all the way down to metaphors: "whenever our 'darker selves' (the President's phrase) threatened, they were easily reordinarinised."[80] Nothing is brighter than the Tribunal it-self, where "the light never altered: it was white neon, skull white, emanating from the walls and ceiling."[81] The skull metaphor underscores the continuities between Enlightenment, white settler colonialism, and nuclear morbidity—so much light upsets the balance of the world. Colonizers' science did not elimi-nate death. It transformed the entire world into a morbid overlit hospital.

The burden of this imbalance is borne by "the original people," the Tangata Moni who refused the ascetic and preordained utopia prescribed by the Tribunal. They were tortured in reordinarination centers, where the otherworlders "can make even your dreams burn your body."[82] They were driven underground, in the city's sewers, hiding in the darkness to survive and preserve history. Women were sterilized and had to "slug their guts out" working in the Tribunal's factory or cleaning their shithouses.[83] When the Tangata Moni died, they couldn't be reincarnated: they were "worn out, a mindless shell the Centres couldn't refill with another identity."[84] And the protagonist's friend, the Tangata Moni named Piwakawaka, concluded: "look where we are: fucking poor, fucking cold, fucking hungry."[85] Why would anyone refuse the comfort, security, peace, and eternal life promised by the Tribunal? wonder the ordinary people who cross paths with the protagonist. What these law-abiding citizens do not realize is that the Tangata Moni's sacrifice is the only bastion of the darkness of the Pō surviving in a world blinded by the awful illumination of atomic power.

In this context, one may surmise that the real quest of the protagonist is not so much to find himself, as he first believes, but rather to restore the lost balance between Ao and Pō. He is given the option to be reincarnated and remain in the world of perpetual light and perpetual life, but he chooses darkness. Like Maui, who sacrificed himself in an attempt to give immortality to humankind, the protagonist sacrifices himself to bring back mortality to humanity. His sacrifice brings back obscurity to this overlit world. In the last paragraphs of the novel, he is seen in his cell, rejoicing at the newfound harmony he finds in his last night before his execution. The obscurity allows him to find peace. Contrasting with his previous traumatic experiences "in the phosphorescent glow of the city," his imminent death coincides with the return of darkness in his cell—a fulfilling, life-filled obscurity.[86] His last words restore balance to the world: "The night is still. I hear it breathing. All is well."[87] This fight for balance postapocalypse is embodied in the titular trope of the black rainbow, an oxymoron combining sun and rain, colors and absence of light, Ao and Pō. As Wendt himself noted, "Ralph [Hotere's *Black Rainbow*] was restoring to the color black or to darkness the Māori or Polynesian view of darkness as being the very fecund and fertile darkness out of which all life comes."[88]

But darkness is not only present in *Black Rainbow* the novel as a thematic trope. It also suffuses the narrative at the metanarrative level, in the form of dark humor. As must be apparent at this point from the excerpts already quoted, *Black Rainbow* is teeming with plays on words, humorous jabs between characters, and witty references to Maui the trickster bringing comic relief throughout the narrative. The young Tangata Moni that the protagonist encounters through his quest provide much of this dark humor, regularly joking about the hero's clumsy rediscovery of his roots: "I thought your suntan was painted on, eh,' laughed Fantail."[89] In a side comment, the characters themselves describe dark humor as the only way to cope with this nuclear-lit dystopia. As the Tangata Moni prepare to break into the Tribunal, they joke around:

"I don't mind admitting I'm scared..." I reached out and put an arm around him. "It's times like this you need..."

"Minties?" Fantail completed his remark.

"No, it's times like this you need a sense of humour."[90]

Such an attitude stands in sharp contrast with that of the narrator's family's behavior at the beginning of the novel. His wife, the Tribunal members, and the president never joke—presumably for the same reason Plato banned humor from his *Republic*. Humor stems from the perception of something being incongruous and off balanced. It thus constitutes a subversive force in an orderly dystopia like post–World War III New Zealand.

Like Tahitian antinuclear artists, Wendt appears to be drawing from traditional comic theater. In this case, he seems to be inspired by the Samoan fale aitu. Samoan American literary scholar Caroline Sinavaiana-Gabbard defines fale aitu (meaning literally the house of spirit) as Samoan comedy sketches satirizing authority figures normally commending respect, like political leaders and pastors... or, in the case of *Black Rainbow*, presidents and tribunals.[91] Traditional Samoan theater also occasionally pokes fun at married couples, "whose relationships are culturally prescribed to be harmonious and cooperative."[92] In Wendt's novel, the protagonist leaves his Tribunal-loving, law-abiding wife to join a group of rebellious teenagers, putting a serious dent in the Tribunal's injunction to live in harmonious and cooperative pairs. The novel thus draws its targets for satire from a long tradition of Samoan theatrical humor.

In addition to aiming at similar targets for its satire, *Black Rainbow* shares much of fale aitu's traditional aesthetics. Sinavaiana-Gabbard notes that fale aitu sketches are "composed and directed by a lead comedian who may conduct the singing and dancing portions of the show as well."[93] *Black Rainbow* similarly draws from multiple genres of performances: where fale aitu performers can alternatively act, sing, and dance, the narrator of *Black Rainbow* alternates between novelistic prose, long descriptions of Ralph Hotere's *Black Rainbow* lithograph, and full-length excerpts of Hone Tuwhare's poems. Fale aitu and Wendt's novel thus share a similar engagement with narrative forms (theater/novel), visual art forms (dancing/painting), and musical art forms (singing/poetry), moving freely from one another. Moreover, in traditional Samoan theater, the lead comedian's acting talents were judged "by how many different characters and voices can be convincingly projected in a single performance."[94] According to this criteria, the protagonist of *Black Rainbow* stands out as a particularly talented lead, since throughout the course of the novel, he goes from being Eric Maile Foster, a banal bank clerk, to rediscovering his talents as a state assassin named Supremo Jones, to reembracing his first identity as a rebellious Tangata Moni named Patimaori Jones, before finally reincarnating as a futuristic self-sacrificing Maui.

Each of these inspirations drawn from fale aitu (targets of satire, shifts in genre, shifts in characters) adds subversive elements to the novel. They allow the narrator, the reader, and the protagonist to escape the orderly structures set in stone by the Tribunal, perhaps not so omnipotent after all. But they challenge the traditional linear, plot-driven narrative of the European realist novel, offering an opportunity to escape the foreign-imposed orderly way to do narrative. In a post–nuclear war context, resorting to traditional forms of Samoan comic thus allows the reader to envision the possibility of playfulness and pleasure even in a postapocalyptic world.

Conclusion: Death, Diseases, and Comedy in the Nuclearized Pacific

Most Pacific narratives about Oceania's nuclearized environmental collapse have taken the form of painful testimonies. From Hone Tuwhare's 1962 eulogy "No Ordinary Sun" to Kathy Jetñil-Kijiner's contemporary spoken-word performances, Pacific creative writers/orators have told the story of the radiation-induced death and diseases that befell Pacific people using tragic, doleful, and angered tones.[95] Such narratives are invaluable to process grief and raise global awareness regarding the issue of nuclear-induced deaths and diseases.[96] There is, however, as shown in this chapter, a less-discussed canon of Pacific nuclear writing: One that refuses pathos in favor of cynicism. One that substitutes tragedy with parody. One that offers to revisit nuclear trauma through caricature. This is the artistic way chosen by artists such as Alexandre Ata, Cronos, Patricia Grace, Bobby Holcomb, Witi Ihimaera, André Marere, THS!, and Albert Wendt.[97] Their decision to adopt a humorous tone to discuss such a tragic topic can seem disconcerting at first. Yet it offers a unique opportunity to draw from traditional forms of Pacific comedy to shed a different light on the present.

Using parody, ironical palimpsests, and caricatures, these writers and artists reclaim the powers of regeneration that characterize Pacific societies. The distinction between resilience and regeneration is an important one, theorized among others by Canadian journalist Naomi Klein. "Resilience—though certainly one of nature's greatest gifts—is a passive process, implying the ability to absorb blows and get back up. Regeneration, on the other hand, is active: we become full participants in the process of maximizing life's creativity."[98] In the fiction and paintings analyzed in this chapter, Isletist texts and imagery become the source of a creative process reasserting Oceanians' ability not only to live but also to laugh, in spite of imperial destruction. Drawing from customary modes of storytelling, such as Ari'oi theater in Tahiti or fale aitu from Samoa, creative artists and writers find the strength to ridicule the colonizers' tropes and myths in traditional artforms transmitted for generations. These writers and artists thus challenge the imperial world order by juxtaposing annihilation and creation, offering as a healing process the disruptive humor of the H-bomb.

5

RADIATION REFUGEES

Rethinking the Age of Mass Migration

If, ontologically, land and people are the same in the indigenous sense,
then what happens when both the people and the land are removed?
—KATERINA MARTINA TEAIWA, *Consuming Ocean Island*

my home . . .
With a sign that said, "Do not return for 25,000 years"
It has been seventy years
We have 24,930 years left . . .
How far do you think she'll be underwater?
—SELINA NEIROK LEEM, "More Than Just a Blue Passport"

How you mourn the loss of a home
that isn't even gone yet.
—TERESA TINEI SIAGATONU, "Atlas"

The twenty-first century is turning out to be, as Edward Said feared, "the age
of the refugee, the displaced person, mass immigration."[1] A rise in 5°C, as fore-
casted by most scientific reports, would radically alter current global modes of
social organization. Some studies project that by 2050, one billion people will
be displaced from their homes because of environmental upheaval.[2] Many human societies yearly adapt to temperature changes of several dozens of degrees,
seamlessly going from 40°C summers to winters with negative temperatures,
but global ecosystems are far less adaptable to temperature shifts than individ-

ual organisms. During the last ice age, twenty thousand years ago, global temperatures were only 5°C lower than the current average.[3] Yet Europe and North America were buried under sheets of ice up to two miles thick, covering what is now New York and London; the oceans lay 120 meters (400 feet) lower than their current level; and Southern Europe had the vegetation seen today in the Siberian tundra. Imagining a planet warmed by five degrees more than preindustrial averages is chilling.

Some optimistic or denialist observers object to these grim projections on the basis that humans adapted to deglaciation twenty thousand years ago. Previous global warmings, however, greatly differ from this current predicament. First, the climate was warming ten times more slowly (by 0.1°C a century) than it is today. Second, humans were not sedentary; they could more easily migrate as the environment transformed. And last but not least, humanity was only a few millions strong and was neither dependent on intensive agriculture and extensive infrastructure for survival nor constrained in its movements by centuries-old geopolitical borders. Relocating billions of sedentary humans today should prove far deadlier than previous climate-induced historical migrations.[4]

In the Global North, climate collapse often triggers fear of mass migration imbued with latent racist tropes. For many, it evokes hordes of southern climate refugees invading Europe and North America. Some environmentalist movements thus lapse into ecofascist undertones. Those movements demand that "Others"—defined on the basis of their skin color, religion, or birthplace—be excluded from certain ecosystems by portraying their presence as a threat to (white) enjoyment and consumption of these environments. Several pioneering environmentalists, by critiquing population growth over the systematic overconsumption of the world's elite, have given credence to these ecofascist tropes and reinforced the widespread fear that stably populated Western countries are threatened by the growing population of the Third World.[5] Even highly regarded environmental trailblazers such as Rachel Carson have mobilized the racist trope of invasive dark-skinned multitudes when discussing environmental issues in North America.[6]

"When people ask me where I'm from / they don't believe me when I say water."[7] These are the words of Samoan American spoken-word performer Terisa Tinei Siagatonu, reflecting on migration in times of climate collapse. Siagatonu is an award-winning poet, mental health educator, and community leader from the Bay Area. She has performed in venues across the world, from the White House in Washington, DC, to the streets of Europe. She performed her poem "Atlas" at the COP21 in Paris. The performance is available on YouTube, while the text of her poem is featured on several digital platforms. In this piece, she reflects on her own condition as a migrant, "a hyphen of a woman: a Samoan-American that carries the weight of both colonizer and colonized, both blade and blood."[8]

For Siagatonu, the threat of having to migrate because of anthropogenic climate change is very real. Both her ancestral home, Samoa, and her birth-place, California, are threatened by water: "California, a state of emergency away from having the drought rid it of all its water. Samoa, a state of emergency away from becoming a saltwater cemetery if the sea level doesn't stop rising."[9] Threatened with the loss of both of her homes within her lifetime, she has come to redefine what it means to belong somewhere:

> When people ask me where I'm from
> what they want is to hear me speak of land
> what they want is to know where I go once I leave here
> the privilege that comes with assuming that home
> is just a destination, and not the panic.
> Not the constant migration that the panic gives birth to.

With these oxymora, Siagatonu offers a dramatic vision of what climate-triggered migration means. But she refuses to act as the prophetic canary in the coal mine, characterized by its silent death in the dark depths of the colliery. She frontally accuses the sedentary carbon addicts responsible for her plight:

> What is it like? To know that home is something
> that's waiting for you to return to it?
> What does it mean to belong to something that isn't sinking?
> What does it mean to belong to what is causing the flood?

The very medium Siagatonu has chosen to share her performance directly implicated her audience. Most of her public is online, and digital technologies are "burning up masses of carbon while shunting activist outrage into impotent feedback loops."[10] The global digital communication system is responsible for 2 percent of global emissions—as much as all the planes in the world. In other words, each viewer, comfortably seated, further contributes to make her homes "broken and butchered places," adding additional weight to her accusations.[11] Refusing to be set up as a symbol of humanity's future, Siagatonu insists that climate-triggered migration is already a reality for too many people:

> So many of us come from water
> but when you come from water
> no one believes you.

At this point, the camera sweeps around to show the hill of Montmartre in the foreground and the skyline of Paris in the background. Siagatonu then asks:

How you mourn the loss of a home
that isn't even gone yet.

The background is highly symbolic. The Paris skyline reminds the viewer that the COP21 participants are there, somewhere, in the background, failing to reach a meaningful agreement to lower greenhouse gas emissions. Yet the foreground also contains hidden meaning. The hill of Montmartre is a lost utopia—a home that is already gone. It was the bastion of the Paris Commune, the first socialist and participative democracy to see the light of day under a capitalist regime. The Commune was bloodily repressed in 1871, and a massive basilica, the Sacré Cœur, was erected where the revolutionaries had taken arms. The enormous church erases both the possibilities of future revolts and the memory that the uprising ever took place. Its sprawling structure does not leave any room for commemorating the fallen communards. Progressives the world over are still mourning the loss of this short-lived utopia, this home where the fruits of the land and of human labor were equitably shared, ever so briefly. Speaking from Montmartre, literally the mount-of-the-martyrs, Siagatonu inscribes current and upcoming losses of homes in historical perspective. Montmartre is a home too much gone; Samoa and California, homes not gone yet. Poised between these two extremes, at the center of the camera shot, Siagatonu asks "how you mourn": which symbols, which words, which temporal frameworks can capture the erasure of place?

Australian philosopher Glenn Albrecht created a neologism to define the particular form of emotional distress that sets in when our home(s) are polluted and altered by extractivism and global warming. He called it solastalgia. It evokes the loss of the solace that can only be found in one's homeland.[12] This chapter explores the poetic practices put in place by Pacific poets to process solastalgia for generations.

Distant islands across Oceania have been connected by trade, wars, and transarchipelagic religious ceremonies for millennia.[13] However, settler colonialism, militarism, and nuclear imperialism have turned this millennia-long saga of oceanic voyaging into a tragic history of forced migration.[14] The second half of the millennia tells over and over again the story of brutal uprooting of Indigenous communities by missionaries, settler colonizers, and slave traders. Yet again, the violent uprooting of Indigenous people from their land took on a different scale under nuclear imperialism. At that point, not only did colonizers exile Pacific people from their islands; they destroyed the basis for life for hundreds of thousands of years. Displaced Pacific artists wrote about the loss of their homes and the resilience of their communities through nuclear violence. These nuclear poems provide contemporary Pacific writers with a point of reference in times of climate collapse. They speak for the need to process the loss of a home that is not even gone yet.

This chapter retraces the history of forced migration in three nuclear colonies: Aelōñ in Ṃajeḷ (the Marshall Islands), Kiribati, and Māʻohi Nui (French-occupied Polynesia). All three countries harbor low-lying atolls now threatened by rising sea levels. I explore the work of three antinuclear artists, Marshallese poet Kathy Jetñil-Kijiner, Māʻohi novelist Chantal T. Spitz, and oral performer Teresia Teaiwa, who traces her lineage back to Fijian, Banaban, Tabiteuean, and African American heritages. Their antinuclear literature contributes to rebuilding a home in the ruins of the nuclear apocalypse and functions as an anchor to address climate-triggered migrations.

Kathy Jetñil-Kijiner's Story Weaving:
From Vaporized Atolls to Artificial Islands

Between 1946 and 1958, the United States detonated sixty-seven devices in Pikinni and Ānewetak (Enewetak). Arguing that these islands were "isolated" and "remote" (without specifying from where), American colonizers set out to create the reality they purported to describe. First, the 166 inhabitants of Pikinni were removed from their atoll and transferred to Roñdik (Rongerik) in 1946, to make way for Operation Crossroad. In a staged ceremony repeated multiple times for national television news, Commodore Ben Wyatt was recorded convincing ri-Pikinni to leave their home by telling them it was "for the good of mankind." Ri-Pikinni were not told that their departure was definitive, nor what their island would be used for. Regardless, refusing to leave was not an option, since there were already thousands of soldiers and scientists on the atoll and dozens of airplanes and ships in the lagoon.[15]

The entire operation was presented to the American public as a humanitarian endeavor. Ri-Pikinni were described in the media as a nomadic group, whose displacement constituted an improvement in their quality of life. US military officials were recorded proclaiming that "the atoll itself is unhealthy" because it "produces little food besides coconut and fish" and arguing that Pikinni and Roñdik looked as alike as two Idaho potatoes.[16] The latter, however, is a sandbar island, with far fewer resources than Pikinni. Within two months, ri-Pikinni faced dramatic shortages of food and water supply. American officials remained unaware of the issue until American anthropologist Leonard

Mason visited the island in 1948. "Imagine," exclaims antinuclear activist Darlene Keju-Johnson, "move someone else from their own home, by your power. Dump them on a little sand. And don't even bother to go back and see how they are doing for a year"![17] Ri-Pikinni were then relocated to Kuwajleen (Kwajalein) and a year later to Kōle (Kili)—an island one-ninth the size of Pikinni with no lagoon. The US Army attempted a repatriation to Pikinni Atoll in the late 1960s, but the detection of unsafe levels of radioactivity in people's bodies after five years of consumption of contaminated food prompted their second and seemingly definitive expulsion from their island.[18]

In December 1946, the US Army evacuated the 142 people of Ānewetak to make room for the bomb codenamed Ivy Mike (seven hundred times more powerful than the bomb that destroyed Hiroshima). Ānewetak's people were displaced to Wūjlañ (Ujelang) atoll. There, they suffered from near starvation, and from polio and measles epidemics triggered by unhealthy living conditions and rat infestations. They had been told they were only leaving for thirty-six months; they remained on Wūjlañ for thirty-three years.[19] In the 1970s, the United States undertook the "decontamination" of Ānewetak. However, the word "decontamination" should always be put in quotes because radioactive waste cannot be cleaned—it can only be displaced, at great environmental, human, and financial cost, to a different site, where it continues to emit its radioactive poison.[20] Radioactive soil and test equipment were thus shoveled onto Runit Island and covered with a concrete dome. Ri-Ānewetak attempted to return home in 1980, although they were only allowed to live on three of the forty islands of their atoll. The other islands were either too radioactive or vaporized.[21]

After having created the "desert" islands on which to detonate its nuclear bombs, the American military proceeded to destroy the surrounding archipelago. In 1954, the United States exploded its largest thermonuclear bomb, codenamed Castle Bravo (one thousand times the power of the bomb that destroyed Hiroshima). Its fallout particularly contaminated Roñḷap (Rongelap), Roñdik (Rongerik), Utrōk (Utrik), and Aelōñin Ae (Ailiginae). The inhabitants of Roñḷap were evacuated after three days of exposure to radioactive fallout, those of Utrōk after four days in nuclear torments. These nuclear refugees were relocated in Kuwajleen for three months, then in Mājro (Majuro) for three years.[22] In 1957, they eventually returned to their atoll, as American researchers saw the resettlement of ri-Majeḷ on irradiated land as "a unique opportunity to study contamination via ingestion."[23] Within twenty years, most people reported miscarriages, abnormal births, various health disorders, and recurring cancers. A radiological assessment conducted in Roñḷap in 1978 concluded that many parts of the island presented dangerous levels of radiation, forcing the inhabitants to seek a way to leave the atoll. As ri-Roñḷap antinuclear activist Lijon Eknilang recalls:

> It wasn't easy to leave Rongelap. We had to give up everything. Our land is our memory of those people we've lost.... But we had to plan ahead for our children. I know it is too late for me and the others, our lives have already been ruined, but it's the future we're thinking about. We don't want our kids to receive all the sickness we are receiving now.[24]

In 1985, ri-Roñḷap sought the assistance of Greenpeace and were relocated to Mejato Island in Kuwajleen atoll aboard the *Rainbow Warrior*. Mejato, however, does not grow enough food, and nuclear refugees have to travel biweekly to Epjā (Ebeye), another island in Kuwajleen atoll, to sell their labor to obtain the necessary supplies to survive.[25] Many ri-Roñḷap ended up settling in Epjā, which is now one of the most crowded islands in the Pacific.[26]

Kuwajleen itself, despite being a refuge for nuclear migrants, has been the site of further displacements imposed by the US nuclear complex. The world's largest atoll, Kuwajleen was used as America's most important site for testing intercontinental ballistic missiles and antiballistic shields since 1959. All of Kuwajleen's inhabitants were expelled to designated parts of the atoll to make room for the missiles. In 1982, a thousand landowners attempted to reoccupy their lands during what became known as "Operation Homecoming." They were evicted by the US Army and deported from the atoll. The movement died down in 1986, when soldiers were instructed to shoot to wound the remaining protestors.[27]

In addition to these forced mass migrations, many individual ri-Majeḷ were forced to spend time in the United States after contracting radio-induced diseases. In 1953, the Atomic Energy Commission launched the controversial Project 4.1, which studied the effects of radiation on human beings in the Marshall Islands. This project involved 539 people, often without their informed consent, and included experimental surgery and injections of chromium-51, radioactive iodine, iron, zinc, and carbon-14.[28] Keju-Johnson denounced: "If a person is found to have a thyroid and it is cancerous and needs to be removed they are sent to either the United States, Hawai'i or Guam. They don't explain to you exactly what they are going to do to your throat. They just say that you are to go. And there is no translator.... They are told not to make any phone calls to any relative or friend."[29] Many ri-Majeḷ were opposed to these forced medical evacuations and have called for better and more affordable medical treatment in their own country.[30]

The fact that these stories of forced migration are little known among American nuclear colonizers is part and parcel of environmental racism. As Kanaka Maoli political scientist Haunani-Kay Trasks highlights, "such are the intended privileges of the so-called American standards of living: ignorance of, and yet power over, one's relations to Native people."[31] Nuclear imperialism does not only annihilate land, it also attempts to erase Indigenous histories.

As noted previously, most nuclear testing facilities in the Pacific are low-lying atolls, which are now some of the first nations threatened to be engulfed by rising sea levels. Marshallese people are thus at risk of experiencing further forced migrations. Such a history of forced migration under nuclear imperialism informs contemporary activists' fight against rising seas. This dynamic is particularly apparent in the work of Kathy Jetñil-Kijiner.

Jetñil-Kijiner is a poet from the Marshall Islands. She comes from a long line of powerful women. Her mother, Hilda Heine, was the first Marshallese to obtain a PhD and the only woman sitting in the Republic of the Marshall Islands (RMI) government.[32] Before her, Jetñil-Kijiner's grandmother Carmen Bigler was the only woman elected in Marshallese Congress in 1965.[33] Jetñil-Kijiner was born in Mājro and raised in Hawai'i. She studied creative writing and Pacific Islands studies, first in California, then in Honolulu. In 2014, she was selected from 544 nominees to speak on behalf of civil society at the United Nations climate summit, in front of hundreds of the world's heads of state. The poem she shared, "Dear Matafele Peinam," was so powerful that it moved world leaders to tears and was met with a standing ovation—an event so rare in the UN General Assembly Hall that it had not happened since the late Nelson Mandela's address.[34] Shortly thereafter, Jetñil-Kijiner was elected "Climate Woman of the Year," and she has been serving as the climate envoy for the Marshall Islands Ministry of Environment. In addition to her performances and advocacy work, Jetñil-Kijiner also taught Pacific studies at the College of the Marshall Islands, and she runs Jo-Jikum, the environmental nonprofit organization that she cofounded. At the time of writing, she is completing a dissertation at the Australian National University.

Her poetry often features her family members and friends affected by the legacy of nuclear imperialism. She lost her ten-year-old cousin to leukemia.[35] Her grandmother has tongue cancer.[36] Her neighbors and friends suffered from sterility, stillbirths, and abnormal pregnancies.[37] The legacy of nuclear imperialism lives on in front of her eyes, in the blood of her kin and the sand of her land. Jetñil-Kijiner addresses the grief brought by nuclear colonialism and carbon imperialism by finding inspiration in traditional Marshallese literary forms. Analyzing Jetñil-Kijiner's oeuvre, American literary scholar Rebecca H. Hogue describes her as taking on the role of a ri-bwebwenato, who are traditionally members of the community passing along knowledge from their kinspeople as well as histories necessary for survival.[38] In a poem titled "Two degrees," Jetñil-Kijiner explores the historical continuities between these two forms of environmental collapse. She performed this piece outside the UN climate summit in 2016 and subsequently published it in her collection of poems, *Iep Jāltok: Poems from a Marshallese Daughter*.

> At a climate change conference
> a colleague tells me 2 degrees
> is just a benchmark for negotiations
> I tell him for my islands 2 degrees
> is a gamble
> at 2 degrees my islands
> will already be under water
> this is why our leaders push
> for 1.5
>
> Seems small
> like 0.5 degrees
> shouldn't matter
> like 0.5 degrees
> are just crumbs
> like the Marshall Islands
> must look
> on a map
> just crumbs you
> dust off the table, wipe
> your hands clean of [39]

Jetñil-Kijiner mobilizes here the very metaphors that have been used by colonizers to justify using the Marshall Islands as nuclear testing sites. "Crumbs you / dust off the table, wipe / your hands clean of" are exactly what Pikinni and Ānewetak were to American military officials. It echoes former statements by Dr. Merrill Eisenbud, first health safety chief of the US Atomic Energy Commission, who compared irradiated ri-Majel to mice.[40] Islands as crumbs, people as mice: with her choice of metaphors, Jetñil-Kijiner shows that mass migration, whether it is triggered by radioactive skies or rising seas, is the result of the same form of environmental racism.

In the following verses, she evokes the fate of the nuclear refugees from Pikinni, many of whom now live exiled on Kōle (Kili) island:

On Kili island
the tides were underestimated
patients sleeping in a clinic with
a nuclear history threaded
into their bloodlines woke
to a wild water world
a rushing rapid of salt
a sewage of syringes and gauze[41]

Here, Jetñil-Kijiner recalls past floods, possibly the 2011 high wave that submerged the whole island, to emphasize that rising sea levels are only adding on to a nuclear history. The stanza is built on alliterations, the rolling consonants emphasizing that she uses here a lexicon usually referring to fresh water to describe salt water: "wild water," "rushing rapid," "sewage of syringes." She thus presents the island's space as a dystopian continuum between land and ocean, just as she presented the island's history as a dystopian continuum between radioactive skies and rising seas.

Jetñil-Kijiner believes her work has "always been about processing the emotional weight of climate change through art."[42] In 2018, she set out to process the grief of losing those islands twice—first to nuclear imperialism, then to carbon imperialism. Sailing on a walap (oceangoing outrigger canoe) to Ānewetak and Pikinni, she aimed to create mourning rituals and bereavement poems. After traveling for five days, her crew reached the Bravo bomb site. They weren't sure what to do once there: "Should there be a ceremony? A prayer perhaps? A poem? I had nothing prepared for the moment. . . . I . . . hadn't given myself any time to reflect on what it would mean to visit this site that was the source of so much pain and legacies of trauma."[43] Crushed by grief at the sight of the vaporized island, she did not perform anything on the spot.

She found a way to address this crushing grief later, while on Runit Dome. As she explains in her blog, "the Runit Dome was once just Runit—one of the islets that make up Enewetak atoll."[44] It was vaporized by American nuclear bombs and reduced to a crater dubbed the "Cactus Crater." During the "cleanup" of the atoll, decades after the explosion, the US Army dumped highly radioactive plutonium-239 waste, 437 plastic bags of plutonium fragments, and more than 104,000 cubic yards of contaminated soil onto the crater before covering it with concrete. The dome is so poorly built that it would not meet today's US standards for the disposal of household trash.[45]

In her mourning piece, titled *Anointed*, Jetñil-Kijiner is filmed climbing the dome. Alternating shots of idyllic scenes of Marshallese life and archival images of nuclear bombs, she can be heard addressing an unnamed island:

How shall we remember you?

You were a whole island, once. You were breadfruit trees heavy with green globes of fruit whispering promises of massive canoes.

. . . .

Then you became testing ground. Nine nuclear weapons consumed you, one by one by one, engulfed in an inferno of blazing heat.[46]

But she is not drowning. She is fighting. While her people lost the island, she presents herself, offers her own body, as a living remnant of it. The vocabulary that she uses to describe the island echoes her own self-description. "You became crater, an empty belly," she tells the island. "Plutonium ground into a concrete slurry filled your hollow cavern. You became tomb. You became concrete shell." She then echoes: "My belly is a crater empty of stories and answers only questions, hard as concrete." The parallelism makes it clear: disfigured and wounded, the land nonetheless lives on in the body of its people.

In this piece, Jetñil-Kijiner mobilizes the gestures of the Marshallese funeral ritual, the eorak, to mourn for the lost island through the motions of her body. The white dome evokes the traditionally white tombs of Marshallese cemeteries, and she follows the custom of reciting the life of the deceased—in this case, the island itself. But a crucial element from the eorak is missing. "There will be no white stones to scatter around this grave," she declares. The cracked dome lacks any of the white coral stones found all over the atoll; it is only an endless expanse of poisonous gray flatness. To get the white stones necessary for the ritual, Jetñil-Kijiner goes to a beach and takes white corals with her to the tomb in a weaved basket made of coconut fronds (see figure 5.1).

The image of this weaved basket is intertwined with other references to weaving as she prepares for the ceremony. Jetñil-Kijiner is filmed braiding her hair and tying her nieded, or jaki (traditional Marshallese woven skirt), around her waist (see figure 5.2). This imagery is important because while she declares that the mourning ritual is impossible to perform on this island ("There will be no white stones to scatter around this grave. There will be no songs to sing"), the video-poem's visual focus on weaving suggests the possibility of healing.

The marvel of weaving, notes Potawatomi biologist and essayist Robin Wall Kimmerer, lies in its power of regeneration. A weaved basket "knows the dual powers of destruction and creation that shape the world. Strands once sepa-

THERE WILL BE NO SONGS TO SING.

FIGURE 5.1. Kathy Jetñil-Kijiner's weaved basket on Runit Dome. Still from *Anointed*.

rated are rewoven into a new whole."[47] Jetñil-Kijiner's woven basket thus embodies her peoples' harmonious relationship with the land. The art of taking only the coconut fronds needed without killing the tree, and of creating a work of art out of separated strands, reads as a symbol of a mutually respectful relationship between the land and its people.

Jetñil-Kijiner further underscores the eloquence of weaving in a Marshallese context in her literary scholarship. Describing the art of aj (traditional Marshallese weaving) as a form of visual text, she argues that weaving designs preserve Marshallese cultural values such as genealogy and relationship to land.[48] Several of the outer layers of a jaki, for example, give information about the wearer's connections to a certain land as inherited matrilocally or patrilocally.[49] While mourning for the lost island, Jetñil-Kijiner thus weaves around her belly and into the film the symbol of Marshallese people's enduring link to and love for the land, as perpetuated in the visual text of her jaki. While Jetñil-Kijiner's oral literature focuses on the pain of mourning, her visual literature suggests the transgenerational vitality of ri-Majeļ's love for the lost island.

Jetñil-Kijiner fears that the forced migration of the people of Āniwetak may not be the last forced displacement undergone by ri-Majeļ. The Marshall Islands are among the four countries, worldwide, that are the most at risk of being engulfed by rising sea levels—along with Kiribati, Tuvalu, and the Maldives. The most pessimistic predictions forecast that oceans will rise above the highest point in the Marshall Islands as early as 2050.[50] High tides and flooding will affect the possibility of keeping the islands inhabitable long before the

PLUTONIUM GROUND INTO A CONCRETE SLURRY

FIGURE 5.2. Kathy Jetñil-Kijiner tying her jaki. Still from *Anointed*.

fatidic day when they go under water. Such high tides have already started endangering communities in low-lying atolls.[51]

Jetñil-Kijiner reports starting to realize that the islands might be lost in July 2018, when University of Hawai'i climate scientist Chip Fletcher announced at a climate change conference that the measures to limit global warming to 1.5 degrees had not been taken in time. Fletcher encouraged his audience to consider adaptation measures such as land reclamation. Marshallese people could choose a few sites to elevate and save from the rising tides. Unfortunately, such projects are expensive and environmentally damaging: due to a global sand shortage, land reclamation comes with environmentally destructive dredging for more sand.[52] As Pacific studies scholar Aimee Bahng denounces, "capitalist development converts scenes of ecological destruction into schemes for more capitalist development."[53]

For Jetñil-Kijiner, land reclamation is no techno-utopian dream: "bulldozed reefs / blasted sands / ... forcing land from an ancient rising sea."[54] She explains, "I can't see this as an opportunity if we have no choice in the matter. Building islands or even just elevating would mean ripping apart our land, and with it the roots of our culture, as well as displacing/uprooting thousands of people in the process, and using processes that could destroy precious reef. It's extreme, and desperate."[55] Nuclear survivors had reached the same conclusion as early as 1954: relocation is not a solution. A petition launched by community leaders Dwight Heine, Atlan Anien, Kabua Kabua, and Dorothy Kabua clearly states that "land means a great deal to the Marshallese. It means more than just a place where you can plant your food crops and build your houses or a place where you can bury your dead. It is the very life of the people. Take away their land and their spirits go also."[56] Artificial islands would only perpetuate the decades-long history of forced migration that Marshallese underwent during the era of nuclear imperialism.

Still, Jetñil-Kijiner draws on Marshallese experience of land loss under nuclear imperialism to confront the threat of forced migration in times of climate collapse. In another poem, titled "Butterfly Thief," she directly addresses the carbon-addicted audiences responsible for this plight:

> I came across a cartoon
> that showed a bumble bee
> cute tubby and smiling
> with a message in a little cartoon bubble
>
> > *If we die*
> > > *we're taking you with us*
>
> Might as well put a Marshallese face
> over that bumble bee
> Because if our islands drown out
> due to the rising sea level
> just who do you think
> will be next
>
> I'm taking you with me[57]

Jetñil-Kijiner performed this poem at the request of the British NGO Clean Energies. In this piece, she departed for the first time from the iconic appeals to hope, solidarity, and resilience that so moved the UN heads of states. Here, she confronts the myth of the welcoming Native, "cute tubby and smiling," to which Pacific people are so often reduced. She links the trope of the smiling Native to the environmental symbol of the bumble bee to *reverse* the hegemonic narrative presenting Oceanians as powerless victims waiting for their imminent demise since the sixteenth century. Addressing her foreign carbon-addicted audience, she threatens back: "I'm taking you with me."

She then continues, recalling the trauma of losing islands to nuclear bombing:

> Another contributing factor
> to the death of bees and butterflies
> are pesticides. For bees, the pesticides cloud their vision.

They lose their way and die
before they reach their home
How many of us
will die before we get to go home
will take a boat to islands that were once whole
once held a hive of community
now reduced to sand and stone

This story was inspired by a visit Jetñil-Kijiner did in 2015 to Mājro atoll. With some friends, she traveled to the island of Kalalen and met a man named Yoster Harris. He pointed to a pile of sand and rocks a few feet away from them and explained that a decade ago, it was a lush island where he would fish and camp. Recurring high tides have now killed all the vegetation. As Jetñil-Kijiner explains in her blog: "He said in Marshallese, 'We've had the funeral for that island—it's over. But you need to save the others.' I came away from the experience feeling the weight of Yoster's appeal, as well as the chilling realization that the pile of sand and rocks that was once an island is exactly what the rest of the Marshall Islands could look like in a few years."[58]

Literary scholar Erin Suzuki argues that Jetñil-Kijiner challenges the mainstream representation of atoll dwellers as paradigmatic victims, showing instead that "Pacific Islanders' moral leadership in global climate discourse springs not from their positions as victims facing the loss of their land but rather from the depths of their generational knowledges gathered from centuries of living with and on the seas."[59] Expanding on Suzuki's insight, it is helpful to highlight how this poem is rooted in transgenerational experiences of loss and regeneration and therefore carries between the lines a celebration of the survival of Marshallese culture through several apocalypses. Indeed, "Butterfly Thief" retraces the genealogy of the land through the Marshallese creation story of Lidrepdrepju and Liwsuonmour, two powerful sisters embodied in basalt stone on the shores of Narño atoll and Aur atoll.[60]

Some stories say our ancestors came from volcano stone
Lidrepdrepju—a basalt rock goddess rooted in reef
Today I keep a basalt rock on my bookshelf
What tokens of our land shall we / will we
store in our selves
inside our honeycomb of chest bones
the buzzing of a shore long gone

I'm taking you with me[61]

Liwsuonmour was thrown into the sea by a proselytizing missionary, and only Lidrepdrepju remains on the rocky shores of Aur.[62] Ri-bwebwenato Alfred Capelle shared with Jetñil-Kijiner that the seemingly unimpressive basalt rock is an important historical site for Marshallese people because Lidredprepju symbolizes permanence. "Eban jako," he said. "It will never be gone."[63] In this context, the poem's leitmotiv takes on a different meaning. The "you" in "I'm taking you with me" may also refer, here, to the land, which remains with the speaker above and below the ocean's surface. Jetñil-Kijiner's poetry thus combines threats to carbon addicts and promises of faithfulness to her land to process solastalgia and threats of further forced displacement.

Prophecies in Kiribati: Teresia Teaiwa's Coconuts

Not far south of Aelōñ in M̧ajel̦ lies the United Kingdom's nuclear playground. The UK's first nuclear tests took place in Australia, in the Montebello Islands, Emu Field, and Maralinga, between 1952 and 1958. During these tests, many Aboriginal people were given one-way train tickets to far-off towns. Others were relocated to a camp in Yalata, on the outskirts of the testing zone. And some people remained on their land, right in the path of the nuclear clouds, a fact known to the Australian government but undisclosed to the public until the 1980s.[64] The Anangu, Tjarutja, and Yankunytjatjara people were disproportionately affected by the fallout and suffer from numerous radiation-related health issues to this day.[65] When the Australian government declined to further collaborate with the United Kingdom's nuclear program, the British government transferred its testing sites to Terapukatea (Malden Island) and Kiritimati (Christmas Island), in the state of Kiribati, then a British protectorate known as the Gilbert and Ellice Islands Colony (GEIC). The series of tests, known as Operation Grapple, were aimed at developing a British thermonuclear bomb.

Just like the American nuclear program, the British nuclear tests resulted in numerous instances of forced migration for Pacific Islanders. As historian Nic Maclellan reports, about 260 i-Kiribati people were living in Kiritimati at the time of Operation Grapple. Originally from Tarawa, they had immigrated to Kiritimati to work on the copra plantations owned by the Australian businessman James Burn. When the British state seized the island, many were hired as laborers on the testing sites.[66] The presence of this large civilian population, with children and elders living directly on the test site, presented a challenge for British authorities. Officials decided to displace them on the day of nuclear tests. "Our present plans are that on firing days, civilians will be embarked in a ship and sailed out of the immediate danger area. They will be landed again on Christmas Island as soon as the burst has taken place," reports Captain Milligan, member of the Grapple Task Force.[67] About two hundred workers and their children were thus relocated to Tabuaeran (Fanning Island) between January and April 1957.

I-Kiribati laborers and their families living in Kiritimati were once again made to move in 1958, when the UK detonated Grapple Y, its largest thermonuclear bomb. Those who were made to stay on Kiritimati, the "Native population . . . required to maintain administration and security," were directly hit by radioactive fallout.[68] Tonga Fou, one of the workers from Tarawa who lived on Kiritimati, reflects back on the imperial obliviousness underpinning these decisions: "Why are they not thinking that human beings are staying on the island?"[69] Those who were able to return to Tarawa at the end of Operation Grapple brought nuclear contamination with them, and many of their descendants are born with congenital disabilities.[70] Many i-Kiribati also continued to live on Kiritimati, despite the fact that the UK Ministry of Defense did not "clean up" the island before 2005.[71]

The people of Rawaki, a group of eight atolls in eastern Kiribati, were also displaced in 1963 and 1964 to Wagina, in the Solomon Islands, ostensibly due to the droughts that were affecting their atolls. Yet as reported by social anthropologist Tammy Tabe, these members of the i-Kiribati diaspora believe that "their forced relocation to the Solomon Islands was a result of Britain's nuclear activities on Christmas Island."[72] They suspect that they were removed from their islands because of the risk of nuclear contamination. Their oral history has not yet been confirmed by colonial archives, which remain fragmented and difficult to access.[73]

These forced migrations, like in Aelōñ in Ṃajeḷ, inform how i-Kiribati activists now apprehend the threat of rising sea levels. Kiribati is one of the four low-lying island nations in the world most threatened to be erased from the map in the coming decades. The country became the center of attention of the global climate movement under the presidency of Anote Tong, a charismatic and dedicated climate activist who crystalized opposition to carbon capitalism during his mandate. But in addition to his efforts at mitigating climate collapse, Tong also considered very seriously the threat of forced displacement. In 2013, Tong's government acquired land on the Fijian island of Vanua Levu and encouraged his fellow citizens to consider relocating there.[74]

How to mourn the loss of a country that isn't lost yet but whose own president acknowledges will very likely disappear? Art offers, here too, unusual perspectives. By considering the poetry of Teresia Teaiwa, we will see that art can mobilize powerful metaphors to draw continuity between different instances of forced mass migration and find symbols of resilience in these recurring tropes.

The late Teresa K. Teaiwa is a leading scholar in Pacific studies, a renowned antinuclear activist, and a popular poet. She is particularly appreciated for her trailblazing scholarship and her mentoring of the next generation of Pacific scholars, and her multifaceted work has been rewarded with numerous prizes, teaching awards, and literary recognition. Daughter of an i-Kiribati father and an African American mother, Teaiwa was born in Honolulu and raised in Fiji. Her family has endured a long history of forced migration. On her father's side, Teresia's relatives were deported from Banaba during World War II and have since remained in exile to facilitate the British extraction of phosphate. On her mother's side, she inherited the memory of the Atlantic slave trade.[75] While Teaiwa found strength in being "deeply connected by genealogy, birth, sweat, and commitment to many parts of [Oceania]," she also remained throughout her career profoundly attuned to the transgenerational traumas of displacement that made her pan-Pacific identity.[76] In fact, in her scholarship, she avoids the words *displacement* or *relocation* to refer to that history. Instead, she uses the arresting neologism *dislocation*.

Teaiwa was very involved against the dislocations triggered by nuclear imperialism and was an active participant in the Nuclear Free and Independent Pacific movement. She has also written groundbreaking scholarship about Kiribati and is considered one of the country's national icons.[77] Yet there is a surprising silence in her work. Her most famous antinuclear pieces do not mention nuclear tests in Kiribati. This silence about the nuked atolls in her country of origin is a surprising void that deserves critical attention.

The first striking example of this trend is her oft-quoted essay on nuclear dislocation, "Bikini and Other S/Pacific N/Oceans," published in 1994. In this piece, she mentions nuclear tests in the Marshall Islands, Australia, and French-occupied Polynesia, but not in Kiribati. The same absence structures her antinuclear poetry. In 2001, she performed a public reading of a collection of poems titled *Coconuts* at the University of Hawai'i at Mānoa. In these poems, both read and sung, she uses the image of a coconut as a metaphor for nuclear-induced and climate-triggered migrations. The sixth poem of her series, titled "bad coconuts" and transformed into a song by Richard Hamasaki and Doug Matsuoka, is dedicated to antinuclear scholar Stewart Firth. Teaiwa explains that she read in Firth's 1987 book, *Nuclear Playground*, that in islands used as nuclear test sites, coconuts have been made radioactive.[78] In an upbeat song using reggae rhythms, Teaiwa invites her audience to sing along:

An apple a day keeps the doctor away [×2]
but a coconut a day will kill you
a coconut a day will kill you [×3]
if you live on Moruroa [×2]
if you visit Fangataufa [×2]
return to Enewetak [×2]
resettle Bikini [×2]
a coconut a day will kill you [×4][79]

The numerous repetitions evoke the countless detonations in these islands, where bombs were exploded over and over and over again for decades. Strikingly enough, however, Teaiwa mentions neither Kiritimati nor Terapukatea in this piece. She lists the test sites of the Marshall Islands and Māʻohi Nui but omits those in Kiribati.

This silence is surprising, given not only her i-Kiribati heritage but also considering the fact that she was brought up in Fiji, the country closest to the British test sites, whose military was tightly involved in Operation Grapple and whose civilians were most directly affected by the subsequent fallout. The Fiji Nuclear Veterans Association was established in 1999 by hundreds of test veterans and family members, and the NGO managed to maintain records on all the test veterans, spouses, and descendants.[80] The same year, the first collection of testimonies of Fijian test veterans came out, edited by Fijian writer Losean Tubanavau-Salaluba and published by a Fijian press.[81] As a scholarly expert on the Republic of Fiji Military Forces (RFMF) who has written extensively on Fijian soldiers' involvement in Malaysia and the Middle East, Teaiwa must have been acutely aware of Fiji's military venture in the neighboring country of Kiribati and is most likely to have consulted this archive.[82]

The absence of Kiribati nuclear dislocation cannot be imputed either to the fact that there were comparatively fewer people affected in Kiribati than in the Marshall Islands or Māʻohi Nui. Teaiwa's antinuclear scholarship was written with the intent to "apprehen[d] generic colonial technologies of marginalization and erasure," to overturn the legacy of Kissinger's dismissal of Pacific suffering on the pretense that it affects only limited numbers of people.[83] She has committed her time and efforts to bring to light the forgotten history of a very small number of people, such as the few dozen women first enlisted in the Fiji Military Forces. The silence surrounding nuclear tests in Kiribati that structures her work must therefore be interpreted as a voluntary choice.

In her early writing, Teaiwa has ventured some explanations for her refusal to focus on i-Kiribati's histories of displacement. In "Scholarship from a Lazy Native" (1995), she denounces the "benevolent ghettoization" that takes place in Pacific studies when Pacific students are encouraged to write only about their specific cultural or national context.[84] Her 2001 dissertation also denounces the trend, dominant in cultural studies at the turn of the century, to privilege analyses of migration, diaspora, and exile. She highlights how this focus on "routes and displacement" only happens at the expense of a study of "roots and home" and tends to marginalize Native studies.[85] Her decision not to dwell on Kiribati's nuclear refugees' routes and displacement may stem from the same radical commitment to speak to all Pacific nuclear injustices, true to her statement that "the Nuclear Free and Independent Pacific operates on the premise that whatever happens in one part of the Pacific Ocean affects that whole ocean."[86]

In addition to these theoretical justifications, I would suggest that this absence in Teaiwa's most quoted article and poetry may also convey the alienation of i-Kiribati in the face of forced displacement. Barred to future generations, Kiribati's nuclear islands are so lost that they cannot even find a way into the prose and song of Kiribati's most iconic writer. In this sense, Teaiwa's performance functions, indirectly, as a mourning song for the country of her ancestors. Her silences are always telling; they reflect unspeakable loss. Sometimes, even the strongest scholar-poet-activists may not be interested in writing about resilience.

Yet in the other pieces of her *Coconut* series, Teaiwa allows herself a more hopeful take on the power of Pacific peoples in the face of forced migration. Her spoken-word performance "Fear of an Estuary," for example, explicitly describes coconuts as a powerful symbol of Pacific people's power in the face of forced migration:

> I think I know what a coconut feels like
> After floating for so long
> in salt water
> And suddenly
> entering
> an estuary
> This ancient feeling
> I'm feeling it again
> This sinking sinking feeling
> Have you ever heard of a coconut drowning?[87]

In this piece, fresh water functions as a metaphor for continental people pouring into the Pacific waters. This poem, however, may have gotten endowed with an additional, latent meaning in times of climate change. It can be read as a prophetic song regarding climate-triggered migration. Sea levels are rising because of melting ice sheets, literally turning the salt water into less dense, fresher waters. Before the icecaps started melting, Pacific people, like coconuts carried by ocean currents, could travel from island to island. As Teaiwa tells her audience, mainly consisting of students from all over Oceania, "If I were a coconut / You would be salt water / In calm or storms / I could float in you / Breathe in you." But the melted fresh water is now threatening to sink the floating fruit: "If I were a coconut / And you were salt water / I would sink / Sink / Sink / When you met / Fresh water."[88] However, the coconut remains in her poetry a symbol of Pacific resilience and of Oceania's power for regeneration. As she says in her concluding sentences: "I would sink / Sink / Sink / But / The wise ones say / I will not / Drown." We can find, in this very poem performed decades before the rise of the Climate Warriors, the prophetic vision of their movement's motto: We are not drowning—we are fighting.

Using the coconut to discuss nuclear poisoning and climate change has important connotations. As Teaiwa explained during a 2001 lecture, "the coconut is very important to Pacific people."[89] In Fiji, where she grew up, the coconut "shapes [people's] consciousness," and in Aotearoa, where she taught, "the word is used pejoratively" to refer to Pacific Islanders.[90] Identifying with the coconut is a way to reendow a term that has been turned into a racial slur with its original ameliorative value. Furthermore, the coconut, brought by oceanic navigators on their voyages to new islands, has long been a powerful symbol of Pacific people's rooted mobility. Indeed, the tree that provides the trunk of the canoe and the fruits that gave water for the voyage symbolize both the voyagers' movement and their rootedness in their original land.[91] According to Pacific studies scholar Candice Steiner, the coconut, prominently used in i-Kiribati video-eco-poetry by the local film company Nei Tabera Ni Kai, is "reminiscent of the spread of life through the islands and of the olive branch–carrying dove in the story of Noah and the Ark—[it] is a very powerful symbol of Islanders' insistence that they will prevail."[92] In her poetry, Teaiwa reappropriates the coconut as a symbol of resilience and regeneration, connecting the first transoceanic voyages, nuclear displacement, and economic and climate-triggered migrations. Focusing on the symbolism of the coconut helps her reflect on the wide diversity of Pacific migrations, "constantly resisting other people's attempts to reduce the Pacific to one thing—to one issue."[93] As she famously underscored, "my job . . . is to remind people of the complexity and not let them try to paint us with a single brush stroke."[94]

Poetry is not Teaiwa's only mode of activism. She has regularly put her body on the line to protest, to educate, and to lead antinuclear and decolonial movements. Yet poetry is a refuge to process the grief inherent in losing islands. Her oral performances help her connect with others and create the community that she fought for. And her metaphors provide powerful tropes: whether radioactive, sinking, or sprouting, coconuts symbolize Pacific peoples' storytelling continuity in the face of nuclear imperialism and carbon imperialism. As the current form of global collective life is about to be shattered by a collapsing climate, such artistic performances underscore an important form of permanence around which to find solace, strength, and inspiration. Teaiwa's poetry provides hope while "interrogating" the concept of hope: it locates hope in the past, as the memory of Pacific people's strength to survive.

Mā'ohi Nui and the Issue of "Voluntary" Migration in Chantal T. Spitz's Writing

The situation in Mā'ohi Nui raises a different issue: the problem of "voluntary" migration under nuclear imperialism. Mā'ohi leadership voluntarily gifted the islands of Moruroa and Fangataufa to France, and thousands of Mā'ohi workers voluntarily abandoned their homeland to work for the Pacific Experimentation Center (CEP). While Aelōñ in Majeḷ and Kiribati are respectively the second and third poorest countries in the Pacific, French-occupied Polynesia is comparatively much richer, its economy bolstered by fifty years of nuclear money.[95] For many Mā'ohi people, the CEP feels like a devil's bargain. Mā'ohi literature processes the feelings of guilt associated with the "voluntary" abandonment of one's land and interrogates the meaning of "freedom" of movement under nuclear imperialism. Such reflections are crucial today, as every day, people "decide" to leave lands rendered uninhabitable by global warming. Mā'ohi writer and antinuclear activist Chantal T. Spitz explores Mā'ohi people's ambivalent complicity in their own system of exploitation, tackling the widespread feeling of guilt that plagues many victims of nuclear imperialism to this day.

Before analyzing Spitz's novel, I should emphasize that not all migrations in Mā'ohi Nui were voluntary. Like the American and the British armies, the French military created by force the allegedly "desert" islands in which they exploded their bombs. Moruroa and Fangataufa are historically and genealogically related to the people of Tureia, an island seventy-five miles north of the nuclear atolls. While Moruroa was uninhabited in the 1960s, it was the birthplace of some of Tureians' ancestors, and it had remained a crucial center of subsistence economy, as Tureians seasonally gathered mother-of-pearl and copra on the atoll. Some have inheritance rights to Moruroa lands.[96] As the nuclear tests continued and gained in intensity, the entire population of Tureia (forty-six people at the time) was relocated to Tahiti in 1968, two years after the beginning of the tests. The French army justified this forced migration by arguing that Tureians had been "invited" to participate in the July festivities of the Heiva.[97] Tragically, these forced displacements were insufficient to prevent radioactive contamination. Tureia buried one-third of its adult population between 1997 and 2002, all victims of cancer.[98] M. Fariki, a survivor of the tests, denounces France's official reports on the contamination of his island: "France has proofs that the nuclear bomb was not poisonous. Not poisonous? Come see my island!"[99]

In addition to relocating Tureians in Tahiti during high-intensity atmospheric tests, the French army regularly displaced the inhabitants of neighboring islands in the Tuamotu and the Gambier archipelagos. Antiradiation shelters were built in Pukarua, Reao, and Mangareva, and the military ordained whole islands to remain confined during radioactive fallout. Again, such limitation of freedom of movement was woefully insufficient to prevent radioactive contamination. The civilian shelters were made of simple corrugated iron, when military shelters on the same islands were in reinforced concrete one meter thick.[100] The shelters were also built belatedly, two years after the beginning of the tests—so after the fallout from Aldebaran on July 2, 1966, which contaminated nearby inhabited islands with levels of radioactivity 142 times higher than at ground zero at Chernobyl. Pacific studies scholar Alex Mawyer describes the Tuamotu and Mangareva as "at once the back of the French state and the back of French Polynesia. The back of the back within the imaginary and the geographical facts of the French nation."[101] Paumotu and Mangarevian people were thus subjected to more drastic forced relocation and mandatory confinement than people of more "central" islands in the country.

Despite these instances of limited freedom of movement, many of the migrations that took place in Māʻohi Nui under nuclear imperialism were strictly voluntary. In 1964, military ships began recruiting workers across the archipelagoes. Many Māʻohi men immediately volunteered to move to Moruroa and Fangataufa. The exact number is unknown; CEP archives report between four thousand and eight thousand local employees, but the antinuclear association Moruroa e Tātou estimates the total number to be closer to fifteen thousand people—one-quarter of the active population at the time.[102] Why did so many men and boys, as young as twelve years old, voluntarily leave for the nuclear atolls? According to an antinuclear activist who wished to remain anonymous, it is because "a man who did not work at Moruroa, who did not manage to find a job, lost status. He was just a poor bugger."[103] The CEP paid 12,000 CFP francs per month (US$110), several times what laborers could make collecting mother-of-pearl or harvesting copra. Many found the prospect of fast and easy money appealing.[104] They were never informed of the health risks the work would induce. Security notices were written in French, a language that most did not speak.[105]

With the working men gone, many families migrated too. As an anonymous worker from Ua Pou notes, "At the CEP they only paid a ticket from Moruroa to Tahiti, but not from Tahiti to [the outer islands]. So to keep your marriage going you arrange for your wife to come over to Tahiti."[106] An exodus ensued. After the tests began, there were eighty-five thousand people in French Polynesia, forty-five thousand of whom lived in Tahiti, a third of whom found shelter in the underserviced suburbs of Pape'ete, Fa'a'ā, Pīra'e, and Arue.[107] By contrast, in the outer islands, depopulation became a stringent issue. In the Henua Enata (Marquesas Islands), for example, the mayor of Ua Pou deplored that after the CEP began recruiting workers, there were only "children and old people" left: "There is now a home of the elderly [in the Marquesas islands] because some people don't have anybody to look after them anymore."[108]

In Tahiti, the rapid influx of migrants from the outer islands came with its own set of issues. "We have social housing projects now, homes for the elderly, we have drugs, urbanization, battered wives; that is Moruroa!... Moruroa not only has contaminated our land but it has also polluted our families, our spirit."[109] Social inequalities widened between rural islanders employed for short-term and underpaid manual labor and the urban national elite working in public service and business sectors. The CEP dramatically increased class inequality, undermined traditional family structures, and created a proletariat impoverished by inflation and real estate speculation. This nuclearization of the economy subtends a widespread sense that local peoples have made a devil's bargain or had it forced on them—a debate that continues to inform local politics to this day.

Many people struggle with the thought that those exiles were voluntarily decided. As reported by a survey of former CEP workers organized by local antinuclear activists, those workers consider themselves active participants in the nuking of their own country: "in their own eyes, [they are] responsible with regard to the possible consequences their actions had for their own health, that of their families and their offspring."[110] This is characteristic of all abusive situations. Feminist scholars have denounced, for example, how victims of sexual assault tend to burden themselves with shame that should be borne by the abuser.[111] Here, victims of nuclear imperialism are consumed with guilt, while the nuclear colonizer still denies its responsibility. While nuclear survivors reproach themselves for their irradiation, the French State refuses to apologize for its nuclear aggression under the pretense that the effects of the radioactivity were not well known (they were) and that colonizer and colonized were similarly exposed (they were not).

Of course, many Tahitian politicians vocally opposed nuclear testing. Pouvanaa a Oopa began collecting signatures in the Tuamotu archipelago as early as 1950, in a contribution to global efforts for the Stockholm peace appeal.[112] In the mid-1960s, representatives Céline Oopa, Francis Sanford, John Teariki, and Felix Tefaatau publicly opposed the CEP at the Tahitian assembly.[113] Yet for two decades, no politician succeeded in centralizing an effective antinuclear movement. Pouvanaa was exiled before the beginning of the tests.[114] Teariki and Sanford's government soon became too financially dependent on CEP money to oppose it successfully.[115] In this difficult political context, it was Mā'ohi orators, writers, and activists who became the vanguard of antinuclear oppositions. It was thus the poet and filmmaker Henri Hiro who organized the first antinuclear marches in the country, before Oscar Temaru coalesced antinuclear and pro-independence sensibilities around his political party in the 1980s. In Hiro's wake, other orators, singers, church leaders, painters, and, of course, Chantal T. Spitz became leading antinuclear voices in the country at the turn of the twentieth century.

Chantal T. Spitz, with whose work I introduced this book, is a novelist, an editor, and a leading figure in Pacific environmental activism. Although a powerful public speaker, she initially rose to fame for her written literature. She has published several novels, romance biographies, short stories, poems, and essays, and she cofounded Tahiti's literary magazine Littérama'ohi. She has spoken on nuclear issues in multiple Pacific countries, such as Australia, Kanaky, Belau, and Fiji. She has also organized and/or participated in several Salon International du Livre Océanien (International Oceanian Literary Salon) and in the Festival International du Film Océanien (International Festival of Oceanian Cinema). Her literature often interrogates Tahiti's upper class's complicity in the ceding of the islands of Moruroa and Fangataufa to the French and explores the prevailing feeling of guilt among many Mā'ohi people.

Spitz was born in Tahiti in 1954, to middle-class parents. Her grandmother was the first of her family to receive a French education, at a time when most Tahitians were schooled in religious institutions and never learned the colonizer's idiom. Spitz's family became part of the elite social class known in Tahiti as the 'āfa or demis (loosely translating as the "half-ones" or the "mixed-race"). This social class, descending from the unions of local nobility and early European immigrants, has historically collaborated closely with colonizers and welcomed the financial manna that accompanied nuclear imperialism. Spitz's grandmother, among others, had decided to make her family draw as many benefits as possible from Westerners' presence. She banned reo tahiti (the Tahitian language) in the family home and ensured that her offspring were given a French education. Spitz grew up to become a teacher, like her father and her grandmother before her. However, the French nuclear testing program and the racial hierarchies plaguing her family led her to jettison her initial career path and to become a leading decolonial voice in her country.[116]

In 1991, when France was still detonating nuclear bombs in Moruroa, Spitz published *L'Île des rêves écrasés*, translated into English in 2007 as *Island of Shattered Dreams*. This book thoroughly transformed the cultural landscape of her time. Not only was it the first novel ever published by a Mā'ohi writer; it was also the first novel written in a nuclear colony to denounce Western nations' nuclear tests in the Pacific. *Island of Shattered Dreams* tells the story of a family in the fictional island of Ruahine.[117] In the novel, three generations of Mā'ohi protagonists fight against expropriation from their island, which has been chosen as the site for the development of France's nuclear experiments. The book, which starts as an ode to the traditional rural Pacific lifestyle, ends in dystopian tones after the protagonists fail to stop the launching of France's first nuclear bomb. The culprits, in Spitz's novel, are not only the evil pāpa'a (white people) who stole the land. Her narrative also prominently features the Mā'ohi politicians "elected to protect [their people] and selling [them] out."[118] They are represented by a character named John Prallet, who deludes the antinuclear protagonists Terii and Tetiare with grand speeches before driving off in his luxury car, "sprawling into his squashy seat for ministerial buttocks."[119] He is the one who voluntarily offers to gift their motu (coral islet) in Ruahine to France: "Let us gift this bit of our territory to the State, thereby participating in the magnificent work of this great Nation to which we belong."[120]

John Prallet is a faintly veiled caricature of a real historical figure, Jacques-Denis Drollet. Drollet played a major role in helping France set up its nuclear testing sites in Mā'ohi Nui. On February 6, 1964, Drollet presided over the deliberation of the Assembly's permanent commission to discuss France's proposed nuclear deal. Going against his former party's desires to rent or sell the atolls to France, he pushed to give away Moruroa and Fangataufa for free. He claims to have hoped that this way, "France would not forget us."[121] His proposition was adopted by the commission, with three votes against two.[122] Drollet subsequently directly benefited from the financial bonanza that the CEP brought to Tahiti. After occupying various posts in the government, he cofounded a local bank and a local airplane company and rose to become a prominent figure in the country's ruling class. Spitz's fictional John Prallet is more Manichean than Jacques-Denis Drollet, as the latter was also a close collaborator of Pouvanaa a Oopa and argues that he gave the atolls to France only after having been threatened with a military coup by Charles de Gaulle himself.[123] Brushing off her original model's inner struggles, Spitz makes her fictional character the embodiment of everything flawed within the Indigenous capitalist class that sold out the country. Yet beyond this caricatural villain, the Mā'ohi are made collectively responsible for their own forced displacement from their land. All the "children of Maeva" are called out for their forced migration:

> Maeva immortelle,
> Aujourd'hui nous te vendons
> Te sacrifiant au Dieu Argent
> Maeva éternelle,
> Aujourd'hui nous te perdons
> Te prostituant à l'étranger.[124]

> Immortal Maeva,
> Today we sell you
> Sacrificing you to the God Money
> Eternal Maeva,
> Today we lose you
> Prostituting you to the foreigner.

Spitz conveys this complex juxtaposing of guilt and victimization in a surprising neologism: "we are being suicided" ("*on nous suicide*").[125]

Spitz's novel thus challenges the binary between passive victims or active agents. As shown by historian David A. Chappell, the debate around whether Oceanians were active agents or passive victims is problematic. "Better descriptions combine fatal impact, imperial domination, active resistance, economic dependency, axial change, and native persistence. One might say, what a mess! Yet the reality . . . is clearly too multifaceted to be encompassed by a simple binary agent-victim construct."[126] This multifaceted reality is better represented in the multilayered psychological struggles featured in Spitz's novel.

At the macrostructural level, Spitz also explores this agent-victim construct in the development of the plot. The male protagonist, Terii, falls in love with Laura, a French nuclear engineer responsible for exploding the missiles. This improbable relationship between the charismatic pro-independence archaeologist and a "stranger raping his land" symbolizes the complex relationship between Mā'ohi Nui and France.[127] After having poisoned the local food supplies with radioactive fallout, France has ensured Mā'ohi dependency on French imported foods and its health care system. Furthermore, like Terii abandoning the barricades for archaeological research, many independence activists focused on cultural revival at the expense of political struggle. Spitz is virulently against this orientation taken by the pro-independence movement in her country. "It has always been our weak point," she says. "To avoid building political movements, we invest in cultural movements. We have the feeling that we are resisting because we are doing cultural things, but it doesn't work."[128]

Perhaps for this reason, Spitz paints a bleak picture of the grassroot antinuclear movements, describing their efforts as somewhat misguided and hopeless. The antinuclear protagonists, Terii and Tetiare, are systematically portrayed by the omniscient narrator as "naïve dreamers."[129] The struggle was unequal and hopeless from the start, as their petitions and delegations are met with state violence:

> *Le jour où débarque le premier contingent deux barrages ont été édifiés aux deux extrémités du motu: troncs de cocotier et de 'aito empilés les uns sur les autres. Ils sont peu nombreux, les défenseurs. Beaucoup de ceux qui ont signé la pétition se sont rendus aux arguments des hommes de confiance des élus politiques locaux.*
>
> *Une courte bataille s'engage et l'histoire une fois encore se répète. Que faire quand on n'a que son corps et son âme à opposer à des soldats de métier? Que faire quand on ne peut rien faire? Inutile combat. Pitoyable affrontement.*[130]

The day when the first military contingent disembarks, two barricades have been built on the two extremities of the motu: trunks of coconut trees and 'aito piled up on top of each other. They are so few, the defenders. Many of those who signed the petition have been convinced by the arguments of local political leaders' man of confidence.

A short battle begins and history once again repeats itself. What to do when one only has one's body and soul to oppose to professional soldiers? What to do when one cannot do anything? Useless struggle. Piteous confrontation.

Two decades later, when I interviewed her in Pape'ete, Spitz reflected on the failures of the antinuclear struggle and their contemporary implications:

> We fought against the nuclear, but in the end we realized that it did not stop because we were listened to. Rather, it stopped because France had decided to stop. It was a slap in the face. It was hard. People protested everywhere in the world, we set the city on fire, we burned down the air-

port, they didn't give a damn! They just stuck to the plan: they do a given number of tests and they stop.[131]

The novel ends on a pessimistic note. After retracing the genealogy of the protagonists across generations, the nuclear bombs interrupt their ancestral lineage. Terii, Eritapeta, and Tetiare's struggle ends with the virtual sterilization of their generation as the three of them remain childless. In the last chapter of the novel, a new character is introduced: an infant born on the day of the first nuclear test. Yet this birth, rather than embodying the hopes of a future generation, does not carry any positive symbolism. It marks the end of a long-lasting custom, enunciated at the beginning of the novel, according to which children are named "from the family's long genealogy, since no one can carry a name that does not belong to their forefathers."[132] That new child is instead christened Charles Voltigeur, in an attempt to link him to Charles de Gaulle and his bomb, the Voltigeuse.[133]

As was the case when creating the character of John Prallet, Spitz took inspiration from historical facts when inventing the character of Charles Voltigeur. On the morning of August 24, 1968, France detonated the nuclear bomb Canopus in Fangataufa. That same morning, a child was born in Mangareva. This child's mother, testifying for Mililani Ganivet and Marie-Hélène Villierme's podcast *Nu/clear Stories*, recalls that France's minister Robert Galley called the local police "to urge [her] to name [her] son Canopus, even though the father of [her] child had already chosen a name."[134] Pressured by the military doctor, the nurse, the mayor, and the police officer who visited her in her labor room, the child's mother agreed to give him the bomb's name.

Far from denoting a multicultural future, the fictional child represents the deculturation awaiting the generation coming in the wake of nuclear imperialism. Deprived both of a proper genealogical identification and of a Māʻohi name, Charles Voltigeur has lost his roots but has not been welcomed by the French in return. As his homonymous godfather Charles de Gaulle "immediately flies away to return to his country," the novel closes on a cultural impasse: "they will never meet."[135] The Māʻohi characters voluntarily unmoored themselves from their own culture, but they were not welcomed on the colonizers' shores.

These critiques resonate harshly in the age of climate collapse. The complacency of global political leaders ominously echoes that of Spitz's corrupt politicians. The inefficiency of antinuclear petitions, barricades, and marches unfortunately brings to mind the current lack of tangible results brought by contemporary climate protests. The collective responsibility bestowed on

Spitz's characters, even those who nominally opposed the nuclear tests, recalls the compromising behavior of carbon-addicted environmentalists the world over. And the interrupted genealogies of the protagonists at the end of the novel evokes an apocalyptic future of entire islands going underwater. The founder of the March for the Climate in Tahiti, Jason Man Sang, highlighted the parallels between nuclear complacency and climate apathy: "It is the same obsession for money, the same denial of scientific warning, nobody comes to the marches. If you all feel bad that you did not join Henri Hiro when he protested the bomb, why is there nobody at the climate marches?"[136] Harshly critical of nuclear traitors and antinuclear activists alike, *Island of Shattered Dreams* can be interpreted as a grim assessment of the potential for collective action to stop either nuclear imperialism or carbon imperialism.

Conclusion: When Hope Lies in the Past

Jetñil-Kijiner, Teaiwa, and Spitz all bring back something that is often lacking in scientific discussions about climate collapse. They bring back emotions. Their poems, songs, and writings share fear, rage, sadness, frustration—along with their tiredness at "the constant reminder that, to the world, we are just a drowning nation; and nothing more."[137] These emotions are crucial. As Chuukese literary scholar Angela Robinson has shown, the vivid emotions portrayed in Pacific climate literature crucially challenge the climate apathy that characterizes the global environmental movement. Pushing people to *feel* environmental collapse can help move the public from climate apathy to climate action.[138]

Australian philosopher Val Plumwood points out that the frequent devaluation of emotions in academic circles, particularly in scientific discussions about climate change, stems from the same hierarchical distinctions between culture and nature *that have led to the climate crisis in the first place*. In thermo-industrial societies, "abstract political and economic relationships subordinate and erase immediate ecological and sensory ones."[139] The recent development of financial capitalism, coming close to denying the necessity of the material world, is but the logical conclusion of the Cartesian division of the world between mind and body, reasons and feelings, men and women, colonizer and colonized, and culture and nature. Carbon addicts are as dependent on land as everyone and everything else, yet they take "the functioning of the 'lower' sphere, the ecological systems which support [them], entirely for granted, needing some grudging support and attention only when they fail to perform as expected."[140] Prioritizing science at the expense of emotion therefore reproduces the very hierarchies that led to environmental collapse. These three Pacific women's demonstration of the political, cultural, and analytical value of emotional and intimate narratives from the Pacific is therefore already, in and of itself, a subversive gesture aimed at undermining the hegemonic Cartesian hierarchy of values. It is only by revaluing emotions on a global scale that genealogies can be perpetuated in the future.

Conclusion

> This is not the end of civilization, but
> a return to one. Only the water insisting
> on what it should always have, spreading
> its liniment over infected wounds. Only
> the water rising above us, reteaching us
> wealth and remembering its name.
> —BRANDY NĀLANI MCDOUGALL, "Water Remembers"

In the Tahitian story of creation, the sky comes from the ruins of a shell. Ta'aroa, the creator god, lived amid emptiness:

> *'Aore ra'i, 'aore fenua, 'aore tai, 'aore marama, 'aore râ, 'aore fetū. . . . 'Aore ta'ata,*
> *'aore pua'a, 'aore 'uri. . . . 'Aore e muhumuhura'a, e pō ana'e ra to vaho.*[1]

There was no sky, no land, no sea, no moon, no sun, no stars. . . . There were no people, no pigs, no dogs. . . . There was no sound, all was darkness outside.

Breaking out of his first shell, tellingly named Rumia (Upset), Ta'aroa used the broken pieces of his former shelter to create the foundation of the sky:

E o taua pa'a o Rumia ra, i vetevete hia i mutaaiho ra, o tona ia fare, te apu o te ra'i atua.[2]

And the shell, Rumia, that he opened first, became his house, the dome of the gods' sky.

As Māori philosopher Te Maire Tau underscores, such stories are not simply records; they are references that communities use as a basis for functioning.[3] This is one of the reasons why the story of the creation of the world by Ta'aroa has been passed down for millennia and continues to be shared in times of nuclear imperialism and carbon imperialism. In Mā'ohi Nui, this narrative helps communities organize around the celebration of the power of life. This cosmogony praises the power of regeneration that can flourish amid ruins, as the upset and broken shell Rumia becomes a solid foundation for the beautiful sky of the gods. In Mā'ohi stories, life is always more powerful than death. Mā'ohi songs, dances, and arts celebrate how life always continues after death through one's descendants, via unbreakable links created across generations by expanding genealogies.[4]

Despite all the suffering shared in the nuclear stories analyzed in this book, these stories are not melancholic narratives of decay. American literary scholar Elizabeth DeLoughrey has warned against Western environmentalists' proclivity to substitute "the unilinear narratives of progress that are constitutive of empire . . . with a narrative of decline [that] still takes a model of single, homogenous, and secular historical time for granted."[5] Pacific (post)apocalyptic stories talk of harrowing tribulations, but they also always talk about regeneration in the wake of imperial apocalypses. Neither tales of progress nor dystopias of decays, they are stories of spiral time—each death connecting to the next life all the way from the original center of the spiral to the outer bounds of time. These are stories celebrating the everlasting capacity of life to reemerge from destruction. As the Hawaiian 'ōlelo no'eau encapsulates, "i ka wā mamua ka wā ma hope."[6]

Sometimes, though, it can be easy to forget that life will prevail. I initially wrote the conclusion for this book where I grew up: in Puna'auia, Tahiti, overlooking ever-warmer waves breaking on a dying reef. The nuclear apocalypse continues to unfold. While the French government recognized—oh so belatedly—that the CEP had a disastrous impact on Mā'ohi people and Mā'ohi land, it fails to meaningfully compensate the victims of its crimes, forcing people who developed radiation-induced cancers to go through a long and arduous administrative process that has rejected the vast majority of victims' claims.[7] The transgenerational damages of the tests are not recognized, and people with radiation-induced diseases who were born after the end of atmospheric tests are routinely attacked online and dismissed in court for fighting for their status as nuclear victims.[8]

Meanwhile, France is modernizing its arsenal to fund its national defense policy of nuclear dissuasion for at least the next seventy years, which as French political scientist Benoît Pelopidas reminds us, is longer than the time that has passed since the first French nuclear test in Algeria.[9] France refuses to sign the Treaty on the Prohibition of Nuclear Weapons and dismisses all calls to dismantle its weapons of mass destruction as naive utopianism.[10] Life in Tahiti is still assaulted by nuclear imperialism, and it is already besieged by carbon imperialism. At the time of this writing, daily news relay new record-breaking heat waves, devastating reports by the Intergovernmental Panel on Climate Change (IPCC), and the renewed militarization of French-occupied Polynesia with the arrival of new rafale planes in the Tahitian skies. It is difficult to convey the feeling of loss and desperation I hear from many activists at Extinction Rebellion Fenua and Te Ora Naho (Fédération des associations de protection de l'environnement [Federation of Environmental Protection Associations]) when I am back home. Our efforts to appeal to the local government, to push the former president Édouard Fritch to declare a state of climate emergency in Māʻohi Nui, have been fruitless. The global movement for climate action has not had better results. This feeling is widely shared across Oceania: As CHamoru poet and lawyer Julian Aguon explains: "I . . . feel like I'm at a funeral when I go home. I see her: [the island], as the fishbowl for so many different kinds of dying. . . . The pipes of everything I wanted desperately to stop are being fitted and laid. Despite how wide our movement has grown, and how fiercely articulate the generation rising to challenge the changing ties, we are losing."[11]

This book does not offer any solutions to avoid environmental collapse. What I hope to do instead is to relate stories by the writers who live(d) through it and hopefully to inspire readers—and myself—to keep fighting for what is left. The Pacific stories, songs, and poems gathered in this book, like Aguon's essays, all have one thing in common: "What connects all of them is not their subject matter but their spirit, which more than anything else is a spirit of insistence. All of them, in their own way, insist on life, no matter the hour, even at the hour of death."[12] Therefore, I see no better way to conclude this book than to turn to the words of wisdom shared by Aguon in his 2021 collection of poems and essays, The Properties of Perpetual Light.

Julian Aguon is a human rights lawyer, activist, and poet from Guahån who has dedicated his life to the fight for human rights. In *Properties of Perpetual Light*, Aguon shares his power to keep on fighting in the name of love, even when the chances of succeeding are becoming slimmer every day. "So much of our story as indigenous peoples," Aguon notes, "has been about shouldering enormous loss and pressing on anyhow, with our hearts broken and our eyes peeled for beauty."[13] Indeed, the poets, writers, and singers discussed in this book all explore the possibilities of grieving what has been lost, while relearning to find beauty, and even, at times, joy and laughter, in a broken and breaking world. These are reminders that it is never too soon nor too late for restoring the land as well as a community's relationship to land. In these cyclical stories of destruction and creation, now is always the right time to mourn and to love more fiercely than ever.

Tellingly, Aguon shared his own experience of mourning at the beginning of his book. Mourning is not to be understood here in a metaphorical sense: in one of the most powerful pieces of his oeuvre, he returns to the trauma of the death of his father, who passed away from cancer when he was only nine years old. This passing shattered his family, plunging his mother, his sister, and himself into sickening depression. Aguon writes,

> The problem, as I see it now, was that each of us mourned *alone*—
>   as opposed to *together*.
> I see us so clearly.
> Each of us an island. All of us at sea.
> We didn't stand a chance.[14]

His first reaction to his loss, as a child, was to hope to escape the place associated with dreadful feelings. "I was envious of everything that could fly," he recalls. "I prayed, without knowing how to, for wings of my own."[15] Yet Aguon ends his narrative of this terrible loss not with his departure from home but with the first instance in which he relearned to bond with his alienated family members.

> When I was ten and [my sister] eleven, I found her outside in the
>   middle of the night, wearing nothing but my dad's old shirt, which
>   she had washed one too many times and which, she said, no longer
>   smelled like him. . . . I could see the emptiness in her eyes.
> I changed my prayer right then and there.
> I prayed for her wings, not mine.[16]

This story ends with one of the rare photographs in the book, captioned as "the only picture I have of my sister Rhea from 1992, the year after our father died, where she's smiling. It is one of my most precious possessions."[17] Aguon's process of mourning includes not only two broken hearts but also two siblings' successful quest for love and solidarity. Even through ruins, Aguon found something—someone—worth fighting for. Today, in the ruins of nuclear imperialism, countless other Pacific writers and artists are finding something, someone, somewhere, worth keeping up the struggle.

Contemporary Pacific literature has been interpreted as a call for "hope in the shadow of sorrow."[18] Yet the search for beauty in a broken—and breaking—world differs sharply from what Craig Santos Perez has aptly denounced as "the emotional labor of hope," too often bestowed on Indigenous peoples.[19] Even Kathy Jetñil-Kijiner, often lauded as "a spoken-word poet for resilience and hope," has shunned this qualification.[20] "With the recent release of IPCC report on 1.5[°C], and the current political climate, even I've begun to reevaluate the meaning of hope, or at least interrogate the discourse of hope," she wrote in 2019.[21] Pacific nuclear literature, as a collection of (post)apocalyptic stories, is not offering any "hope" for a better future. It is offering an expertise in what Anna Lowenhaupt Tsing and her coeditors have eloquently called the "arts of living on a damaged planet."[22]

Emphasizing the importance of mourning and of the prevailing power of life within the movement from climate justice does not in any way imply that the fight for a less catastrophic future should be given up. Letting carbon-addicted communities continue on their current self-destructive trajectory would mean that the world could be warmed by up to 9°C by the end of the century—a rise in temperatures that would lead to unqualifiable suffering for most living beings, human and other-than-human alike. Each decimal of a degree not warmed, each ton of greenhouse gas not released in the atmosphere, each family not driven from their home by rising seas or scorched land, each fish not smothered, each plant not withered, each mountaintop not dynamited is worth fighting for. Taking the time to mourn and finding the strength to fight are not incompatible; in fact, they are both necessary to overcome the pain affecting so many environmental-justice activists. It is time to go beyond the sterile opposition between resistance and resilience, mitigation and adaptation, agency and victimhood. Pacific (post)apocalyptic stories recount the tale of contemporary Oceanian climate activists who have both a broken heart and eyes peeled for beauty. Oceania has been put on fire, yet fierce love of her islands will continue to prompt those who love her to fight for her through cyclical time. As Aguon concludes—or begins: "Our broken world is waiting."[23]

Notes

INTRODUCTION. "WE ARE NOT DROWNING — WE ARE FIGHTING"

1   Seasteading Institute, "Floating City Project," September 17, 2018. https://www
.seasteading.org/floating-city-project/.

2   Seasteaders wanted to install their prototype in Tahiti's lagoon rather than in
international waters primarily because they wanted access to the island's internet
undersea cable, Honotua (Pascal Ortega, physics professor at the University
of French Polynesia and vice president in charge of research, consulted on the
Floating Island Project, conversation in Puna'auia, February 23, 2018).

3   Seasteading Institute and the Government of French Polynesia, "Memorandum
of Understanding," January 13 2017, https://firebasestorage.googleapis.com/v0/b
/blue-frontiers.appspot.com/o/docs%2FMemorandum_of_Understanding.pdf
?alt=media&token=9509af2a-643d-470f-9e2a-7538d61b1a15.

4   Naomi Klein, *No Is Not Enough: Resisting Trump's Shock Politics and Winning the World
We Need* (Chicago: Haymarket, 2017).

5   Arif Dirlik, "Asia-Pacific Studies in an Age of Global Modernity," in *Remaking Area
Studies: Teaching and Learning across Asia and the Pacific*, ed. Terence Wesley-Smith
and Jon Goss (Honolulu: University of Hawai'i Press, 2010), 16.

6   Tahiti, a high island, is not predicted to be engulfed by water. However, as most
arable and habitable land is concentrated on its low-lying coastal rim, rising sea
waters will have a devastating impact on its population, food production, and
economy. For more on the impact of sea level rise on various Pacific Islands, see
Vicente R. Barros and Christopher B. Fields, eds., *Climate Change 2014: Impacts,
Adaptation, and Vulnerability: Working Group II Contribution to the Fifth Assessment
Report of the Intergovernmental Panel on Climate Change*, pt. B, *Regional Aspects*
(Cambridge: Cambridge University Press, 2014), 1613–42.

7   France also tested fifteen nuclear devices in the nearby atoll of Fangataufa.

8   On September 11, 1963, President Charles de Gaulle assured a delegation of
Tahitian politicians in Paris, "There will be no danger.... We shall make the tests
only when the wind blows in the right direction." Charles de Gaulle, quoted in

Stewart Firth and Karin Von Strokirch, "A Nuclear Pacific," in *The Cambridge History of the Pacific Islanders*, ed. Donald Denoon, Stewart Firth, Jocelyn Linnekin, Malama Meleisea, and Karen Nero (Cambridge: Cambridge University Press, 1998), 342; and in Bengt Danielsson and Marie-Thérèse Danielsson, *Moruroa, notre bombe coloniale: Histoire de la colonisation nucléaire de la Polynésie française* (Paris: L'Harmattan, 1993), 217.

9   Admiral Jean Lichère, director of the Pacific Experimentation Center (CEP), quoted in Miriam Kahn, *Tahiti beyond the Postcard: Power, Place, and Everyday Life* (Seattle: University of Washington Press, 2011), 86.

10 Seasteading Institute and the Government of French Polynesia, "Memorandum of Understanding," 7; Darlene Keju-Johnson, "Micronesia," in *Pacific Women Speak: Why Haven't You Known?*, ed. Women Working for an Independent and Nuclear-Free Pacific (Oxford: Green Line, 1987), 6; Sasha Davis, *The Empires' Edge: Militarization, Resistance, and Transcending Hegemony in the Pacific* (Athens: University of Georgia Press, 2015), 63.

11 Sam Amaru, "'Ia ora na tout le monde," Facebook, January 30, 2018, https://www .facebook.com/AssociationTAOANOTAHITI/posts/1196002240552045.

12 Turo a Raapoto, *Te pinainai o te àau* (Puna'auia, Tahiti: Tupuna éditions, 1990), 14.

13 Chantal T. Spitz, "J'eus un pays," *Littérama'ohi*, no. 24 (2018): 46. The short story was later republished with some modifications in her latest collection of stories, *et la mer pour demeure* (Pīra'e, Tahiti: Au vent des îles, 2022), 35–44.

14 Helen Scales, *The Brilliant Abyss: Exploring the Majestic Hidden Life of the Deep Ocean, and the Looming Threat That Imperils It* (New York: Atlantic Monthly Press, 2021), 222.

15 Spitz, "J'eus un pays," 46.

16 Tilman Ruff, "The Humanitarian Impact and Implications of Nuclear Test Explosions in the Pacific Region," *International Review of the Red Cross* 97, no. 899 (2015): 792.

17 Commission d'Enquête sur les conséquences des essais nucléaires (CESCEN), "Les Polynésiens et les essais nucléaires: Indépendance nationale et dépendance polynésienne" (Pape'ete, Tahiti: Assemblée de la Polynésie française, 2006), 167.

18 Gabriel Tetiarahi, "The Society Islands: Squeezing Out the Polynesians," in *Land Tenure in the Pacific*, 3rd ed. (Suva, Fiji: University of the South Pacific Press, 1987), 46.

19 CESCEN, "Les Polynésiens et les essais nucléaires," 133.

20 John Taroanui Doom, *A he'e noa i te tau: Mémoires d'une vie partagée* (Pape'ete, Tahiti: Haere Pō, 2016), 164.

21 "Hagards et perdus d'avoir oublié jusqu'au nom de la lune qui les a vus naître. Amputés de mémoire. Hébétés de certitudes grotesques et étrangères, ils erreront orphelins de sein et de plasma nourriciers." Peu, *Pina*, 101 (translated by Jeffrey Zuckerman).

22 Spitz, "J'eus un pays," 48–49.

23 Kyle Powys Whyte, "Our Ancestors' Dystopia Now: Indigenous Conservation and the Anthropocene," in *The Routledge Companion to the Environmental Humanities*, ed. Ursula Heise, Jon Christensen, and Michelle Niemann (New York: Routledge, 2017), 207.

24 Kimberly M. Blaeser, *Gerald Vizenor: Writing in the Oral Tradition* (Norman: University of Oklahoma Press, 1996), and Susan Berry Brill de Ramírez, *Contemporary American Indian Literatures and the Oral Tradition* (Tucson: University of Arizona Press, 1999), both cited in Craig Santos Perez, *Navigating CHamoru Poetry: Indigeneity, Aesthetics, and Decolonization* (Tucson: University of Arizona Press, 2022), 146.

25 Candace Fujikane, *Mapping Abundance for a Planetary Future: Kanaka Maoli and Critical Settler Cartographies in Hawai'i* (Durham, NC: Duke University Press, 2021), 3.

26 Kyle Powys Whyte, "Indigenous Science (Fiction) for the Anthropocene: Ancestral Dystopias and Fantasies of Climate Change Crises," *Environment and Planning E: Nature and Space* 1, nos. 1–2 (2018): 226. For more on climate change as the latest instantiation of various attacks on Indigenous peoples and their lands, see Otto Heim, "How (Not) to Globalize Oceania: Ecology and Politics in Contemporary Pacific Island Performance Arts," *Commonwealth Essays and Studies* 41, no. 1 (2018): 131–45; and Christina Veran, "Oceania Rising," *Cultural Survival Quarterly Magazine* 37, no. 2 (2013): 12–13.

27 Elizabeth M. DeLoughrey, *Allegories of the Anthropocene* (Durham, NC: Duke University Press, 2019), 7.

28 Mililani Ganivet and Marie-Hélène Villierme, *Nu/Clear Stories* (Onesia S/pacific Storytellers, 2023), podcast, episode 1, May 2023.

29 Albert Wendt, "Novelists and Historians and the Art of Remembering," in *Class and Culture in the South Pacific*, ed. Anthony Hooper (Suva, Fiji: Centre for Pacific Studies, University of Auckland, and Institute of Pacific Studies, University of the South Pacific, 1987), 87.

30 For more on hegemonic apocalypse narratives, see Claire Colebrook, *Essays on Extinction*, vol. 1, *Death of the PostHuman* (Ann Arbor, MI: Open Humanities, 2014); and Pablo Servigne and Gauthier Chapelle, *L'Entraide: L'Autre loi de la jungle* (Paris: Les liens qui libèrent, 2019).

31 Mililani Ganivet and Marie-Hélène Villierme, "Re-membering Nuclear Stories from a Maohi Lens," *Experiment* (blog), December 13, 2021, https://experiment.com /projects/re-membering-nuclear-stories-from-a-maohi-lens.

32 Quoted in Serge Massau, *Paroles d'un autochtone: Entretiens avec le sénateur Richard Ariihau Tuheiava* (Pape'ete, Tahiti: Haere Pō, 2011), 16, 82.

33 Whyte, "Indigenous Science (Fiction)," 236.

34 Nick Estes, *Our History Is the Future: Standing Rock versus the Dakota Access Pipeline, and the Long Tradition of Indigenous Resistance* (New York: Verso, 2019).

35 Rebecca Priestley, *Mad on Radium: New Zealand in the Atomic Age* (Auckland: Auckland University Press, 2012), 49.

36 Paul Quilès, Jean-Marie Collin, and Michel Drain, *L'Illusion nucléaire: La Face cachée de la bombe atomique* (Paris: Éditions Charles Léopold Mayer, 2018), 93.

37 For more on how nuclear testing began "the age of ecology," see Elizabeth DeLoughrey, "Postcolonialism," in *The Oxford Handbook of Ecocriticism*, ed. Greg Garrard (Oxford: Oxford University Press, 2014), 331; Donald Worster, *Nature's*

Economy: A History of Ecological Ideas (Cambridge: Cambridge University Press, 1994), 342; and Ralph H. Lutts, "Chemical Fallout: Rachel Carson's *Silent Spring*, Radioactive Fallout, and the Environmental Movement," in *No Birds Sing: Rhetorical Analyses of Rachel Carson's "Silent Spring,"* ed. Craig Waddell (Carbondale: Southern Illinois University Press, 2000), 17–42.

38 Shine Choi and Catherine Eschle, "Rethinking Global Nuclear Politics, Rethinking Feminism," *International Affairs* 98, no. 4 (2022): 1132.

39 Daniel Immerwahr, *How to Hide an Empire: A History of the Greater United States* (New York: Farrar, Straus and Giroux, 2019), 18.

40 Anaïs Maurer and Rebecca H. Hogue, "Introduction: Transnational Nuclear Imperialisms," *Journal of Transnational American Studies* 11, no. 2 (2020): 25–43.

41 Jan Zalasiewicz et al., "When Did the Anthropocene Begin? A Mid-Twentieth Century Boundary Level Is Stratigraphically Optimal," *Quaternary International* 383 (October 2015): 196–203.

42 Maxime Robin, "Aux États-Unis, des écologistes séduits par le nucléaire," *Le Monde diplomatique*, August 1, 2022, 20–21.

43 Christophe Blain and Jean-Marc Jancovici, *Le Monde sans fin, miracle énergétique et dérive climatique* (Paris: Dargaud, 2021), 133–52.

44 La Parisienne Libérée, *Le Nucléaire, c'est fini* (Paris: La fabrique éditions, 2019), 41–57.

45 It is no coincidence that the biggest institutional contributor to global carbon emissions, the US Army, is also the main initiator of the nuclear arms race. See Elizabeth DeLoughrey, "Toward a Critical Ocean Studies for the Anthropocene," *English Language Notes* 57, no. 1 (2019): 21–36.

46 Stewart Firth, *Nuclear Playground* (Honolulu: University of Hawai'i Press, 1987).

47 The same is true of Great Britain, which detonated twenty-one bombs in Australia and Kiribati with a total payload of 8 megatons, compared to twenty-four bombs in the United States' Nevada test site with a yield of "only" 1.3 megatons. The situation is even more clear-cut for France, which detonated 93 percent of its bombs and 100 percent of its thermonuclear devices in Moruroa and Fangataufa. For more on the yield of nuclear tests, see Beverly Deepe Keever, *News Zero: The New York Times and the Bomb* (Monroe, ME: Common Courage, 2004), 10–12; and Viktor Mikhailov, ed., *Catalog of Worldwide Nuclear Testing* (New York: Begell House, 1999).

48 Jessica Hurley, *Infrastructures of Apocalypse: American Literature and the Nuclear Complex* (Minneapolis: University of Minnesota Press, 2020), 6.

49 S. Davis, *The Empires' Edge*, 52.

50 The United States tested its Pacific devices in Pikinni (23 tests, 1946–58), Ānewetak (43 tests, 1948–58), Kalama atoll (12 tests, 1958–62), Kiribati (24 tests, 1962), and in open waters (4 tests, 1955–62). The United Kingdom tested 21 bombs in the Pacific: 12 in Australia (1952–58) and 9 in Kiribati (1957–58). France tested 193 bombs in Moruroa and Fangataufa between 1966 and 1996.

51 Marie-Hélène Aubert and Michèle Rivasi, *The French Nuclear Tests in Polynesia: Demanding the Truth and Proposals for the Future: Proceedings of the Symposium, 20th*

February 1999 (Lyon: Centre de documentation et de recherche sur la paix et les conflits, 1999).

52 Oceania is also scarred with the Great Pacific Garbage Patch, also known as the "plastic continent," constituted almost exclusively of waste produced by Asian and North American countries, slowly dissolving into a smog of toxic microplastic particles. Scientists have warned that if nothing is done to stop this new form of imperial invasion, the Pacific could become constituted of 50 percent fish and 50 percent plastic within a mere thirty years. World Economic Forum, "The New Plastics Economy: Rethinking the Future of Plastics," January 19, 2016, 7.

53 The New York investment firm KVR has targeted Palmyra and Wake islands for plutonium disposal, while US firm Babcock and Wilcox Environmental Service Inc. and the Taiwanese corporation Taipower have turned to Aelōñ in M̧ajel̨ for similar purposes. See Valerie Kuletz, "The Movement for Environmental Justice in the Pacific Islands," in *The Environmental Justice Reader: Politics, Poetics, and Pedagogy*, ed. Joni Adamson, Mei Mei Evans, and Rachel Stein (Tucson: University of Arizona Press, 2002), 131–36.

54 Carol Farbotko, "Wishful Sinking: Disappearing Islands, Climate Refugees and Cosmopolitan Experimentation," *Asia Pacific Viewpoint* 51, no. 1 (2010): 54.

55 Tony Crook and Peter Rudiak-Gould, *Pacific Climate Cultures: Living Climate Change in Oceania* (Warsaw: De Gruyter, 2018), 9.

56 Farbotko, "Wishful Sinking."

57 The concept was invented by the French anthropologist Alban Bensa to refer specifically to the ideology underpinning the colonization of Kanaky, which presupposed that the local population would wither away in contact with white peoples. Alban Bensa, *Chroniques kanak: L'Ethnologie en marche* (Paris: Ethnies, 1995), 116. The expression, however, can be extended to refer to all of Oceania. For more on racial power dynamics in Kanaky (New Caledonia), see Bensa, *Chroniques kanak*; Isabelle Merle, *Expériences coloniales: La Nouvelle-Calédonie, 1853–1920* (Paris: Belin, 1995); Jean-Marie Tjibaou, *La Présence kanak* (Paris: Éditions Odile Jacob, 1996); David A. Chappell, *The Kanak Awakening: The Rise of Nationalism in New Caledonia* (Honolulu: University of Hawai'i Press, 2013); and Eric Waddell, *Jean-Marie Tjibaou, Kanak Witness to the World: An Intellectual Biography* (Honolulu: Pacific Islands Development Program, East-West Center, 2008).

58 Hone Tuwhare, "Three Poems by Hone Tuwhare," *Te Ao Hou*, September 1959, 17. The poem was later republished and widely circulated in a 1962 collection of poems. See Hone Tuwhare, *No Ordinary Sun: Poems* (Auckland: Blackwood and J. Paul, 1962).

59 Talei Luscia Mangioni, "Fighting for a Nuclear Free Pacific," *Funambulist: Politics of Space and Bodies* 39, no. 1 (2022): 46.

60 Excerpt performed and translated to French by Lagikula Kasitano and Tenisio Lagikula. Quoted in Raymond Mayer, "'Convoitise mondialisée et réactivité océanienne d'après les actualités chantées et dansées à Wallis et Futuna,'" in *L'Océanie convoitée: Actes des colloques, Paris, septembre 2015, Punaauia (UPF), novembre 2016* (Paris: CNRS éditions, 2017), 310–11.

61 Raymond Mayer, Malino Nau, Eric Pambrun, and Christophe Laurent, "Chanter la guerre à Wallis ('Uvea)," *Journal de la Société des Océanistes*, nos. 122–23 (December 2006): 155.

62 Elizabeth DeLoughrey, "Heliotropes: Solar Ecologies and Pacific Radiations," in *Postcolonial Ecologies: Literatures of the Environment*, ed. Elizabeth DeLoughrey and George B. Handley (New York: Oxford University Press, 2011), 236.

63 Priestley, *Mad on Radium*, 49.

64 Frédéric Angleviel, *Les Missions à Wallis et Futuna au XIXe siècle* (Bordeaux: Université Michel de Montaigne, 1994), 57–58.

65 Father Pierre Bataillon, 1936, quoted in Angleviel, *Les Missions*, 9; commandant of the *Vire*, 1876, quoted in Angleviel, *Les Missions*, 156.

66 Angleviel, *Les Missions*, 119.

67 Marc Soulé, "Relations coutume, État, Église à Wallis et Futuna 1837–1961," *Outre-Mers: Revue d'histoire* 92, no. 348 (2005): 122.

68 Mayer, "Convoitise mondialisée," 311.

69 Alexandre Poncet, *Histoire de l'île Wallis*, vol. 2, *Le Protectorat français* (Paris: Société des océanistes, 2013), 162–81.

70 Caroline Sinavaiana-Gabbard, "Literature and the Wheel of Time: Cartographies of Vā," *Sympokē* 26, no. 1 (2018): 33.

71 Kathy Jetñil-Kijiner, "Iep Jāltok: A History of Marshallese Literature" (master's thesis, University of Hawai'i at Mānoa, 2014), 11.

72 Sunnie Kaikala Mākua, Manulani Aluli Meyer, and Lynette Lokelani Wakinekona, "Mo'olelo: Continuity, Stories, and Research in Hawai'i," in *Applying Indigenous Research Methods*, ed. Sweeney Windchief and Timothy San Pedro (New York: Routledge, 2019), 142.

73 Brandy Nālani McDougall, *Finding Meaning: Kaona and Contemporary Hawaiian Literature* (Tucson: University of Arizona Press, 2016), 16.

74 Perez, *Navigating CHamoru Poetry*, 33–34; Teresia K. Teaiwa, "What Remains to Be Seen: Reclaiming the Visual Roots of Pacific Literature," *PMLA* 125, no. 3 (2010): 734.

75 Albert Wendt, *Nuanua: Pacific Writing in English since 1980* (Honolulu: University of Hawai'i Press, 1995), 3.

76 Julia Frengs, *Corporeal Archipelagos: Writing the Body in Francophone Oceanian Women's Literature* (Lanham, MD: Lexington, 2017), 7.

77 Jamaica Heolimeleikalani Osorio, *Remembering Our Intimacies: Mo'olelo, Aloha 'Āina, and Ea* (Minneapolis: University of Minnesota Press, 2021), 32.

78 Moetai Brotherson, *Le Roi absent* (Pīra'e, Tahiti: Au vent des îles, 2013); Moetai Brotherson, personal communication, Faa'ā, July 8, 2015.

79 Chantal T. Spitz, *L'Île des rêves écrasés* (Pīra'e, Tahiti: Au vent des îles, 1991), 159.

80 Craig Santos Perez, *Habitat Threshold* (Oakland, CA: Omnidawn, 2020), 56.

81 Teaiwa, "What Remains to Be Seen," 730–31.

82 See Agnes Quigg, "History of the Pacific Islands Studies Program at the University of Hawaii: 1950–1986" (master's thesis, University of Hawai'i at Mānoa, 1987), 7–8.

83 Albert Wendt, "Towards a New Oceania," in *Writers in East-West Encounter: New Cultural Bearings*, ed. Guy Amirthanayagam (London: Palgrave Macmillan UK,

1982), 202-15; Vicente M. Diaz and J. Kēhaulani Kauanui, "Native Pacific Cultural Studies on the Edge," *Contemporary Pacific* 13, no. 2 (2001): 327; Teresia Teaiwa, "For or Before an Asia Pacific Studies Agenda? Specifying Pacific Studies," in *Remaking Area Studies: Teaching and Learning across Asia and the Pacific*, ed. Terence Wesley-Smith and Jon Goss (Honolulu: University of Hawai'i Press, 2010), 115-16; Haunani-Kay Trask, "Writing in Captivity: Poetry in a Time of Decolonization," *Wasafiri* 12, no. 25 (1997): 42-43.

84 Rob Nixon, *Slow Violence and the Environmentalism of the Poor* (Cambridge, MA: Harvard University Press, 2011), 2.

85 Keju-Johnson, "Micronesia," 7.

86 Amitav Ghosh, *The Great Derangement: Climate Change and the Unthinkable* (Chicago: University of Chicago Press, 2016), 9.

87 Léopold Lambert, *États d'urgence: Une histoire spatiale du continuum colonial français* (Toulouse: Premiers matins de novembre, 2021).

88 Maurer and Hogue, "Introduction: Transnational Nuclear Imperialism," 34-35.

89 Whyte, "Indigenous Science (Fiction)," 238.

90 Pauline Reynolds and Vehia Wheeler, "Mā'ohi Methodologies and Frameworks for Conducting Research in Mā'ohi Nui," *AlterNative* 18, no. 4 (2022), 488-95.

91 The terms refer to First Nations people respectively in Guåhan (Guam), Kiribati, Kanaky (New Caledonia), Hawai'i, Mā'ohi Nui (French Polynesia), Aotearoa (New Zealand), Vanuatu, Aelōñ in Ṃajeḷ (Marshall Islands), Samoa, and 'Uvea.

CHAPTER 1. ISLETISM

1 For more on the Tureians' displacement, see Bruno Barrillot, *Les Irradiés de la République: Les Victimes des essais nucléaires français prennent la parole* (Lyon: Complexe, 2003), 203; and Commission d'Enquête sur les conséquences des essais nucléaires (CESCEN), "Les Polynésiens et les essais nucléaires: Indépendance nationale et dépendance polynésienne" (Pape'ete, Tahiti: Assemblée de la Polynésie française, 2006), 84.

2 Service Mixte de Sécurité Radiologique, "Rapport Secret SMSR 2720," 1966.

3 Traci Brynne Voyles, *Wastelanding: Legacies of Uranium Mining in Navajo Country* (Minneapolis: University of Minnesota Press, 2015), 9.

4 Alban Bensa, *Chroniques kanak: L'Ethnologie en marche* (Paris: Ethnies, 1995), 116.

5 For more on the use of Marshallese people as human experiments, see Holly M. Barker, *Bravo for the Marshallese: Regaining Control in a Post-nuclear, Post-colonial World* (Belmont, CA: Wadsworth, 2013), 41-42; and Barbara Rose Johnston and Holly M. Barker, *Consequential Damages of Nuclear War: The Rongelap Report* (Walnut Creek, CA: Left Coast, 2008).

6 See Tilman Ruff, "The Humanitarian Impact and Implications of Nuclear Test Explosions in the Pacific Region," *International Review of the Red Cross* 97, no. 899 (2015): 778; and Stewart Firth and Karin Von Strokirch, "A Nuclear Pacific," in *The Cambridge History of the Pacific Islanders* (Cambridge: Cambridge University Press, 1998), 324-58.

7   Sasha Davis, *The Empires' Edge: Militarization, Resistance, and Transcending Hegemony in the Pacific* (Athens: University of Georgia Press, 2015), 18.

8   Marie-Claude Beaudeau, dir., *Les Essais nucléaires et la santé, actes de la conférence du 19 janvier 2002 au Sénat* (Lyon: Centre de documentation et de recherche sur la paix et les conflits, 2002), 34.

9   Barrillot, *Les Irradiés de la République*, 212.

10 Alain Babadzan, "Une Perspective pour deux passages: Notes sur la représentation traditionnelle de la naissance et de la mort en Polynésie," *L'Homme* 23, no. 3 (1983): 81–99.

11 For more on the history of medical human experimentation, see Anita Guerrini, *Experimenting with Humans and Animals: From Galen to Animal Rights* (Baltimore: Johns Hopkins University Press, 2003).

12 Michel-Rolph Trouillot, *Silencing the Past: Power and the Production of History* (Boston: Beacon, 1995), 74.

13 Anne McClintock, *Imperial Leather: Race, Gender, and Sexuality in the Colonial Conquest* (New York: Routledge, 1995), 46.

14 Immanuel Wallerstein, *European Universalism: The Rhetoric of Power* (New York: W. W. Norton, 2006), 3.

15 Peter Hulme, *Colonial Encounters: Europe and the Native Caribbean, 1492–1797* (New York: Methuen, 1986); Richard Grove, *Green Imperialism: Colonial Expansion, Tropical Island Edens and the Origins of Environmentalism, 1600–1860* (New York: Cambridge University Press, 1995); Richard Drayton, *Nature's Government: Science, Imperial Britain, and the "Improvement" of the World* (New Haven, CT: Yale University Press, 2000); Rod Edmond and Vanessa Smith, eds., *Islands in History and Representation* (New York: Routledge, 2003).

16 Robert Bernasconi, "With What Must the Philosophy of World History Begin? On the Racial Basis of Hegel's Eurocentrism," *Nineteenth-Century Contexts* 22, no. 2 (2000): 186–90.

17 Michael Hoffheimer, "Hegel, Race, Genocide," *Southern Journal of Philosophy* 39, no. S1 (2001): 36.

18 "Hegelianism" has since become synonymous with this racist hierarchization of ethnicities. Scholar-activist Noam Chomsky thus described the mass mortality brought by nineteenth-century imperialism as caused by "the Hegelian assumption that [victims] are 'mere things,' whose lives have 'no value.'" Noam Chomsky, *Radical Priorities* (Oakland, CA: AK, 1981), 305.

19 Even in Algeria, France moved its nuclear tests to the region of Tamazgha, Algeria's Indigenous peoples land. The Imazighen, Indigenous people of North Africa, sometimes describe themselves as fighting both European and Arab imperialism and denounce being persecuted by both for valuing their own Indigenous culture and language. Kahina Nuunja, "Free People: The Imazighen of North Africa," *Intercontinental Cry* (blog), March 12, 2013, https://intercontinentalcry.org/free-people-the-imazighen-of-north-africa/. Again, the same rhetoric of "isolation" and "remoteness" was used to install nuclear testing facilities on Indigenous lands, far from (sub)imperial centers.

20   Davis, *The Empires' Edge*, 18.

21   Chantal Spitz, personal communication, Pape'ete, Tahiti, February 10, 2017.

22   Even if scholars still debate the precise size of the population before Europeans' arrival, the death toll of even the lowest estimates is still of the order of 50 to 75 percent—enough to thoroughly shatter existing socioeconomic structures. For specific national statistics, see David Chappell, "Violences coloniales à Hawaii," in *Violences océaniennes*, ed. Frédéric Angleviel (Paris: L'Harmattan, 2004), 70; Walter Lini, *Beyond Pandemonium: From the New Hebrides to Vanuatu* (Wellington: Asia Pacific, 1980), 247; Michelle Keown, *Pacific Islands Writing: The Postcolonial Literatures of Aotearoa / New Zealand and Oceania* (New York: Oxford University Press, 2007), 40; Bengt Danielsson and Marie-Thérèse Danielsson, *Moruroa, notre bombe coloniale: Histoire de la colonisation nucléaire de la Polynésie française* (Paris: L'Harmattan, 1993), 133; Bruno Saura, *Des Tahitiens, des Français: Leurs représentations réciproques aujourd'hui* (Pira'e, Tahiti: Au vent des îles, 2011), 15; Haunani-Kay Trask, *From a Native Daughter: Colonialism and Sovereignty in Hawai'i* (Honolulu: University of Hawai'i Press, 1999), 7.

23   Ciara Lacy, dir., *American Masters | Jamaica Heolimeleikalani Osorio: This Is the Way We Rise* (Firelight Media, 2020).

24   Teresia Teaiwa, *Sweat and Salt Water: Selected Works* (Honolulu: University of Hawai'i Press, 2021), 75–76.

25   Robert Nicole, *The Word, the Pen, and the Pistol: Literature and Power in Tahiti* (Albany: State University of New York Press, 2001), 108.

26   Historians have debated how frequent the use of bacterial warfare has been during the Native American genocide, but there is no controversy surrounding the assertion that it occurred at least once, in 1763, in Pennsylvania. For more, see Elizabeth A. Fenn, "Biological Warfare in Eighteenth-Century North America: Beyond Jeffery Amherst." *Journal of American History* 86, no. 4 (2000): 1552–80.

27   Kalama'okaina Niheu, "Reclaiming the Sacred 'Aina (Land)," in *Pacific Women Speak Out for Independence and Denuclearization*, ed. Zohl dé Ishtar (Annandale: Raven, 1998), 11.

28   Philippe Bachimon, *Tahiti, entre mythes et réalités: Essai d'histoire géographique* (Paris: Éditions du comité des travaux historiques et scientifiques, 1990), 245–49.

29   Alexandre Poncet, *Histoire de l'île Wallis*, vol. 2, *Le Protectorat français* (Paris: Société des océanistes, 2013), 162–81.

30   Moira Fontin, "The Performance of Memory in Rapa Nui Theatre," *Pacific Dynamics: Journal of Interdisciplinary Research* 2, no. 2 (2018): 106.

31   Matt K. Matsuda, *Pacific Worlds: A History of Seas, Peoples, and Cultures* (New York: Cambridge University Press, 2012), 227.

32   Diego Muñoz Azócar, "Diaspora Rapanui (1871–2015): L'Île de Pâques, le Chili continental et la Polynésie française" (PhD diss., École des Hautes Etudes en Sciences Sociales, Paris, 2017); Jean Bessière and Sylvie André, eds., *Littératures du Pacifique insulaire: Nouvelle-Calédonie, Nouvelle-Zélande, Océanie, Timor Oriental: Approches historiques, culturelles et comparatives* (Paris: Honoré Champion, 2013), 21–26.

33 Michel Foucault, "L'étatisation du biologique," in *Il faut défendre la société: Cours au collège de France, 1975-1976* (Paris: Gallimard/Seuil, 1997), 213.

34 Robert Fletcher, "The Art of Forgetting: Imperialist Amnesia and Public Secrecy," *Third World Quarterly* 33, no. 3 (2012): 423-39.

35 Jodi A. Byrd, "Fracturing Futurity: Colonial Agnosia and the Untimely Indigenous Present" (lecture, University of New Mexico, Albuquerque, October 25, 2012); Manu Vimalassery, Juliana Hu Pegues, and Alyosha Goldstein, "Introduction: On Colonial Unknowing," *Theory and Event* 19, no. 4 (2016).

36 Susanne C. Moser, "Getting Real about It: Meeting the Psychological and Social Demands of a World in Distress," in *Environmental Leadership: A Reference Handbook*, ed. Deborah Rigling Gallagher (Thousand Oaks, CA: SAGE, 2012), 907.

37 Tony de Brum, quoted in Alex Pashley, "Climate Change Migration Is 'Genocide,' Says Marshall Islands Minister," Climate Home News, October 5, 2015, https://climatechangenews.com/2015/10/05/climate-change-migration-is-genocide-says-marshall-islands-minister/.

38 Cathie Dunsford, *Manawa Toa: Heart Warrior* (Melbourne: Spinifex, 2000), 128-29.

39 John R. Gillis, *Islands of the Mind: How the Human Imagination Created the Atlantic World* (New York: Palgrave Macmillan, 2004); Jean-Marc Tera'ituatini Pambrun, *L'Île aux anthropologues* (Paris: Le manuscrit, 2010), 21-22.

40 John R. Gillis, "Taking History Offshore: Atlantic Islands in European Minds, 1400-1800," in *Islands in History and Representation*, ed. Rod Edmond and Vanessa Smith (New York: Routledge, 2003), 24.

41 Rousseau, Jean-Jacques. *Émile, ou de l'éducation* (Francfort: Cengage Gale London, 1762), 145-46.

42 Teuira Henry and John Muggridge Orsmond, *Ancient Tahiti* (Honolulu: Bernice P. Bishop Museum, 1928), 5.

43 Quoted in Serge Massau, *Paroles d'un autochtone: Entretiens avec le sénateur Richard Ariihau Tuheiava* (Pape'ete, Tahiti: Haere Pō, 2011), 46.

44 Serge Tcherkézoff, *Tahiti 1768: Jeunes filles en pleurs, la face cachée des premiers contacts et la naissance du mythe occidental* (Pīra'e, Tahiti: Au vent des îles, 2004).

45 For more on the long history of Westerners' presence in the Pacific before the late eighteenth century, see Matsuda, *Pacific Worlds*, 49-126.

46 Tcherkézoff, *Tahiti 1768*.

47 For more on the rahui system, see Tamatoa Bambridge, *The Rahui: Legal Pluralism in Polynesian Traditional Management of Resources and Territories* (Canberra: ANU Press, 2016).

48 Louis-Antoine de Bougainville, *Voyage autour du monde par la frégate La Boudeuse et la flûte L'Étoile* (1771, repr., Paris: La découverte, 2006), 170.

49 For more on Bougainville's role in the invention of the myth of the South Seas, see Etienne Taillemite, ed., *Bougainville et ses compagnons autour du monde: 1766-1769, journaux de navigation* (Paris: Imprimerie nationale, 1977); and Eric Vibart, *Tahiti: Naissance d'un paradis* (Brussels: Éditions complexe, 1987), 96.

50 "Infesté . . . les malheureuses compagnes de vos plaisirs" with "funestes caresses."

Denis Diderot, *Supplément au voyage de Bougainville* (1772; repr., Paris: Pocket, 2004), 22–25.

51 "Elles sont condamnées à périr"; the "aimables suppliantes... embrassai[en]t ses genoux." Diderot, *Supplément*, 25, 31.

52 Trouillot, *Silencing the Past*, 81.

53 Teresia Teaiwa, "Reading Gauguin's *Noa Noa* with Hau'ofa's *Kisses in the Nederends*: 'Militourism,' Feminism, and the 'Polynesian' Body," in *Inside Out: Literature, Cultural Politics, and Identity in the New Pacific* (Lanham, MD: Rowman and Littlefield, 1999), 252.

54 Such missionaries' narratives include William Ellis, *Polynesian Researches, during a Residence of Nearly Eight Years in the Society and Sandwich Islands* (New York: J. and J. Harper, 1833); John Davies, *The History of the Tahitian Mission, 1799–1830* (Cambridge, UK: Hakluyt Society at the University Press, 1961); Honoré Laval, *Mémoires pour servir à l'histoire de Mangareva, ère chrétienne, 1834–1871* (Paris: Musée de l'homme, 1968). Spanish Catholic missionaries had begun proselytizing some parts of the western Pacific, but that region had not crystallized in the pre-Enlightenment European collective imagination as an idyllic heaven.

55 See administrative reports such as J.-A. Moerenhout, *Voyages aux îles du Grand océan* (Paris: Arthus-Bertrand, 1837); Edmond De Bovis, *État de la société tahitienne à l'arrivée des Européens* (Paris: Revue coloniale, 1855); and Marc Le Goupils, *Comment on cesse d'être colon: Six années en Nouvelle-Calédonie* (Paris: Bernard Grasset, 1910).

56 Victor Hugo, "La Fille d'O-Taïti," in *Les Orientales* (Paris: Ollendorf, 1829), 200–202; Herman Melville, *Typee: A Peep at Polynesian Life* (London: J. Murray, 1846); Herman Melville, *Omoo: Adventures in the South Seas* (Project Gutenberg Online Catalog, 1847); Herman Melville, *Mardi, and a Voyage Thither* (Boston: Page, 1949); Pierre Loti, *Le Mariage de Loti* (Paris: Calmann Lévy, 1878); Robert Louis Stevenson, *South Sea Tales* (New York: Oxford University Press, 1893); Robert Louis Stevenson, *The Beach of Falesà* (North Hollywood: Aegypan, 1892); Robert Louis Stevenson, *The Ebb-Tide* (London: Penguin Classics, 1894).

57 Paul Gauguin, *Noa Noa* (1901; repr., Paris: A. Balland, 1966); Victor Segalen, "Cycle Polynésien," in *Les Immémoriaux* (Paris: Librairie générale française, 1907), reprinted in *Œuvres complètes* (Paris: Robert Laffont, 1995), 99–523; Jack London, *South Sea Tales* (New York: Macmillan, 1911); Somerset Maugham, *The Moon and Sixpence* (New York: Viking Penguin, 1919); Jean Giraudoux, *Suzanne et le Pacifique* (Paris: Grasset, 1921); Jean Giraudoux, *Supplément au voyage de Cook; pièce en un acte* (Paris: Grasset, 1936); Henry Matisse, *Window in Tahiti* (painting, 1935); Georges Simenon, *Touriste de bananes* (Paris: Folio, 1938).

58 "Races primitives qui s'éteignent tout doucement au contact des races civilisées, et qu'un siècle prochain trouvera probablement disparues." Loti, *Le Mariage*, 53.

59 Teresia Teaiwa, "Bikinis and Other S/Pacific N/Oceans," *Contemporary Pacific* 6, no. 1 (1994): 87.

60 A. D. G., main representative of the French National Front in Kanaky, wrote a compromising novel. Reverzy was a close sympathizer of the far-right journal *L'Action Française* at the time of his Oceanian writing. Their works feature

offensive racist language, targeting Kanak, Māʻohi, and Chinese communities. See A. D. G., *Les Billets nickelés* (Paris: Gallimard, 1988); and Jean Reverzy, *Le Passage* (1954; repr., Paris: Les éditions du sonneur, 2014).

61 Pablo Neruda, *La Rosa separada* (Buenos Aires: Editorial Losada, 1973); J.-M. G. Le Clézio, *Raga: Approche du continent invisible* (Paris: Éditions du seuil, 2006); Aldous Huxley, *Island* (New York: Harper Perennial Modern Classics, 1962).

62 "Patria sin voz," "un vacío oceánico." Neruda, *La Rosa separada*, 8, 34.

63 "Obra[s] que labraron las manos del aire, los guantes del cielo." Neruda, *La Rosa separada*, 16.

64 Madi Williams, *Polynesia, 900–1600* (Leeds, UK: Arc Humanities, 2021), 30.

65 Williams, *Polynesia*, 72–73.

66 Jared M. Diamond, *Collapse: How Societies Choose to Fail or Succeed* (New York: Viking, 2005). For more on critiques of Diamond's 2005 best seller and analyses of the contemporary Rapa Nui diaspora, see Muñoz Azócar, "Diaspora Rapanui," 48–49.

67 The first swimmer to come back from the nearby islet of Motu Nui with a frigate egg makes his leader the chief for the next year. For more on the Rapa Nui cultural renaissance, see Fontin, "The Performance of Memory," 107–11; and Dan Bendrups, *Singing and Survival: The Music of Easter Island* (New York: Oxford University Press, 2019), 123–25.

68 Fontin, "The Performance of Memory," 110.

69 "Para que no las viera sino el mar." Neruda, *La Rosa separada*, 22.

70 Neruda, *La Rosa separada*, 2.

71 See Merril Eisenbud, head of the US Atomic Energy Commission, quoted in Ruff, "The Humanitarian Impact," 805, 778.

72 Neruda, *La Rosa separada*, 22.

73 Neruda, *La Rosa separada*, 22.

74 Grant McCall, "El pasado en el presente de Rapanui (Isla de Pascua)," in *Etnografía: Sociedades indígenas contemporáneas y su ideología*, ed. Jorge Hidalgo (Santiago: Editorial A. Bello, 1996), 17–48.

75 Quoted in Marisol Galilea, "Rapa Nui, isla histórica: Una lectura de *La Rosa separada* de Pablo Neruda," *Alpha (Osorno)*, no. 46 (2018): 9–31.

76 Galilea, "Rapa Nui, isla histórica," 18–19.

77 Galilea, "Rapa Nui, isla histórica," 14.

78 Danielsson and Danielsson, *Moruroa*, 338.

79 I asked nuclear physicist Sébastien Philippe, who works on reconstructing nuclear clouds from declassified French archives, whether these speculations were correct. He confirmed that despite the lack of available measurements, it seemed likely that Rapa Nui was heavily exposed (personal correspondence, November 15, 2021).

80 Patrick Chastel and Philippe Lemaire, *Le Sourire du tiki* (Pīraʻe, Tahiti: Au vent des îles, 2001), 64; Le Clézio, *Raga*, 82; Patrice Guirao, *Lyao-Ly* (Pīraʻe, Tahiti: Au vent des îles, 2013), 19; Claudine Jacques, *Le Cri de l'acacia* (Pīraʻe, Tahiti: Au vent des îles, 2007), 21; Jean-Claude Lama, *Regards: Une vie polynésienne* (Pīraʻe, Tahiti: Au vent des îles, 1999), 74.

81 Chantal Kerdiles, *Voyance sous les tropiques* (Pīra'e, Tahiti: Au vent des îles, 1997), 40; Anne-Catherine Blanc, *Moana blues* (Pīra'e, Tahiti: Au vent des îles, 2002), 126; Claudine Jacques, *L'Homme-lézard* (Nîmes: HB éditions, 2002), 71; Claudine Jacques, *Le Cri de l'acacia*, 31–40; Claudine Jacques, *Nouméa mangrove* (Pīra'e, Tahiti: Au vent des îles, 2010), 66, 159; Bernard De La Vega, *Angélus en terre lointaine* (Pīra'e, Tahiti: Au vent des îles, 2013), 68; Marc Frémy, *Te Pō rumaruma: Les Histoires de la terrasse* (Pape'ete, Tahiti: Marc Frémy, 2003), 12; Christian Hyvernat, *Opération TNT* (Pīra'e, Tahiti: Au vent des îles, 2005), 219; Le Clézio, *Raga*, 34; Nicolas Kurtovitch, *Good night friend* (Pīra'e, Tahiti: Au vent des îles, 2006), 68; Marc Cizeron, *Tonton Grand-Frère* (Pape'ete, Tahiti: Haere Pō, 2006), 82; Marc Stephan, *Pakepakeha: Le Fantôme du Hauraki golf* (Pīra'e, Tahiti: Au vent des îles, 2013), 262; Roland Rossero, *Corps à corps* (Nouméa, New Caledonia: Éditions humanis, 2015), 139.

82 Mario Vargas Llosa, *El paraíso en la otra esquina* (Bogotá: Alfaguara, 2003).

83 "La disponibilité extrême de la vahine." Reverzy, *Le Passage*, 48.

84 "Les filles des îles avai[en]t gardé du temps jadis cette propension à jouir du temps présent, à profiter d'un bel homme." Marc Frémy, *Trois papiers aux clous, un amour chinois* (Pīra'e, Tahiti: Au vent des îles, 2000), 35.

85 Homi K. Bhabha, *The Location of Culture* (New York: Routledge, 2004), 107.

86 Teaiwa, "Reading Gauguin's Noa Noa," 251.

87 Teaiwa, "Bikinis and Other S/Pacific N/Oceans," 95.

88 Jean-Christophe Gay, "Les Îles du Pacifique dans le monde du tourisme," *Hermès, La Revue*, no. 65 (2013): 84–88.

89 Tahitian photographer Teva Sylvain, quoted in Kahn, *Tahiti beyond the Postcard*, 26.

90 Chantal Spitz, "Cannibalisme identitaire," *Littérama'ohi*, no. 23 (2013): 35–40.

CHAPTER 2. OCEANITUDE

1 "Écoutons, lisons maintenant de l'océanitude: Henri Hiro, Chantal Spitz, Déwé Gorodé, Grâce Molisa et tous les autres qui nous montrent le chemin de l'importance du vivre-ensemble." Paul Tavo, *Quand le cannibale ricane* (Port Vila: Alliance française du Vanuatu, 2015), 536.

2 Epeli Hau'ofa, *We Are the Ocean: Selected Works* (Honolulu: University of Hawai'i Press, 2008), 32.

3 Hau'ofa, *We Are the Ocean*, 32.

4 Paul Tavo, personal correspondence, January 3, 2020.

5 Souleymane Bachir Diagne, "Négritude," in *The Stanford Encyclopedia of Philosophy*, ed. Edward N. Zalta (Stanford: Metaphysics Research Lab, Stanford University, 2018), https://plato.stanford.edu/archives/sum2018/entries/negritude/.

6 Maile Renee Arvin, *Possessing Polynesians: The Science of Settler Colonial Whiteness in Hawai'i and Oceania* (Durham, NC: Duke University Press, 2019).

7 For more on Polynesians' fluctuating identification with Blackness, see Robbie Shilliam, *The Black Pacific: Anti-colonial Struggles and Oceanic Connections* (London: Bloomsbury Academic, 2015); and Quito Swan, *Pasifika Black: Oceania, Anti-colonialism, and the African World* (New York: New York University Press, 2022).

8   Arvin, *Possessing Polynesians*, 27.

9   Joyce Lindsay Pualani Warren, "Theorizing Pō: Embodied Cosmogony and Polynesian National Narratives" (PhD diss., University of California, Los Angeles, 2017), 70.

10 Nālani Wilson-Hokowhitu and Manulani Aluli Meyer, "I Ka Wā Mamua, The Past before Us," in *The Past before Us: Moʻokūʻauhau as Methodology*, ed. Nālani Wilson-Hokowhitu (Honolulu: University of Hawaiʻi Press, 2019), 1.

11 Jolie Liston and Melson Miko, "Oral Tradition and Archaeology: Palau's Earth Architecture," in *Pacific Island Heritage: Archaeology, Identity and Community*, ed. Jolie Liston, Geoffrey Clark, and Dwight Alexander (Canberra: ANU Press, 2011), 185.

12 Forrest Wade Young, "Rapa Nui," *Contemporary Pacific* 29, no. 1 (2017): 173; Peter H. Buck, *Vikings of the Pacific* (Chicago: University of Chicago Press, 1938), 228–36.

13 For more, see Andreas Hejnol, "Ladders, Trees, Complexity, and Other Metaphors in Evolutionary Thinking," in *Arts of Living on a Damaged Planet: Ghosts and Monsters of the Anthropocene* (Minneapolis: University of Minnesota Press, 2017), 91.

14 Manulani Aluli Meyer, "Written Direct Testimony of Dr. Manulani Aluli Meyer as a Witness at the Conservation District Use Application for Permit of the Thirty Meter Telescope (TMT)," available at *Sacred Mauna Kea* blog, November 7, 2017, https://dlnr.hawaii.gov/mk/files/2016/10/B.05a-wdt-Meyer.pdf.

15 Tavo, *Quand le cannibale ricane*, 536.

16 Representatives of Pacific Countries and Territories, Aotearoa–New Zealand, Australia, Cook Islands, Federated States of Micronesia, Fiji, French Polynesia, Hawaii, Kiribati, Niue, New Caledonia, Palau, Papua New Guinea, Rapa Nui, Samoa, Solomon Islands, and Tonga, "The Ocean Declaration of Maupiti" (UNESCO World Heritage Workshop of the Pacific Islands, Maupiti, November 7, 2009).

17 Teresia Kieuea Teaiwa, *Sweat and Salt Water: Selected Works* (Honolulu: University of Hawaiʻi Press, 2021), 71.

18 Teaiwa, quoted in Dale Husband, "Teresia Teaiwa: You Can't Paint the Pacific with Just One Brush Stroke," *E-Tangata* (blog), October 24, 2015, https://e-tangata.co.nz/korero/you-cant-paint-the-pacific-with-just-one-brush-stroke/.

19 Paul Tavo, *L'Âme du kava* (Port Vila: Alliance française du Vanuatu, 2011).

20 Tavo, *Quand le cannibale ricane*, 5.

21 "Une excellente poubelle à ciel ouvert qui recevra les déchets toxiques des pays industrialisés." Tavo, *Quand le cannibale ricane*, 6.

22 "Déversant . . . sur les rivages hostiles des continents." Tavo, *Quand le cannibale ricane*, 529. In the Pacific context, Japan, whose empire once stretched from Guåhan in the north to Kiribati in the south, and who long sought to dump its radioactive waste in the Mariana Trench, stands out as a colonial power in its own right.

23 Margaret Rodman, "Boundary and a Bridge: Women's Pig Killing as a Border-Crossing between Spheres of Exchange in East Aoba," in *Vanuatu: Politics, Economics and Ritual in Island Melanesia*, ed. Michael Allen (New York: Academic Press, 1981), 72–74.

24   Mildred Sope and Mikaela Nyman, "A Conversation about Poetry and Politics," in
      Sista, Stanap Strong! A Vanuatu Women's Anthology, ed. Mikaela Nyman and Rebecca
      Tobo Olul-Hossen (Wellington: Victoria University Press, 2021), 31.

25   Traci Brynne Voyles, *Wastelanding: Legacies of Uranium Mining in Navajo Country*
      (Minneapolis: University of Minnesota Press, 2015).

26   Quoted in Women Working for an Independent and Nuclear-Free Pacific
      (WWINFP), *Pacific Women Speak: Why Haven't You Known?* (Oxford: Green Line,
      1987), 27.

27   Claude Meillassoux, *Femmes, greniers et capitaux* (Paris: F. Maspero, 1975), 119.

28   "Il était le seul à pouvoir trouver un boulot de merde à Port-Vila pour pourvoir sa
      famille de ces choses-là." Tavo, *Quand le cannibale ricane*, 367.

29   "Le lendemain il réintégrerait la vie aliénante de la ville, mais il était désormais
      prêt à l'affronter." Tavo, *Quand le cannibale ricane*, 524.

30   Tavo, *Quand le cannibale ricane*, 527–28.

31   Claude Lévi-Strauss, *Tristes tropiques* (Paris: Plon, 1955), 27.

32   Paul Gardissat and Nicolas Mezzalira, *Nabanga: An Illustrated Anthology of the Oral
      Traditions of Vanuatu* (Port Vila: Vanuatu National Cultural Council, 2005), 13.

33   Joël Bonnemaison, *Gens de pirogue et gens de la terre: Les Fondements géographiques
      d'une identité. L'archipel du Vanuatu. Essai de géographie culturelle* (Paris: Éditions de
      l'ORSTOM, 1996), 435.

34   Tavo, *Quand le cannibale ricane*, 529.

35   Pablo Servigne, Raphaël Stevens, and Gauthier Chapelle, *Une autre fin du monde est
      possible* (Paris: Éditions du seuil, 2018), 248.

36   Masashi Soga and Kevin J. Gaston, "Extinction of Experience: The Loss of
      Human–Nature Interactions," *Frontiers in Ecology and the Environment* 14, no. 2
      (2016): 94–101.

37   Tavo, *Quand le cannibale ricane*, 530.

38   Craig Santos Perez and Justyn Ah Chong, "Praise Song for Oceania," YouTube
      video (Honolulu: Olanā Media, 2017), https://www.youtube.com/watch?v=t6fme
      BerLZc&ab_channel=craigsantosperez; Terisa Tinei Siagatonu, "Atlas" (poem
      recited for the COP21, Paris, December 10, 2015, https://www.youtube.com/watch?v
      =mZMgGzD1—g&ab_channel=FastforClimate).

39   Hauʻofa, *We Are the Ocean*, 58.

40   Teaiwa, quoted in Hauʻofa, *We Are the Ocean*, 41.

41   "Une étendue de gouttes lacrymales a débordé de la surface de nos îles et de nos
      atolls. Si vous pensiez que c'était l'océan, vous vous trompiez." Ariirau, "Tristesse
      s'agrippe à moi, 720 fois Hiroshima en mon pays," *Littérama'ohi*, no. 16 (2009): 69.

42   John Puhiatau Pule, "100 Love Poems," Mana Moana Pasifika Voices (Sharm El
      Sheikh: United Nations Framework Convention of Climate Change COP-26, 2022),
      https://www.manamoana.co.nz/artwork/100-love-poems/.

43   Valérie Gobrait, *Matari'i: La Légende de Matari'i* (Pape'ete, Tahiti: Valérie Gobrait,
      2008), 72 ("hommes-poissons"); Alexandre Moeava Ata, *Voyage en OGM (Océanie
      Génétiquement Modifiée)* (Pape'ete, Tahiti: Haere Pō, 2010), 22 ("gens de la mer");
      James George, *Ocean Roads* (Wellington: Huia, 2007), 117; Ariirau, *Matamimi ou la*

vie nous attend (Pīraʻe, Tahiti: Au vent des îles, 2006), 112 ("humanité océanienne"); Luc Énoka Camoui and Waixen Wayewol, *Pue Tiu, au cœur de la parole: Poèmes et poésies kanak de la Nouvelle-Calédonie* (Nouméa, New Caledonia: L'Herbier de feu, 2011), 14 ("l'humanité de l'océanité").

44 Jamaica Heolimeleikalani Osorio, *Remembering Our Intimacies: Moʻolelo, Aloha ʻĀina, and Ea* (Minneapolis: University of Minnesota Press, 2021), 97.

45 Cutcha Risling Baldy, "Coyote Is Not a Metaphor: On Decolonizing, (Re)Claiming and (Re)Naming 'Coyote,'" *Decolonization: Indigeneity, Education and Society* 4, no. 1 (2015): 5.

46 Candace Fujikane, *Mapping Abundance for a Planetary Future: Kanaka Maoli and Critical Settler Cartographies in Hawaiʻi* (Durham, NC: Duke University Press, 2021), 8.

47 Henri Bergson, *L'Evolution créatrice* (Paris: Librairie H. Le Soudier, 1907), 156.

48 Bergson, *L'Évolution créatrice*, 166.

49 Aimé Césaire, "Discours sur l'art africain," *Études littéraires* 6, no. 1 (1966), reprinted in *Gradhiva: Revue d'anthropologie et d'histoire des arts*, no. 10 (November 4, 2009): 209.

50 Diagne, "Négritude."

51 Bergson, *L'Évolution créatrice*, 136. Bergson has been reclaimed by Senghor as a Negritude thinker.

52 Césaire, "Discours sur l'art africain," 209.

53 Aimé Césaire, *Cahier d'un retour au pays natal* (Paris: Présence africaine, 1983), 44.

54 Senghor has been most criticized for writing that "emotion is Negro, as reason is Hellenic" ("*l'émotion est nègre, comme la raison héllène*"). Léopold Sédar Senghor, *Liberté I: Négritude et humanisme* (Paris: Éditions du seuil, 1964), 288.

55 Souleymane Bachir Diagne, *Bergson postcolonial: L'Élan vital dans la pensée de Léopold Sédar Senghor et de Mohamed Iqbal* (Paris: CNRS éditions, 2011); Souleymane Bachir Diagne, "Senghor et la révolution de 1889," *Romanic Review* 100, nos. 1–2 (March 2009): 103–11.

56 Senghor, *Liberté*, 43.

57 Bergson, *L'Évolution créatrice*, 88.

58 "Aussi déraciné qu'une touffe d'herbe végétant sur du sable." Tavo, *Quand le cannibale ricane*, 285.

59 Tavo, *Quand le cannibale ricane*, 527.

60 Senghor, *Liberté*, 38.

61 Kathy Jetñil-Kijiner, *Iep Jāltok: Poems from a Marshallese Daughter* (Tucson: University of Arizona Press, 2017), 67.

62 ʻUmi Perkins, "Moʻokūʻauhau and Mana," in *The Past before Us: Moʻokūʻauhau as Methodology*, ed. Nālani Wilson-Hokowhitu (Honolulu: University of Hawaiʻi Press, 2019), 69–80.

63 David Uahikeaikaleiʻohu Maile, "Science, Time, and Mauna a Wākea: The Thirty-Meter Telescope's Capitalist-Colonialist Violence," *Red Nation* (blog), May 13 and 20, 2015 (pts. 1 and 2), http://therednation.org/science-time-and-mauna-a-wakea-the-thirty-meter-telescopes-capitalist-colonialist-violence-an-essay-in-two-parts/.

64 Maile, "Science, Time, and Mauna a Wākea," May 20, 2015 (pt. 2).

65 Leon Noʻeau Peralto, "Mauna a Wakea: Hanau Ka Mauna, the Piko of Our Ea," in *A Nation Rising: Hawaiian Movements for Life, Land, and Sovereignty*, ed. Noelani Goodyear-Kaʻōpua, Ikaika Hussey, and Erin Kahunawaikaʻala Wright (Durham, NC: Duke University Press, 2014), 233.

66 Hiʻilei Julia Hobart, "At Home on the Mauna: Ecological Violence and Fantasies of Terra Nullius on Maunakea's Summit," *Native American and Indigenous Studies* 6, no. 2 (2019): 34.

67 Wilson-Hokowhitu and Meyer, "I Ka Wā Mamua," 3.

68 Pua Case and Amy Goodman, "'We Are Not Anti-Science': Why Indigenous Protectors Oppose the Thirty Meter Telescope at Mauna Kea," *Democracy Now!*, July 22, 2019, https://www.democracynow.org/2019/7/22/why_indigenous _protectors_oppose_the_thirty.

69 Osorio, *Remembering Our Intimacies*, 151.

70 Aanchal Saraf, "'We'd Rather Eat Rocks': Contesting the Thirty Meter Telescope in a Struggle over Science and Sovereignty in Hawaiʻi," *Journal of Transnational American Studies* 11, no. 1 (2020): 159.

71 Case and Goodman, "'We Are Not Anti-Science.'"

72 Haunani-Kay Trask, *From a Native Daughter: Colonialism and Sovereignty in Hawaiʻi* (Honolulu: University of Hawaiʻi Press, 1999), 247–48.

73 Tulsi Gabbard, "Ua Mau Ke Ea o Ka ʻāina i Ka Pono," Twitter, July 19, 2019, https://twitter.com/TulsiGabbard/status/1152350291481595905.

74 Tavo, *Quand le cannibale ricane*, 529.

75 Hobart, "At Home on the Mauna," 31.

76 Quoted in Maile, "Science, Time, and Mauna a Wakea," May 20, 2015 (pt. 2).

77 Case and Goodman, "'We Are Not Anti-Science.'"

78 Lanikala Mangauil, quoted in Erin Suzuki, *Ocean Passages: Navigating Pacific Islander and Asian American Literatures* (Philadelphia: Temple University Press, 2021), 164.

79 Bruno Latour, *Où atterrir? Comment s'orienter en politique* (Paris: La découverte, 2017), 86.

80 "Open Letter Opposing Criminalization of Maunakea Protectors," 2019, https:// docs.google.com/document/u/2/d/1YR8M4eboRjJSsfvVtmukb6dDgUonDBdmj9 AUohirkmY/.

81 Kahikina de Silva, quoted in Candace Fujikane, "Introduction: Asian Settler Colonialism in the U.S. Colony of Hawaiʻi," in *Asian Settler Colonialism: From Local Governance to the Habits of Everyday Life in Hawaiʻi* (Honolulu: University of Hawaiʻi Press, 2008), 15.

82 Saraf, "'We'd Rather Eat Rocks,'" 162.

83 Kathy Jetñil-Kijiner, "Iep Jāltok: A History of Marshallese Literature" (master's thesis, University of Hawaiʻi at Mānoa, 2014), 69.

84 Manulani Aluli Meyer, Ngahiraka Mason, and Luana Busby-Neff, "Manulani Aluli Meyer: Kapu Aloha for Maunakea, a Discipline of Compassion," UH Hilo Stories, University of Hawaiʻi, April 13, 2015, https://hilo.hawaii.edu/chancellor/stories /2015/04/13/kapu-aloha/.

85 For more on kapu aloha, see the educational handout printed by the local environmental group Mauna Kea Anaina Hau, accessed September 12, 2019, https://maunakeaanainahou.org/kapu-aloha/.

86 Manulani Aluli Meyer, "Ekolu Mea Nui: Three Ways to Experience the World," *Canadian Journal of Native Studies* 31, no. 2 (2017): 15; Meyer, "Written Direct Testimony."

87 Meyer, Mason, and Busby-Neff, "Manulani Aluli Meyer."

88 Anaïs Maurer, "Océanitude: Repenser le tribalisme occidental au prisme des nationalismes océaniens," *Francosphères* 8, no. 2 (2019): 109–25.

CHAPTER 3. ATOMIC ANIMALS

1 Craig Santos Perez, *Habitat Threshold* (Oakland, CA: Omnidawn, 2020), 36.

2 The original palimpsest is an excerpt from Alison Hawthorne Deming, *Zoologies: On Animals and the Human Spirit* (Minneapolis: Milkweed, 2014).

3 Ransom A. Myers and Boris Worm, "Rapid Worldwide Depletion of Predatory Fish Communities," *Nature* 423, no. 6937 (May 2003): 282.

4 Callum Roberts, *The Ocean of Life: The Fate of Man and the Sea* (New York: Penguin, 2013), 41.

5 Robert S. Emmett and David E. Nye, *The Environmental Humanities: A Critical Introduction* (Cambridge, MA: MIT Press, 2017), 168.

6 Robert R. Dunn et al., "The Sixth Mass Coextinction: Are Most Endangered Species Parasites and Mutualists?," *Proceedings of the Royal Society B: Biological Sciences* 276, no. 1670 (2009): 3037–45.

7 David Archer, *The Long Thaw: How Humans Are Changing the Next 100,000 Years of Earth's Climate*, rev. ed. (Princeton, NJ: Princeton University Press, 2016), 108–12.

8 Ursula K. Heise, *Imagining Extinction: The Cultural Meanings of Endangered Species* (Chicago: University of Chicago Press, 2016).

9 Kyle Powys Whyte, "Our Ancestors' Dystopia Now: Indigenous Conservation and the Anthropocene," in *The Routledge Companion to the Environmental Humanities* (New York: Routledge, 2017), 208.

10 Kyle Powys Whyte, "Indigenous Science (Fiction) for the Anthropocene: Ancestral Dystopias and Fantasies of Climate Change Crises," *Environment and Planning E: Nature and Space* 1, nos. 1–2 (2018): 226.

11 Alfred W. Crosby, *Ecological Imperialism: The Biological Expansion of Europe, 900–1900* (New York: Cambridge University Press, 2004).

12 There are notable exceptions, such as Albert Wendt, *Black Rainbow* (Honolulu: University of Hawaiʻi Press, 1995); and Keri Hulme, *Stonefish* (Wellington: Huia, 2007).

13 Whyte, "Indigenous Science (Fiction)," 236.

14 Raʻi Chaze, personal communication, Punaʻauia, Tahiti, August 6, 2016. All subsequent quotes by Chaze are from this interview.

15 Henri Hiro, quoted in Jean-Marc Teraʻituatini Pambrun, *Henri Hiro, héros polynésien* (Moorea: Puna Honu, 2010), 37.

16 Vehia Jennifer Wheeler, "Climate Change, Watershed Management, and

Resiliency to Flooding: A Case Study of Papeno'o Valley, Tahiti Nui (French Polynesia)" (master's thesis, University of Hawai'i at Mānoa, 2018), 5.

17 Epeli Hau'ofa, *We Are the Ocean: Selected Works* (Honolulu: University of Hawai'i Press, 2008), 68–72.

18 Bruno Saura, *Mythes et usages des mythes: Autochtonie et idéologie de la Terre Mère en Polynésie* (Paris: Peeters, 2013), 234.

19 Ra'i Chaze, *Vai: La Rivière au ciel sans nuages* (Pape'ete, Tahiti: Self-published, CreateSpace, 1990), 41.

20 Chaze, *Vai*, 43.

21 "Le feu t'aura, petit poisson!... Le feu qui fait des vagues et des raz-de-marée." Chaze, *Vai*, 42.

22 Nic Maclellan, "Nuclear Testing and Racism in the Pacific Islands," in *The Palgrave Handbook of Ethnicity*, ed. Steven Ratuva (London: Palgrave Macmillan, 2019), 4.

23 Bengt Danielsson, "Under a Cloud of Secrecy: The French Nuclear Tests in the Southeastern Pacific," in *French Polynesia: A Book of Selected Readings* (Suva, Fiji: Institute of Pacific Studies of the University of the South Pacific, 1988), 266.

24 Danielsson, "Under a Cloud of Secrecy," 266.

25 Bruno Barrillot, *Les Irradiés de la République: Les Victimes des essais nucléaires français prennent la parole* (Lyon: Éditions complexe, 2003), 208.

26 Mililani Ganivet and Marie-Hélène Villierme, *Nu/Clear Stories* (Onesia S/pacific Storytellers, 2023), podcast, episode 2, June 2023.

27 Pieter De Vries and Han Seur, *Moruroa and Us: Polynesians' Experiences during Thirty Years of Nuclear Testing in the French Pacific* (Lyon: Centre de documentation et de recherche sur la paix et les conflits, 1997), 77.

28 De Vries and Seur, *Moruroa and Us*, 103.

29 Lucas Paeamara, *Mangareva: Taku Akaereere* (Pīra'e, Tahiti: Au vent des îles, 2005), 94–96.

30 De Vries and Seur, *Moruroa and Us*, 50.

31 Ganivet and Villierme, *Nu/Clear Stories*, episode 2.

32 De Vries and Seur, *Moruroa and Us*, 52.

33 Ra'i Chaze, personal communication, August 6, 2016.

34 Chaze, *Vai*, 43.

35 Chaze, *Vai*, 43.

36 Chaze, *Vai*, 44.

37 Teuira Henry and John Muggridge Orsmond, *Ancient Tahiti* (Honolulu: Bernice P. Bishop Museum, 1928), 439–43. For a comparative analysis of different versions of this etiological story, see Bruno Saura, *Un poisson nommé Tahiti: Mythes et pouvoirs aux temps anciens polynésiens* (Pīra'e, Tahiti: Au vent des îles, 2020).

38 Hau'ofa, *We Are the Ocean*, 75.

39 Harriet Bulkeley, "Common Knowledge? Public Understanding of Climate Change in Newcastle, Australia," *Public Understanding of Science* 9, no. 3 (2000): 313–33.

40 Stanley Cohen, *States of Denial: Knowing about Atrocities and Suffering* (Cambridge, UK: Polity, 2001), 8.

41 Cohen, *States of Denial*, 9.

42 Chaze, *Vai*, 44.

43 Chaze, *Vai*, 44.

44 Witi Ihimaera, *The Whale Rider* (Orlando: Harcourt, 1987), 84.

45 Ihimaera, *The Whale Rider*, 90–92.

46 Ihimaera, *The Whale Rider*, 44.

47 Ihimaera, *The Whale Rider*, 45.

48 Ihimaera, *The Whale Rider*, i.

49 Nuclear Free and Independent Pacific Conference and Pacific Concerns Resource Centre, *No Te Parau Tia, No Te Parau Mau, No Te Tiamaraa = For Justice, Truth and Independence: Report of the 8th Nuclear Free and Independent Pacific (NFIP) Conference, Arue, Tahiti, Te Ao Maohi (French Polynesia), 20–24 September 1999* (Suva, Fiji: Pacific Concerns Resource Centre, 2000), 18–19.

50 Maclellan, "Nuclear Testing and Racism," 4.

51 Hau'ofa, *We Are the Ocean*; Maclellan, "Nuclear Testing and Racism"; and Talei Luscia Mangioni, "Fighting for a Nuclear Free Pacific," *Funambulist: Politics of Space and Bodies* 39, no. 1 (2022): 42–47.

52 Bengt Danielsson and Marie-Thérèse Danielsson, *Moruroa, notre bombe coloniale: Histoire de la colonisation nucléaire de la Polynésie française* (Paris: L'Harmattan, 1993), 197.

53 Anare Bakale, quoted in Nic Maclellan, *Grappling with the Bomb: Britain's Pacific H-Bomb Tests* (Canberra: ANU Press, 2017), 230.

54 Paul Ah Poy, quoted in Maclellan, *Grappling with the Bomb*, 139.

55 Brigadier General J. W. White and Rear Admiral G. S. Patrick, quoted in Maclellan, *Grappling with the Bomb*, 214.

56 Commissariat à l'énergie atomique (CEA), *Les Atolls de Mururoa et Fangataufa, le milieu vivant et son évolution* (Paris: Masson, 1993), 241.

57 Jean Chesneaux and Nic Maclellan, *La France dans le Pacifique: De Bougainville à Moruroa* (Paris: La découverte, 1992), 98.

58 Maclellan, "Nuclear Testing and Racism," 16–18.

59 Barrillot, *Les Irradiés de la République*, 118.

60 Francis Ariioehau Sanford, quoted in Yves Haupert, *Francis Sanford à cœur ouvert* (Pīra'e, Tahiti: Au vent des îles, 1998), 140–41.

61 Ihimaera, *The Whale Rider*, 44–46.

62 Ihimaera, *The Whale Rider*, 44–45.

63 Hau'ofa, *We Are the Ocean*, 31.

64 Ihimaera, *The Whale Rider*, 93–94.

65 Jean Rostand, "Avant-Propos," in *Folie nucléaire* (Paris: Éditions de l'Épi, 1966), 28.

66 Ihimaera, *The Whale Rider*, 94.

67 Ihimaera, *The Whale Rider*, 99.

68 Ihimaera, *The Whale Rider*, 5.

69 Albert Wendt, "Tatauing the Post-colonial Body," in *Inside Out: Literature, Cultural Politics, and Identity in the New Pacific*, ed. Vilsoni Hereniko and Rob Wilson (Lanham, MD: Rowman and Littlefield, 1999), 403.

70   David R. Simmons, *Ta Moko: The Art of Maori Tattoo* (Rosedale, New Zealand: Raupo, 2009).

71   'Umi Perkins, "Pono and the Koru: Toward Indigenous Theory in Pacific Island Literature," *Hūlili* 4, no. 1 (2007): 59.

72   Elizabeth DeLoughrey, "The Spiral Temporality of Patricia Grace's 'Potiki,'" ARIEL: *A Review of International English Literature* 30, no. 1 (1999): 68.

73   Ihimaera, *The Whale Rider*, 4, 100.

74   Ihimaera, *The Whale Rider*, 101.

75   Ihimaera, *The Whale Rider*, 119.

76   Ihimaera, *The Whale Rider*, 78.

77   The most moderate estimates suggest that the population went from eighty-six thousand in 1769 to forty-two thousand in 1896. See James Belich, *Making Peoples: A History of the New Zealanders from Polynesian Settlement to the End of the Nineteenth Century* (Honolulu: University of Hawai'i Press, 2002), 178.

78   Ihimaera, *The Whale Rider*, 115.

79   Craig Santos Perez, *From Unincorporated Territory [Guma']* (Richmond, CA: Omnidawn, 2014), 40.

80   Guam Legislature Archives, "30th Guam Legislature—Resolutions," list of resolutions in electronic format, December 30, 2010, http://www.guamlegislature .com/30th_res.htm.

81   Pablo Servigne and Raphaël Stevens, *Comment tout peut s'effondrer: Petit manuel de collapsologie à l'usage des générations présentes* (Paris: Éditions du seuil, 2015).

82   Perez, *Habitat Threshold*, 35.

83   Perez, *Habitat Threshold*, 57.

84   Craig Santos Perez, *Navigating CHamoru Poetry: Indigeneity, Aesthetics, and Decolonization* (Tucson: University of Arizona Press, 2021), 131.

85   David Atienza De Frutos and Alexandre Coello De la Rosa, "Death Rituals and Identity in Contemporary Guam (Mariana Islands)," *Journal of Pacific History* 47, no. 4 (2012): 467.

86   Perez, *Navigating CHamoru Poetry*, 138.

87   Perez, *Navigating CHamoru Poetry*, 134–39.

88   Perez, *Habitat Threshold*, 35.

89   Perez, *Navigating CHamoru Poetry*, x.

90   Collier Nogues, "'With [Our] Entire Breath': The US Military Buildup on Guåhan (Guam) and Craig Santos Perez's Literature of Resistance," *Shima* 12, no. 1 (2018): 21.

91   Committee on Energy and Natural Resources, "Military Build-Up on Guam: Hearing before the Committee on Energy and Natural Resources, Unites States Senate 110th Congress" (US Government Printing Office, May 1, 2008), https:// www.govinfo.gov/content/pkg/CHRG-110shrg44544/html/CHRG-110shrg44544 .htm.

92   Perez, *From Unincorporated Territory*, 24.

93   Paul Lai, "Discontiguous States of America: The Paradox of Unincorporation in Craig Santos Perez's Poetics of Chamorro Guam," *Journal of Transnational American Studies* 3, no. 2 (2011): 9–10; Valerie Solar Woodward, "'I Guess They Didn't

Want Us Asking Too Many Questions': Reading American Empire in Guam,"
Contemporary Pacific 25, no. 1 (2013): 84.

94   Perez, *From Unincorporated Territory*, 88.

95   Perez, *From Unincorporated Territory*, 24.

96   Amy Kaplan, quoted in Nogues, "With [Our] Entire Breath," 23.

97   Aimee Bahng, "The Pacific Proving Grounds and the Proliferation of Settler Environmentalism," *Journal of Transnational American Studies* 11, no. 2 (2020): 45–73.

98   Cheryl Lousley, "Ecocriticism and the Politics of Representation," in *The Oxford Handbook of Ecocriticism* (Oxford: Oxford University Press, 2014), 160.

99   Perez, *From Unincorporated Territory*, 63. The poem is a quote from William Mullen, "One of the World's Most Endangered Species, Guam Kingfishers Live on in Zoos in Struggle to Survive," *Chicago Tribune*, June 27, 2010.

100   Perez, *From Unincorporated Territory*, 31.

101   Perez, *From Unincorporated Territory*, 22–23.

102   Craig Santos Perez, "Habitat Threshold Book Talk" (book talk series at the Greenhouse: An environmental humanities research group at the University of Stavanger, Stavanger, Norway, November 17, 2020).

103   Perez, *From Unincorporated Territory*, 31, 62, 63.

104   Whyte, "Our Ancestors' Dystopia Now," 207.

105   Robin Wall Kimmerer, *Braiding Sweetgrass: Indigenous Wisdom, Scientific Knowledge and the Teachings of Plants* (Minneapolis: Milkweed, 2015), 327.

106   Kimmerer, *Braiding Sweetgrass*, 328.

CHAPTER 4. THE H-BOMB AND HUMOR

1   Ebola, HIV, Zika, MERS-Cov, H5N1, and most recently SARS-Cov-2, to name only a few, have ravaged human communities across the world. The majority of these new microbial pathogens originate in the bodies of animals: pets, livestock, and—overwhelmingly—wildlife. Ebola came from bats, HIV from monkeys, MERS from dromedary camels, H5N1 from chickens, and scientists struggle to find the culprit for coronavirus (a bat? a pangolin? a snake?). Yet the animals themselves are not to blame. Industrial capitalism is. Habitat destruction, expanding towns, and sprawling industrial activity create pathways for microbial pathogens to cross over to human bodies. See Sonia Shah, "Contre les pandémies, l'écologie," *Le Monde diplomatique*, March 1, 2020.

2   As the climate warms, deadly mosquito-borne diseases are likely to spread up larger territories, bringing malaria, dengue, chikungunya, West Nile virus, yellow fever, filariasis, and Zika to millions more people. Diseases that had disappeared will come back: climate change is melting permafrost soils that have been frozen for thousands of years, and as the ice melts, it releases ancient viruses and bacteria that spring back to life. Anthrax released from the permafrost has already infected communities in the arctic circle in 2016. Smallpox, bubonic plague, and Spanish flu buried in Siberia are likely to reappear next. See BBC News, "Russia Anthrax Outbreak Affects Dozens," August 2, 2016, sec. Europe, https://www.bbc.com/news

/world-europe-36951542; and Jeffery K. Taubenberger, Johan V. Hultin, and David M. Morens, "Discovery and Characterization of the 1918 Pandemic Influenza Virus in Historical Context," *Antiviral Therapy* 12, no. 4, pt. B (2007): 581–91.

3   World Health Organization, "Antibiotic Resistance," World Health Organization, accessed July 31, 2020, https://www.who.int/news-room/fact-sheets/detail/antibiotic-resistance.

4   Vicki Brower, "Back to Nature: Extinction of Medicinal Plants Threatens Drug Discovery," *JNCI: Journal of the National Cancer Institute* 100, no. 12 (2008): 838–39.

5   Pablo Servigne and Raphaël Stevens, *Comment tout peut s'effondrer: Petit manuel de collapsologie à l'usage des générations présentes* (Paris: Éditions du seuil, 2015), 122–23.

6   Bengt Danielsson and Marie-Thérèse Danielsson, *Moruroa, notre bombe coloniale: Histoire de la colonisation nucléaire de la Polynésie française* (Paris: L'Harmattan, 1993), 648; Bruno Barrillot, *Les Irradiés de la République: Les Victimes des essais nucléaires français prennent la parole* (Lyon: Éditions complexe, 2003), 8.

7   Tilman A. Ruff, "The Humanitarian Impact and Implications of Nuclear Test Explosions in the Pacific Region," *International Review of the Red Cross* 97, no. 899 (2015): 792; Commission d'Enquête sur les conséquences des essais nucléaires (CESCEN), "Les Polynésiens et les essais nucléaires: Indépendance nationale et dépendance polynésienne" (Pape'ete, Tahiti: Assemblée de la Polynésie française, 2006), 173.

8   Pieter De Vries and Han Seur, *Moruroa and Us: Polynesians' Experiences during Thirty Years of Nuclear Testing in the French Pacific* (Lyon: Centre de documentation et de recherche sur la paix et les conflits, 1997), 101; Holly M. Barker, *Bravo for the Marshallese: Regaining Control in a Post-nuclear, Post-colonial World* (Belmont, CA: Wadsworth, 2013).

9   Ruff, "The Humanitarian Impact," 800.

10 Research on Chernobyl's biosphere has shown that exposure to radioactivity produces recessive genetic mutations that slowly spread into the species' genome, and the likelihood that a given individual will combine two recessive genes may reach its apex generations after radiation exposure. The incidence of radio-induced diseases and birth defects in Mā'ohi Nui is already twice to twenty-six times higher than the French national average. See Alain Dubois, *Jean Rostand, un biologiste contre le nucléaire* (Paris: Berg International, 2012); Commission d'Enquete sur les consequences des essais nucleaires (CESCEN), "Les Polynésiens et les essais nucléaires," 49; and Béatrice Le Vu et al., "Cancer Incidence in French Polynesia 1985–95," *Tropical Medicine and International Health* 5, no. 10 (2000): 722–31.

11 For more on the Runit Dome, see Michael Gerrard, "America's Forgotten Nuclear Waste Dump in the Pacific," *SAIS Review of International Affairs* 35, no. 1 (2015): 89.

12 Florence Parly, "Communiqué de presse: Inauguration du système Telsite 2," Ministère des armées, Salle de presse, June 21, 2018, accessed January 17, 2019, https://www.defense.gouv.fr/salle-de-presse/communiques/communiques-de-florence-parly/cp_inauguration-du-systeme-telsite-2.

13 French geographers Brice Martin and Carine Heitz also noted the incongruency of monitoring only Moruroa, when Fangataufa had been judged so unstable by the

French military that all underground tests stopped on that atoll for more than a decade. Brice Martin and Carine Heitz, "Un 'tsunami d'eau radioactive'? Réalité et perception des risques sismiques," in *Des Bombes en Polynésie: Les Essais nucléaires français dans le Pacifique*, ed. Renaud Meltz and Alexis Vrignon (Paris: Éditions vendémiaire, 2022), 37–90.

14 Ray Acheson, *Banning the Bomb, Smashing the Patriarchy* (Lanham, MD: Rowman and Littlefield, 2021), 57.

15 Acheson, *Banning the Bomb*, 57.

16 Bruno Saura and Dorothy Levy, *Bobby: L'Enchanteur du Pacifique* (Pīra'e, Tahiti: Au vent des îles, 2013), 259.

17 Saura and Levy, *Bobby*, 259.

18 Miriam Kahn, "Tahiti Intertwined: Ancestral Land, Tourist Postcard, and Nuclear Test Site," *American Anthropologist* 102, no. 1 (2000): 7–26.

19 Roger Baléras, quoted in Renaud Meltz, "Pourquoi la Polynésie?," in *Des Bombes en Polynésie: Les Essais nucléaires français dans le Pacifique*, ed. Renaud Meltz and Alexis Vrignon (Paris: Éditions vendémiaire, 2022), 68.

20 Meltz, "Pourquoi la Polynésie?," 68.

21 Danielsson and Danielsson, *Moruroa*, 175–77.

22 Quoted in Danielsson and Danielsson, *Moruroa*, 177.

23 Charles Teriiteanuanua Manu-Tahi, *Te parau itea ore hia: Pehepehe: Poèmes* (Pape'ete, Tahiti: Te hiroa maohi tumu, 1979), 11 (my emphasis).

24 Goenda Turiano-Reea, "Le Comique dans la tradition orale et la littérature contemporaine tahitiennes—vision du rire, vision du monde" (PhD diss., Université de la Polynésie française, 2016), 17.

25 Turiano-Reea, "Le Comique," 17.

26 Turiano-Reea, "Le Comique," 17.

27 For a detailed account of antinuclear activists' exile and censorship, see John Taroanui Doom, *A he'e noa i te tau: Mémoires d'une vie partagée* (Pape'ete, Tahiti: Haere Pō, 2016), 45, 55, 101.

28 Saura and Levy, *Bobby*, 259.

29 Paul Gauguin, *Lettres de Paul Gauguin à Georges-Daniel de Monfreid* (Paris: Éditions Georges Crès et Cie, 1918), 152.

30 "[Ces mythes qui] nous établissent dans une identité immuable immobile nous réduisent au silence à l'absence nous laissent sans voix sans consistance.... Peuple insonore." Chantal Spitz, *Pensées insolentes et inutiles* (Pape'ete, Tahiti: Éditions Te Ite, 2006), 130.

31 Diana Looser, "A Piece 'More Curious Than All the Rest': Re-encountering Pre-colonial Pacific Island Theatre, 1769–1855," *Theatre Journal* 63, no. 4 (2011): 526–30.

32 James Cook, *The Journals of Captain James Cook on His Voyages of Discovery*, vol. 2, ed. John Beaglehole (Cambridge: Hakluyt Society, 1955), appendix 5, p. 8, quoted in Looser, "A Piece 'More Curious Than All the Rest,'" 528–29.

33 Vilsoni Hereniko, *Woven Gods: Female Clowns and Power in Rotuma* (Honolulu: University of Hawai'i Press, 1995), 130.

34 Heinui le Caill, personal communication, June 24, 2022.

35 Adolphe Sylvain, *Sylvain's Tahiti* (Cologne: Taschen, 2001).

36 Hereniko, *Woven Gods*, 152.

37 Hereniko, *Woven Gods*, 152; Looser, "A Piece 'More Curious,'" 530.

38 "Décomposition, vautours et charognards avaient proprement fait leur œuvre." Alexandre Moeava Ata, *Tautai ou le ruisseau de Bali* (Pape'ete, Tahiti: Haere Pō, 2011), 7.

39 Ata, *Tautai*, 29.

40 Denis Diderot, *Supplément au voyage de Bougainville* (1772; repr., Paris: Pocket, 2004), 20.

41 "Leurs prénoms avaient traversé les océans et se transmettaient comme des passeports de volupté." Ata, *Tautai*, 20.

42 "[Son] regard s'attardait plutôt sur d'autres anatomies que la sienne." Ata, *Tautai*, 47.

43 "Société en cours de mutation." Ata, *Tautai*, 71.

44 "Une suite saccadée de palpitations." Ata, *Tautai*, 75.

45 "La diabétie," "des lèpres de goudron." Ata, *Tautai*, 76–77.

46 Victor Segalen, *Les Immemoriaux* (Paris: Librairie Générale Française, 1907).

47 "Des missionnaires spécialement chargés de noyauter ... une société civile somnolente ... répandaient la bonne parole." Ata, *Tautai*, 58–69.

48 "Le temple mormon d'Orovini n'est plus ..., la vénérable demeure de Tekau Pomare, délabrée, exhale un *au secours*! Pitoyable." Ata, *Tautai*, 76–77.

49 Before Pomare I won the Fei Pi battle against the Teva dynasty in 1815, Tahiti was ruled by many leaders (ari'i), each one in charge of a chiefdom (mata'eina'a). Pomare I was the first ari'i to unite an entire island under his rule, which greatly facilitated Westerners' impositions of new legislations. In 1819, a new set of laws known as the Pomare Code marks the beginning of an entirely new socioeconomic order in the island.

50 Bruno Saura, *Histoire et mémoire des temps coloniaux en Polynésie française* (Pīra'e, Tahiti: Au vent des îles, 2015), 107–11.

51 Klaus Neumann, "'In Order to Win Their Friendship': Renegotiating First Contact," in *Voyaging through the Contemporary Pacific*, ed. Geoffrey M. White and David Hanlon (Lanham, MD: Rowman and Littlefield, 2000), 190.

52 There are notable exceptions. See Louise Peltzer, *Lettre à Poutaveri* (Pīra'e, Tahiti: Au vent des îles, 1995); and Losana Natuman, "The Bitterness of Sugar Cane," in *Sista, Stanap Strong! A Vanuatu Women's Anthology*, ed. Mikaela Nyman and Rebecca Tobo Olul-Hossen (Wellington: Victoria University Press, 2021), 19–24.

53 Stéphanie Vigier, *La Fiction face au passé: Histoire, mémoire et espace-temps dans la fiction littéraire océanienne contemporaine* (Limoges, France: Presses universitaires de Limoges et du Limousin, 2012), 287.

54 Spitz, *Pensées insolentes et inutiles*, 84.

55 "L'aéroport militaire allait enfin offrir des retombées entièrement bénéfiques, touristiques cette fois. Drôle d'époque en vérité!" Ata, *Tautai*, 58.

56 Ata, *Tautai*, 59.

57 "Nouveau missionnaire de lendemains enchanteurs, le médecin fut foudroyé d'une leucémie." Ata, *Tautai*, 59.

58   Ata, *Tautai*, 59.

59   Subramani, "A Promise of Renewal: An Interview with Epeli Hauʻofa," in *Inside Out: Literature, Cultural Politics, and Identity in the New Pacific*, ed. Vilsoni Hereniko and Rob Wilson (Lanham, MD: Rowman and Littlefield, 1999), 42.

60   Vilsoni Hereniko and David Hanlon, "An Interview with Albert Wendt," in *Inside Out: Literature, Cultural Politics, and Identity in the New Pacific*, ed. Vilsoni Hereniko and Rob Wilson (Lanham, MD: Rowman and Littlefield, 1999), 92.

61   Albert Wendt, *Black Rainbow* (Honolulu: University of Hawaiʻi Press, 1995), 97.

62   Wendt, *Black Rainbow*, 77.

63   Wendt, *Black Rainbow*, 98.

64   Paul Sharrad, *Albert Wendt and Pacific Literature: Circling the Void* (Manchester: Manchester University Press, 2003), 206–7; Elizabeth M. DeLoughrey, *Routes and Roots: Navigating Caribbean and Pacific Island Literatures* (Honolulu: University of Hawaiʻi Press, 2007), 196–229; Teresa Shewry, *Hope at Sea: Possible Ecologies in Oceanic Literature* (Minneapolis: University of Minnesota Press, 2015), 147–66; Julia A. Boyd, "Black Rainbow, Blood-Earth: Speaking the Nuclearized Pacific in Albert Wendt's *Black Rainbow*," *Journal of Postcolonial Writing* 52, no. 6 (2016): 672–86; Rebecca H. Hogue, "Decolonial Memory and Nuclear Migration in Albert Wendt's *Black Rainbow*," *Modern Fiction Studies* 66, no. 2 (2020): 325–48.

65   Wendt, *Black Rainbow*, 12–13.

66   Wendt, *Black Rainbow*, 16–17.

67   Wendt, *Black Rainbow*, 245.

68   Wendt, *Black Rainbow*, 82, 231, 241.

69   Wendt, *Black Rainbow*, 241.

70   Wendt, *Black Rainbow*, 116.

71   Wendt, *Black Rainbow*, 113.

72   Wendt, *Black Rainbow*, 100.

73   Wendt, *Black Rainbow*, 100.

74   Wendt, *Black Rainbow*, 263.

75   Rebecca Priestley, *Mad on Radium: New Zealand in the Atomic Age* (Auckland: Auckland University Press, 2012), 3.

76   DeLoughrey, *Routes and Roots*, 249.

77   Theodor Adorno and Max Horkheimer, quoted in DeLoughrey, *Routes and Roots*, 249–50.

78   Hone Tuwhare, *Mihi: Collected Poems* (Auckland: Penguin, 1987), quoted in Wendt, *Black Rainbow*, 196.

79   Jean-Marc Teraʼituatini Pambrun, *L'Allégorie de la natte, ou, Le Tahuʼa-parau-tumu-fenua dans son temps* (Papeʼete, Tahiti: Ed. by author, 1993), 12.

80   Wendt, *Black Rainbow*, 218.

81   Wendt, *Black Rainbow*, 22.

82   Wendt, *Black Rainbow*, 159.

83   Wendt, *Black Rainbow*, 143.

84   Wendt, *Black Rainbow*, 144.

85   Wendt, *Black Rainbow*, 122–23.

86 Wendt, *Black Rainbow*, 264.

87 Wendt, *Black Rainbow*, 265.

88 Wendt, quoted in Hogue, "Decolonial Memory," 337.

89 Wendt, *Black Rainbow*, 234.

90 Wendt, *Black Rainbow*, 235.

91 Caroline Sinavaiana-Gabbard, "Where the Spirits Laugh Last: Comic Theater in Samoa," in *Inside Out: Literature, Cultural Politics, and Identity in the New Pacific*, ed. Vilsoni Hereniko and Rob Wilson (Lanham, MD: Rowman and Littlefield, 1999), 200.

92 Sinavaiana-Gabbard, "Where the Spirits Laugh Last," 200.

93 Sinavaiana-Gabbard, "Where the Spirits Laugh Last," 183.

94 Sinavaiana-Gabbard, "Where the Spirits Laugh Last," 187.

95 Hone Tuwhare, *No Ordinary Sun: Poems* (Auckland: Blackwood and J. Paul, 1962); Kathy Jetñil-Kijiner, *Iep Jāltok: Poems from a Marshallese Daughter* (Tucson: University of Arizona Press, 2017); Kathy Jetñil-Kijiner, dir., *Monsters* (Genbaku Dome, Hiroshima, 2017).

96 I offer one possible analysis of the aesthetics structuring this type of representation of radio-induced death and diseases in Francophone Pacific literature in "Nukes and Nudes: Counter-hegemonic Identities in the Nuclearized Pacific," *French Studies: A Quarterly Review* 72, no. 3 (2018): 394–411; and in "Snaring the Nuclear Sun: Decolonial Ecologies in Titaua Peu's *Mutismes: E 'Ore te Vāvā*," *Contemporary Pacific* 32, no. 2 (2020): 371–97.

97 Not discussed in this chapter but using a similar narrative strategy are Patricia Grace's cosmogonic caricature "Sun's Marbles" and Witi Ihimaera's journalistic parody "Wiwi." See Patricia Grace, "Sun's Marbles," in *The Sky People* (London: Penguin, 1994), 10–16; and Witi Ihimaera, "Wiwi (or, If New Zealand Was the Center of the World)," in *Below the Surface: Words and Images in Protest at French Testing on Moruroa*, ed. Ambury Hall (Auckland: Random House New Zealand, 1995), 62–64. I have discussed these works in "'Qui ne mourrait pas de cancer dans nos îles?' La créativité poétique des océaniens antinucléaires," in *Des Bombes en Polynésie: Les Essais nucléaires français dans le Pacifique*, ed. Renaud Meltz and Alexis Vrignon (Paris: Éditions vendémiaire, 2022), 549–67.

98 Naomi Klein, *This Changes Everything: Capitalism vs. the Climate* (Toronto: Vintage Canada, 2014), 447.

CHAPTER 5. RADIATION REFUGEES

1 Edward W. Said, *Reflections on Exile and Other Essays* (Cambridge, MA: Harvard University Press, 2000), 137–38.

2 Lower estimates only consider migrations triggered by climate issues such as rising sea levels, floods, droughts, wildfires, heat waves, etc. They do not account for the mass population movements that will come with diseases, wars, nuclear accidents, toxic spills, and industrial pollution. See Susanne Melde, "Data on Environmental Migration: How Much Do We Know?" (International

Organization for Migration: Knowledge Platform on People on the Move in a Changing Climate, 2016), https://environmentalmigration.iom.int/data -environmental-migration-how-much-do-we-know.

3 David Archer, *The Long Thaw: How Humans Are Changing the Next 100,000 Years of Earth's Climate*, rev. ed. (Princeton, NJ: Princeton University Press, 2016), 65.

4 Jean-Marc Jancovici, *Dormez tranquilles jusqu'en 2100: Et autres malentendus sur le climat et l'énergie* (Paris: Éditions Odile Jacob, 2015), 50–52.

5 Michael E. Zimmerman, "The Threat of Ecofascism," *Social Theory and Practice* 21, no. 2 (1995): 207–38; Kev Smith, "Ecofascism: Deep Ecology and Right-Wing Co-optation," *Synthesis/Regeneration* 2, no. 21 (2003): 1–25; Bernhard Forchtner, ed., *The Far Right and the Environment: Politics, Discourse and Communication*, Routledge Studies in Fascism and the Far Right (New York: Routledge, 2020).

6 Jennifer Wenzel, "Reading Fanon Reading Nature," in *What Postcolonial Theory Doesn't Say*, ed. Anna Bernard, Ziad Elmarsafy, and Stuart Murray (New York: Routledge, 2015), 194–96.

7 Terisa Tinei Siagatonu, "Atlas" (poem recited for the COP21, Paris, December 10, 2015, https://www.youtube.com/watch?v=mZMgGzD1–g&ab_channel=Fastfor Climate).

8 Siagatonu, "Atlas."

9 Siagatonu, "Atlas."

10 Roy Scranton, *Learning to Die in the Anthropocene: Reflections on the End of a Civilization* (San Francisco: City Lights, 2015), 68.

11 Siagatonu, "Atlas."

12 Glenn Albrecht, "Solastalgia: A New Concept in Health and Identity," *PAN: Philosophy, Activism, Nature*, no. 3 (2005): 41–55.

13 Since the sixteenth century, Pacific voyaging has even become global. In the eighteenth and nineteenth centuries, Pacific voyagers explored China, Europe, Peru, the Philippines, and the United States. For more on Pacific global history at that time, see Nicholas Thomas, *Islanders: The Pacific in the Age of Empire* (New Haven, CT: Yale University Press, 2012), 2–24.

14 Rebecca H. Hogue, "Decolonial Memory and Nuclear Migration in Albert Wendt's *Black Rainbow*," *Modern Fiction Studies* 66, no. 2 (2020): 326.

15 Darlene Keju-Johnson, "Micronesia," in *Pacific Women Speak: Why Haven't You Known?*, by Women Working for an Independent and Nuclear-Free Pacific (WWINFP) (Oxford: Green Line, 1987), 6.

16 Sasha Davis, *The Empires' Edge: Militarization, Resistance, and Transcending Hegemony in the Pacific* (Athens: University of Georgia Press, 2015), 63.

17 Keju-Johnson, "Micronesia," 6.

18 Pikinni is now a scuba-diving center for rich tourists wishing to explore the shipwrecks of Operation Crossroad.

19 Beverly Keever, *News Zero: The New York Times and the Bomb* (Monroe: Common Courage, 2004), 15.

20 On the need to decontaminate our nuclear vocabulary, see La Parisienne Libérée, *Le Nucléaire, c'est fini* (Paris: La fabrique éditions, 2019), 215–23.

21   Stewart Firth and Karin Von Strokirch, "A Nuclear Pacific," in *The Cambridge History of the Pacific Islanders* (Cambridge: Cambridge University Press, 1998), 331.

22   Barbara Rose Johnston and Holly M. Barker, *Consequential Damages of Nuclear War: The Rongelap Report* (Walnut Creek, CA: Left Coast, 2008).

23   Quoted in Holly M. Barker, *Bravo for the Marshallese: Regaining Control in a Post-nuclear, Post-colonial World* (Belmont, CA: Wadsworth, 2013), 90.

24   Quoted in WWINFP, *Pacific Women Speak*, 19.

25   WWINFP, *Pacific Women Speak*, 18.

26   For more on relocation in Kuwajleen, see Greg Dvorak, *Coral and Concrete: Remembering Kwajalein Atoll between Japan, America, and the Marshall Islands* (Honolulu: University of Hawai'i Press, 2018).

27   Stewart Firth, *Nuclear Playground* (Honolulu: University of Hawai'i Press, 1987), 65–67.

28   Tilman A. Ruff, "The Humanitarian Impact and Implications of Nuclear Test Explosions in the Pacific Region," *International Review of the Red Cross* 97, no. 899 (2015): 775–813.

29   Keju-Johnson, "Micronesia," 9.

30   This feeling is captured by the letter that Nelson Anjain, a magistrate of Rongelap, wrote in 1975 to the American doctor Robert Conard: "I realize now that your entire career is based on our illness. We are far more valuable to you, than you are to us. . . . We do not want to see you again. We want medical care from doctors who care about us, not about collecting information for the US government's war makers." Nelson Anjain, quoted in Johnston and Barker, *Consequential Damages of Nuclear War*, 139.

31   Haunani-Kay Trask, *From a Native Daughter: Colonialism and Sovereignty in Hawai'i* (Honolulu: University of Hawai'i Press, 1999), 179.

32   Kathy Jetñil-Kijiner, "A Word about My Mother," *Kathy Jetñil-Kijiner* (blog), February 20, 2014, https://jkijiner.wordpress.com/2014/02/20/a-word-about-my-mother/.

33   Kathy Jetñil-Kijiner, "Iep Jāltok: A History of Marshallese Literature" (master's thesis, Hawai'i, University of Hawai'i at Mānoa, 2014), 74.

34   For more on Jetñil-Kijiner's performance at the UN, see Monica C. Labriola, "Marshall Islands," *Contemporary Pacific* 28, no. 1 (2016): 195; and Angela L. Robinson, "Of Monsters and Mothers: Affective Climates and Human-Nonhuman Sociality in Kathy Jetñil-Kijiner's 'Dear Matafele Peinam,'" *Contemporary Pacific* 32, no. 2 (2020): 323.

35   "There had been a war / raging inside Bianca's six year old bones / white cells had staked their flag / they conquered the territory of her tiny body / they saw it as her destiny / they said it was manifested." Kathy Jetñil-Kijiner, *Iep Jāltok: Poems from a Marshallese Daughter* (Tucson: University of Arizona Press, 2017), 25.

36   ("Words / are ripped / from the belly / of her throat / before they can be born / . . . an unturned layer of earth I / can no longer cultivate." Jetñil-Kijiner, *Iep Jāltok*, 42.

37   "Netta gave birth to something resembling the eggs of a sea turtle / And Flora gave birth to something like the intestines / She told this to a committee of men /

who washed their hands of their sin." Kathy Jetñil-Kijiner, dir., *Monsters* (Genbaku Dome, Hiroshima, 2017).

38 Rebecca H. Hogue, "Nuclear Normalizing and Kathy Jetñil-Kijiner's 'Dome Poem," *Amerasia Journal* 47, no. 2 (2021): 210.

39 Jetñil-Kijiner, *Iep Jāltok*, 76–77.

40 "While it is true that these people do not live, I would say, the way Westerners do, civilized people, it is nevertheless also true that these people are more like us than mice." Quoted in Ruff, "The Humanitarian Impact," 805.

41 Jetñil-Kijiner, *Iep Jāltok*, 78.

42 Kathy Jetñil-Kijiner, "Bulldozed Reefs and Blasted Sands: Rituals for Artificial Islands," *Kathy Jetñil-Kijiner* (blog), February 7, 2019, https://www.kathyjetnilkijiner .com/bulldozed-reefs-and-blasted-sands-rituals-for-artificial-islands/.

43 Kathy Jetñil-Kijiner, "Dome Poem Part II: Of Islands and Elders," *Kathy Jetñil-Kijiner* (blog), March 2, 2018, https://www.kathyjetnilkijiner.com/dome-poem-part-ii-of -islands-and-elders/.

44 Kathy Jetñil-Kijiner, "New Year, New Monsters, New Poems," *Kathy Jetñil-Kijiner* (blog), January 25, 2018, https://www.kathyjetnilkijiner.com/new-year-new -monsters-and-new-poems/.

45 Michael B. Gerrard, "America's Forgotten Nuclear Waste Dump in the Pacific," *SAIS Review of International Affairs* 35, no. 1 (2015): 89.

46 Kathy Jetñil-Kijiner and Dan Lin, dirs., *Annointed* (Runit Dome, Marshall Islands, 2018).

47 Robin Wall Kimmerer, *Braiding Sweetgrass: Indigenous Wisdom, Scientific Knowledge and the Teachings of Plants* (Minneapolis: Milkweed, 2015), 256.

48 Jetñil-Kijiner, "Iep Jāltok," 34.

49 Dirk H. R. Spennemann, *Tattooing in the Marshall Islands* (Majuro: Republic of the Marshall Islands Historic Preservation Office, 1992), quoted in Kathy Jetñil- Kijiner, "Iep Jāltok," 33–34.

50 Scranton, *Learning to Die*, 15–16.

51 Evelyn Flores, "The Caregiver's Story," *The Missing Slate*, October 1, 2017.

52 Laleh Khalili, *Sinews of War and Trade: Shipping and Capitalism in the Arabian Peninsula* (New York: Verso, 2020), 52–53.

53 Aimee Bahng, "The Pacific Proving Grounds and the Proliferation of Settler Environmentalism," *Journal of Transnational American Studies* 11, no. 2 (2020): 47.

54 Kathy Jetñil-Kijiner, Aka Niviâna, and Dan Lin, dirs., *Rise* (Greenland, Marshall Islands, 2018).

55 Jetñil-Kijiner, "Bulldozed Reefs."

56 Marshallese People, "Petition from the Marshallese People concerning the Pacific Islands: Complaint regarding Explosions of Lethal Weapons within Our Home Islands to United Nations Trusteeship Council" (United Nations Trusteeship Council, April 20, 1954), https://www.osti.gov/opennet/servlets/purl/16364835.pdf.

57 Kathy Jetñil-Kijiner, "'Butterfly Thief' and Complex Narratives of Disappearing Islands," *Kathy Jetñil-Kijiner* (blog), April 30, 2017, https://www.kathyjetnilkijiner .com/butterfly-thief-and-complex-narratives-of-disappearing-islands/.

58 Jetñil-Kijiner, "'Butterfly Thief.'"

59   Erin Suzuki, *Ocean Passages: Navigating Pacific Islander and Asian American Literatures* (Philadelphia: Temple University Press, 2021), 70.

60   Jetñil-Kijiner, "Iep Jāltok," 43.

61   Jetñil-Kijiner, "'Butterfly Thief.'"

62   Jack A. Tobin, *Stories from the Marshall Islands: Bwebwenato Jan Aelon Kein* (Honolulu: University of Hawai'i Press, 2001), 54.

63   Jetñil-Kijiner, "Iep Jāltok," 65.

64   Nic Maclellan, *Grappling with the Bomb: Britain's Pacific H-Bomb Tests* (Canberra: ANU Press, 2017), 30.

65   Ruff, "The Humanitarian Impact."

66   Maclellan, *Grappling with the Bomb*, 233.

67   Letter from Group Captain F. M. Milligan, Headquarters Task Force Grapple, to G. A. C. Witheridge, Ministry of Supply, August 9, 1957, quoted in Maclellan, *Grappling with the Bomb*, 238.

68   "Evacuation of native population," memo from Air Vice Marshall Wilfred Oulton, Headquarters Grapple Task Force, March 29, 1957, GRA/6/5/AIR, marked "restricted," CO1036/281, quoted in Maclellan, *Grappling with the Bomb*, 248.

69   Tonga Fou, August 1, 2008, quoted in Maclellan, *Grappling with the Bomb*, 255.

70   Maclellan, *Grappling with the Bomb*, 254–56.

71   Maclellan, *Grappling with the Bomb*, 276.

72   Tammy Tabe, "Climate Change Migration and Displacement: Learning from Past Relocations in the Pacific," *Social Sciences* 8, no. 7 (2019): 5.

73   Becky Alexis-Martin, Matthew Breay Bolton, Dimity Hawkins, Sydney Tisch, and Talei Luscia Mangioni, "Addressing the Humanitarian and Environmental Consequences of Atmospheric Nuclear Weapon Tests: A Case Study of UK and US Test Programs at Kiritimati (Christmas) and Malden Islands, Republic of Kiribati," *Global Policy* 12, no. 1 (2021): 112.

74   Klaus-Gerd Giesen, "Autonomies politiques et dépendances économiques en Océanie," in *L'Océanie Convoitée: Actes des colloques*, ed. Sémir Al Wardi and Jean-Marc Regnault (Pape'ete, Tahiti: Self-published, CreateSpace, 2017), 330.

75   For more on the forced displacement undergone by her father, John Teaiwa, see Katerina Martina Teaiwa, *Consuming Ocean Island: Stories of People and Phosphate from Banaba* (Bloomington: Indiana University Press, 2014).

76   Katerina Teaiwa, April K. Henderson, and Terence Wesley-Smith, introduction to *Sweat and Salt Water*, by Teresia K. Teaiwa (Honolulu: University of Hawai'i Press, 2021), xvi. While she found a home in Fiji, for example, she is very critical of foreign reporters commenting on the ease of Banabans' displacement: "I want to . . . ram down that white man's throat the pleasure of being relocated from an island you know like the back of your hand, having your hand amputated and having someone else's hand sewn in its place." Teaiwa, *Sweat and Salt Water*, 197.

77   Teaiwa, Henderson, and Wesley-Smith, introduction to *Sweat and Salt Water*, xvi. For Teaiwa's scholarship on Kiribati, see Teresia K. Teaiwa, "Yaqona/Yagoqu: Roots and Routes of a Displaced Native," *Cultural Studies and New Writing* 4, no. 2 (1998): 92–106.

78 Teresia Teaiwa and Sia Figiel, *Terenesia: Amplified Poetry and Songs*, Hawai'i Dub Machine (Honolulu: 'Elepaio, 2000).

79 Teresia Teaiwa, "Bad Coconuts" (song), feat. H. Doug Matsuoka and Richard Hamasaki, in Teaiwa and Figiel, *Terenesia*.

80 Alexis-Martin et al., "Addressing the Humanitarian and Environmental Consequences," 115.

81 Losean Tubanavau-Salaluba, ed., *Kirisimasi: Na sotia kei na lewe ni mataivalu e wai ni viti e na vakatovotovo iyaragi nei peritania mai Kirisimasi* (Suva, Fiji: Pacific Concerns Resource Centre, 1999), cited in Alexis-Martin et al., "Addressing the Humanitarian and Environmental Consequences," 115.

82 For more on Teaiwa's scholarship on the Fiji military, see Teaiwa, *Sweat and Salt Water*, 127–87.

83 Teresia K. Teaiwa, "Bikinis and Other S/Pacific N/Oceans," *Contemporary Pacific* 6, no. 1 (1994): 96.

84 Teaiwa, *Sweat and Salt Water*, 216–17.

85 Teresia K. Teaiwa, "Militarism, Tourism and the Native: Articulations in Oceania" (PhD diss., University of California, Santa Cruz, 2001), 47–48.

86 Teaiwa, *Sweat and Salt Water*, 119.

87 Teresia Teaiwa, "Fear of an Estuary" (spoken-word performance), in Teaiwa and Figiel, *Terenesia*.

88 Teaiwa, "Fear of an Estuary."

89 Teaiwa, "Fear of an Estuary."

90 Teaiwa, "Fear of an Estuary."

91 See, for example, Elizabeth M. DeLoughrey, *Routes and Roots: Navigating Caribbean and Pacific Island Literatures* (Honolulu: University of Hawai'i Press, 2007); and Joël Bonnemaison, *Gens de pirogue et gens de la terre: Les Fondements géographiques d'une identité. L'archipel du Vanuatu. Essai de géographie culturelle* (Paris: Éditions de l'ORSTOM, 1996).

92 Candice Elanna Steiner, "A Sea of Warriors: Performing an Identity of Resilience and Empowerment in the Face of Climate Change in the Pacific," *Contemporary Pacific* 27, no. 1 (2015): 162.

93 Dale Husband, "Teresia Teaiwa: You Can't Paint the Pacific with Just One Brush Stroke," *E-Tangata* (blog), October 24, 2015, https://e-tangata.co.nz/korero/you -cant-paint-the-pacific-with-just-one-brush-stroke/.

94 Husband, "Teresia Teaiwa."

95 Although French-occupied Polynesia is relatively richer than other Pacific countries, it has a weaker social safety net than France, with no unemployment benefits, no Universal Basic Income (Revenu de Solidarité Active, or RSA), a smaller minimum wage, smaller family allowances, etc. For more on economic disparity between France and French-occupied Polynesia, see Jean-Marc Regnault, *Le Pouvoir confisqué en Polynésie française: L'Affrontement Temaru-Flosse* (Paris: Les Indes savantes, 2005); Jean Chesneaux, ed., *Tahiti après la bombe: Quel avenir pour la Polynésie?* (Paris: L'Harmattan, 1995); and Sémir Al Wardi and Jean-Marc Régnault, *Tahiti en crise durable: Un lourd héritage* (Moorea: Les éditions de Tahiti, 2011).

96 Commission d'Enquête sur les conséquences des essais nucléaires (CESCEN), "Les Polynésiens et les essais nucléaires: Indépendance nationale et dépendance polynésienne" (Pape'ete, Tahiti: Assemblée de la Polynésie française, 2006), 251.

97 Bengt Danielsson and Marie-Thérèse Danielsson, *Moruroa, notre bombe coloniale: Histoire de la colonisation nucléaire de la Polynésie française* (Paris: L'Harmattan, 1993), 260; Bruno Barrillot, *Les Irradiés de la République: Les victimes des essais nucléaires français prennent la parole* (Lyon: Éditions complexe, 2003), 203.

98 Marie-Claude Beaudeau, ed., *Les Essais nucléaires et la santé, actes de la conférence du 19 janvier 2002 au Sénat* (Lyon: Centre de documentation et de recherche sur la paix et les conflits, 2002), 34.

99 CESCEN, "Les Polynésiens et les essais nucléaires," 251.

100 Danielsson and Danielsson, *Moruroa*, 264.

101 Alexander Mawyer, "The Maladie du Secret: Witnessing the Nuclear State in French Polynesia" (lecture, Pacific Islands Political Science Association, Mānoa, June 2014).

102 CESCEN, "Les Polynésiens et les essais nucléaires," 113.

103 Pieter De Vries and Han Seur, *Moruroa and Us: Polynesians' Experiences during Thirty Years of Nuclear Testing in the French Pacific* (Lyon: Centre de documentation et de recherche sur la paix et les conflits, 1997), 70.

104 Danielsson and Danielsson, *Moruroa*, 149.

105 De Vries and Seur, *Moruroa and Us*, 70.

106 De Vries and Seur, *Moruroa and Us*, 29.

107 Danielsson and Danielsson, *Moruroa*, 148.

108 De Vries and Seur, *Moruroa and Us*, 198.

109 De Vries and Seur, *Moruroa and Us*, 70.

110 De Vries and Seur, *Moruroa and Us*, 66.

111 Laurie Penny, *Sexual Revolution: Modern Fascism and the Feminist Fightback* (London: Bloomsbury, 2022), 17.

112 Nic Maclellan, "Nuclear Testing and Racism in the Pacific Islands," in *The Palgrave Handbook of Ethnicity*, ed. Steven Ratuva (London: Palgrave Macmillan, 2019), 4.

113 Alfred René Grand, "Pouvanaa a Oopa et nationalisme à Tahiti" (Thèse de 3e cycle, Université Paris 1 Panthéon-Sorbonne, 1981), 361–66.

114 Historians still debate whether Pouvanaa a Oopa's exile should be attributed to a French conspiracy in view of the upcoming nuclear tests or simply to colonial administrators in Pape'ete being unwilling to relinquish their power. While Jean Guiart claims that Paris was too absorbed with the Algerian war to orchestrate the arson and the trial that led to Pouvanaa's exile, Jean-Marc Regnault and Catherine Vannier have argued that the Metua's condemnation was orchestrated by French officials to clear the way for the CEP. In 2022, Alexis Vrignon seconded Guiart's thesis, reviving the controversy. For more on the Pouvanaa affair, see Jean-Marc Regnault and Catherine Vannier, *Le Metua et le Général: Un combat inégal* (Moorea: Les éditions de Tahiti, 2009); Jean Guiart, *Le Bêtisier océanien: Ce qu'il faut savoir de l'Océanie et dictionnaire des erreurs accumulées* (Nouméa, New Caledonia: Le Rocher-à-la-Voile; Pape'ete, Tahiti: Te pito o te fenua, 2012), 238–39; Bruno Saura, *Histoire*

et *mémoire des temps coloniaux en Polynésie française* (Pīra'e, Tahiti: Au vent des îles, 2015), 281–95; and Bruno Saura, *Pouvanaa a Oopa: Père de la culture politique tahitienne* (Pīra'e, Tahiti: Au vent des îles, 2012), 310–72.

115 See Yves Haupert, *Francis Sanford à cœur ouvert* (Pīra'e, Tahiti: Au vent des îles, 1998), 141; Saura, *Histoire et mémoire*, 310.

116 Spitz, personal communication, Pape'ete, Tahiti, February 10, 2017.

117 Ruahine stands for both the island of Huahine, where Spitz witnessed transnational corporations organize land expropriations, and the island of Moruroa, the main site of nuclear testing.

118 "Ils sont élus pour nous protéger et ils nous vendent!" Chantal T. Spitz, *L'Île des rêves écrasés* (Pīra'e, Tahiti: Au vent des îles, 1991), 112.

119 "En s'enfonçant dans son siège moelleux pour postérieur gouvernemental." Spitz, *L'Île des rêves écrasés*, 111.

120 "Offrons ce bout de notre territoire à l'État, participant ainsi à l'œuvre magnifique de cette grande Nation dont nous faisons partie." Spitz, *L'Île des rêves écrasés*, 116.

121 Jacques-Denis Drollet, quoted in CESCEN, "Les Polynésiens et les essais nucléaires," 36.

122 Rosa Raoult, Alexandre Legayic, and Drollet himself voted in favor, while Charles Lehartel and Félix Tefaatau voted against it. The most vocal antinuclear parliamentarians, John Teariki and Francis Sanford, were not included in the commission. CESCEN, "Les Polynésiens et les essais nucléaires," 36.

123 Testifying in front of the CESCEN, Drollet maintains that he was summoned by De Gaulle: "He made me understand that, for national security, he was ready to declare that French Polynesia would become a 'strategic military territory' with a military government if we did not acquiesce to his transfer demand. And since this general does not have a reputation as a jester, I took this threat or this blackmail very seriously. We had struggled and lost so much to acquire our democratic rights that in my mind, I thought about making concessions to avoid the yoke of a military government." Quoted in CESCEN, "Les Polynésiens et les essais nucléaires," 33.

124 Spitz, *L'Île des rêves écrasés*, 99.

125 Spitz, *L'Île des rêves écrasés*, 160.

126 David A. Chappell, "Active Agents versus Passive Victims: Decolonized Historiography or Problematic Paradigm?," in *Voyaging through the Contemporary Pacific* (Lanham, MD: Rowman and Littlefield, 2000), 314.

127 "Elle est un de ces étrangers qui viole sa terre." Spitz, *L'Île des rêves écrasés*, 135.

128 Spitz, personal communication, Pape'ete, Tahiti, February, 10, 2017.

129 "Pauvre naïf" and "pauvre rêveuse." Spitz, *L'Île des rêves écrasés*, 109.

130 Spitz, *L'Île des rêves écrasés*, 117.

131 Spitz, personal communication, Pape'ete, Tahiti, February 10, 2017.

132 "[Les enfants sont nommés] dans la longue généalogie de sa famille, car nul ne peut porter un nom qui n'appartient à ses pères." Spitz, *L'Île des rêves écrasés*, 31.

133 Historically the Betelgeuse, but the Voltigeuse in the novel.

134 Mililani Ganivet and Marie-Hélène Villierme, *Nu/Clear Stories* (Onesia S/pacific Storytellers, 2023), podcast, episode 1, May 2023. Translated by Mililani Ganivet and Marie-Hélène Villierme.

135 "S'envole aussitôt pour regagner son pays"; "Ils ne se rencontreront jamais." Spitz, *L'Île des rêves écrasés*, 186, 187.

136 Jason Man Sang, public intervention after the performance of *Les Champignons de Paris — Te Mau tuputupua a Paris*, Te Fare Tauhiti Nui, May 21, 2022, from the play by Émilie Génaédig and Emma Faua-Tufariua, *Les Champignons de Paris — Te mau tuputupua a Paris* (Pape'ete, Tahiti: Haere Pō, 2017).

137 Kathy Jetñil-Kijiner, "A Moment of Clarity—Why I'm Going to Paris COP21," *Kathy Jetñil-Kijiner* (blog), November 22, 2015, https://jkijiner.wordpress.com/2015/11/22/a-moment-of-clarity-why-im-going-to-paris-cop21/.

138 Robinson, "Of Monsters and Mothers," 326.

139 Val Plumwood, *Environmental Culture: The Ecological Crisis of Reason* (New York: Routledge, 2001), 97.

140 Plumwood, *Environmental Culture*, 99.

CONCLUSION. "WITH OUR HEARTS BROKEN
AND OUR EYES PEELED FOR BEAUTY"

1 Teuira Henry and John Muggridge Orsmond, *Ancient Tahiti* (Honolulu: Bernice P. Bishop Museum, 1928), 336–37.

2 Henry and Orsmond, *Ancient Tahiti*, 337.

3 Te Maire Tau, *The Oral Traditions of Ngāi Tahu: Ngā Pikitūroa o Ngāi Tahu* (Dunedin, NZ: University of Otago Press, 2003), 259, quoted in Madi Williams, *Polynesia, 900–1600* (Leeds, UK: Arc Humanities, 2021), 22.

4 Bruno Saura, *Des Tahitiens, des Français*, vol. 2, *Essai sur l'assimilation culturelle en situation coloniale consentie* (Pīra'e, Tahiti: Au vent des îles, 2021), 189–90.

5 Elizabeth M. DeLoughrey, *Allegories of the Anthropocene* (Durham, NC: Duke University Press, 2019), 8.

6 This 'ōlelo no'eau can be loosely translated as "through the past is the future" (more literally, "through the time in front is the time behind").

7 Between 2010 and 2018, the French-led Comité d'indemnisation des victimes des essais nucléaires (CIVEN, Committee of Compensation of Victims of Nuclear Tests) rejected 98 percent of all demands for compensation. In recent years, about 50 percent of applications are still rejected. Léna Lenormand, chairwoman of the Association 193 Women's Committee, personal communication, Puna'auia, June 29, 2022. See also Association 193, *The Nuclear Fact and Its Consequences* (Faa'ā, Tahiti: Association 193, 2014).

8 Hinamoeura Morgant-Cross, representative of the Mā'ohi nuclear victims activists group Association 193 at the 2022 Meeting of States Party regarding the Treaty on the Prohibition of Nuclear Weapons, personal communication, Puna'auia, May 18, 2022; and Béatrice Mou Sang Teinauri, *Je m'appelle Airuarii* (Pape'ete, Tahiti: Publication indépendante, 2022).

9 Benoît Pélopidas, *Repenser les choix nucléaires: La Séduction de l'impossible* (Paris: Les presses de Sciences Po, 2022), 16.

10 Marco De Jung, Nic Maclellan, Carla Cantagallo, Dimity Hawkins, and Pam Kingfisher, "Challenging Nuclear Secrecy: A Discussion of Ethics, Hierarchies, and Barriers to Access in Nuclear Archives." Nuclear Truth Project, July 31, 2023, p. 29. https://nucleartruthproject.org/resources/.

11 Julian Aguon, *The Properties of Perpetual Light* (Mangilao: University of Guam Press, 2021), 19. I am not here equating my modest work at Extinction Rebellion Fenua with Aguon's inspiring lifelong dedication to climate justice but simply emphasizing the commonalities shared by many people invested in limiting environmental damage.

12 Aguon, *The Properties of Perpetual Light*, 3.

13 Aguon, *The Properties of Perpetual Light*, 98.

14 Aguon, *The Properties of Perpetual Light*, 34.

15 Aguon, *The Properties of Perpetual Light*, 35.

16 Aguon, *The Properties of Perpetual Light*, 36.

17 Aguon, *The Properties of Perpetual Light*, 37.

18 Teresa Shewry, *Hope at Sea: Possible Ecologies in Oceanic Literature* (Minneapolis: University of Minnesota Press, 2015), 1.

19 Craig Santos Perez, "This Changes Everything," Facebook, November 2, 2017, http://www.facebook.com.

20 Ruha Fifita, "Kathy Jetñil-Kijiner: A Spoken-Word Poet for Resilience and Hope," QAGOMA *Blog*, May 9, 2019, https://blog.qagoma.qld.gov.au/apt9-kathy-jetnil-kijiner-a-spoken-word-poet/.

21 Kathy Jetñil-Kijiner, "Bulldozed Reefs and Blasted Sands: Rituals for Artificial Islands," *Kathy Jetñil-Kijiner* (blog), February 7, 2019, https://www.kathyjetnilkijiner.com/bulldozed-reefs-and-blasted-sands-rituals-for-artificial-islands/.

22 Anna Lowenhaupt Tsing, Nils Bubandt, Elaine Gan, and Heather Anne Swanson, eds., *Arts of Living on a Damaged Planet: Ghosts and Monsters of the Anthropocene* (Minneapolis: University of Minnesota Press, 2017).

23 Aguon, *The Properties of Perpetual Light*, 82.

Bibliography

Acheson, Ray. *Banning the Bomb, Smashing the Patriarchy*. Lanham, MD: Rowman and Littlefield, 2021.

A. D. G. *Les Billets nickelés*. Paris: Gallimard, 1998.

Aguon, Julian. *The Properties of Perpetual Light*. Mangilao: University of Guam Press, 2021.

Albrecht, Glenn A. "Solastalgia: A New Concept in Health and Identity." *PAN: Philosophy, Activism, Nature*, no. 3 (2005): 41–55.

Alexis-Martin, Becky, Matthew Breay Bolton, Dimity Hawkins, Sydney Tisch, and Talei Luscia Mangioni. "Addressing the Humanitarian and Environmental Consequences of Atmospheric Nuclear Weapon Tests: A Case Study of UK and US Test Programs at Kiritimati (Christmas) and Malden Islands, Republic of Kiribati." *Global Policy* 12, no. 1 (2021): 106–21.

Al Wardi, Sémir, and Jean-Marc Régnault. *Tahiti en crise durable: Un lourd héritage*. Moorea: Les éditions de Tahiti, 2011.

Angleviel, Frédéric. *Les Missions à Wallis et Futuna au XIXe siècle*. Bordeaux: Université Michel de Montaigne, 1994.

Archer, David. *The Long Thaw: How Humans Are Changing the Next 100,000 Years of Earth's Climate*. Rev. ed. Princeton, NJ: Princeton University Press, 2016.

Ariirau. *Matamimi ou la vie nous attend*. Pīra'e, Tahiti: Au vent des îles, 2006.

Ariirau. "Tristesse s'agrippe à moi, 720 fois Hiroshima en mon pays." *Littérama'ohi*, no. 16 (2009): 66–69.

Arvin, Maile Renee. *Possessing Polynesians: The Science of Settler Colonial Whiteness in Hawai'i and Oceania*. Durham, NC: Duke University Press, 2019.

Association 193. *The Nuclear Fact and Its Consequences*. Faa'ā, Tahiti: Association 193, 2014.

Ata, Alexandre Moeava. *Tautai ou le ruisseau de Bali*. Pape'ete, Tahiti: Haere Pō, 2011.

Ata, Alexandre Moeava. *Voyage en OGM (Océanie Génétiquement Modifiée)*. Pape'ete, Tahiti: Haere Pō, 2010.

Aubert, Marie-Hélène, and Michèle Rivasi. *The French Nuclear Tests in Polynesia: Demanding the Truth and Proposals for the Future: Proceedings of the Symposium, 20th February 1999*. Lyon: Centre de documentation et de recherche sur la paix et les conflits, 1999.

Babadzan, Alain. "Une Perspective pour deux passages: Notes sur la représentation traditionnelle de la naissance et de la mort en Polynésie." *L'Homme* 23, no. 3 (1983): 81–99.

Bachimon, Philippe. *Tahiti, entre mythes et réalités: Essai d'histoire géographique.* Paris: Éditions du comité des travaux historiques et scientifiques, 1990.

Bahng, Aimee. "The Pacific Proving Grounds and the Proliferation of Settler Environmentalism." *Journal of Transnational American Studies* 11, no. 2 (2020): 45–73.

Baldy, Cutcha Risling. "Coyote Is Not a Metaphor: On Decolonizing, (Re)Claiming and (Re)Naming 'Coyote.'" *Decolonization: Indigeneity, Education and Society* 4, no. 1 (2015): 1–20.

Bambridge, Tamatoa. *The Rahui: Legal Pluralism in Polynesian Traditional Management of Resources and Territories.* Canberra: ANU Press, 2016.

Barker, Holly M. *Bravo for the Marshallese: Regaining Control in a Post-nuclear, Post-colonial World.* Belmont, CA: Wadsworth, 2013.

Barrillot, Bruno. *Les Irradiés de la République: Les Victimes des essais nucléaires français prennent la parole.* Lyon: Éditions complexe, 2003.

Barros, Vicente R., and Christopher B. Fields, eds. *Climate Change 2014: Impacts, Adaptation, and Vulnerability: Working Group II Contribution to the Fifth Assessment Report of the Intergovernmental Panel on Climate Change.* Pt. B, *Regional Aspects.* Cambridge: Cambridge University Press, 2014.

BBC News. "Russia Anthrax Outbreak Affects Dozens." August 2, 2016, sec. Europe. https://www.bbc.com/news/world-europe-36951542.

Beaudeau, Marie-Claude, dir. *Les Essais nucléaires et la santé, actes de la conférence du 19 janvier 2002 au Sénat.* Lyon: Centre de documentation et de recherche sur la paix et les conflits, 2002.

Belich, James. *Making Peoples: A History of the New Zealanders from Polynesian Settlement to the End of the Nineteenth Century.* Honolulu: University of Hawai'i Press, 2002.

Bendrups, Dan. *Singing and Survival: The Music of Easter Island.* New York: Oxford University Press, 2019.

Bensa, Alban. *Chroniques kanak: L'Ethnologie en marche.* Paris: Ethnies, 1995.

Bergson, Henri. *L'Évolution créatrice.* Paris: Librairie H. Le Soudier, 1907.

Bernasconi, Robert. "With What Must the Philosophy of World History Begin? On the Racial Basis of Hegel's Eurocentrism." *Nineteenth-Century Contexts* 22, no. 2 (2000): 171–201.

Bessière, Jean, and Sylvie André, eds. *Littératures du Pacifique insulaire: Nouvelle-Calédonie, Nouvelle-Zélande, Océanie, Timor Oriental: Approches historiques, culturelles et comparatives.* Paris: Honoré Champion, 2013.

Bhabha, Homi K. *The Location of Culture.* New York: Routledge, 2004.

Blaeser, Kimberly M. *Gerald Vizenor: Writing in the Oral Tradition.* Norman: University of Oklahoma Press, 1996.

Blain, Christophe, and Jean-Marc Jancovici. *Le Monde sans fin, miracle énergétique et dérive climatique.* Paris: Dargaud, 2021.

Blanc, Anne-Catherine. *Moana blues.* Pira'e, Tahiti: Au vent des îles, 2002.

Bonnemaison, Joël. *Gens de pirogue et gens de la terre: Les Fondements géographiques d'une identité. L'archipel du Vanuatu. Essai de géographie culturelle.* Paris: Éditions de l'ORSTOM, 1996.

Bougainville, Louis-Antoine de. *Voyage autour du monde par la frégate* La Boudeuse *et la flûte* L'Étoile. 1771. Reprint, Paris: La découverte, 2006.

Boyd, Julia A. "Black Rainbow, Blood-Earth: Speaking the Nuclearized Pacific in Albert Wendt's *Black Rainbow.*" *Journal of Postcolonial Writing* 52, no. 6 (2016): 672–86.

Brotherson, Moetai. *Le Roi absent.* Pīra'e, Tahiti: Au vent des îles, 2013.

Brower, Vicki. "Back to Nature: Extinction of Medicinal Plants Threatens Drug Discovery." *JNCI: Journal of the National Cancer Institute* 100, no. 12 (2008): 838–39.

Buck, Peter H. *Vikings of the Pacific.* Chicago: University of Chicago Press, 1938.

Bulkeley, Harriet. "Common Knowledge? Public Understanding of Climate Change in Newcastle, Australia." *Public Understanding of Science* 9, no. 3 (2000): 313–33.

Byrd, Jodi A. "Fracturing Futurity: Colonial Agnosia and the Untimely Indigenous Present." Lecture presented at the University of New Mexico, Albuquerque, October 25, 2012.

Camoui, Luc Énoka, and Waixen Wayewol. *Pue Tiu, au cœur de la parole: Poèmes et poésies kanak de la Nouvelle-Calédonie.* Nouméa, New Caledonia: L'Herbier de feu, 2011.

Case, Pua, and Amy Goodman. "'We Are Not Anti-Science': Why Indigenous Protectors Oppose the Thirty Meter Telescope at Mauna Kea." *Democracy Now!,* July 22, 2019. https://www.democracynow.org/2019/7/22/why_indigenous_protectors_oppose _the_thirty.

Césaire, Aimé. *Cahier d'un retour au pays natal.* Paris: Présence africaine, 1983.

Césaire, Aimé. "Discours sur l'art africain." *Études littéraires* 6, no. 1 (1966): 99–109. Reprinted in *Gradhiva: Revue d'anthropologie et d'histoire des arts,* no. 10 (November 4, 2009): 208–15.

Chappell, David A. "Active Agents versus Passive Victims: Decolonized Historiography or Problematic Paradigm?" In *Voyaging through the Contemporary Pacific,* edited by David Hanlon and Geoffrey M. White, 303–26. Lanham, MD: Rowman and Littlefield, 2000.

Chappell, David A. *The Kanak Awakening: The Rise of Nationalism in New Caledonia.* Honolulu: University of Hawai'i Press, 2013.

Chappell, David A. "Violences coloniales à Hawaii." In *Violences océaniennes,* edited by Frédéric Angleviel, 63–75. Paris: L'Harmattan, 2004.

Chastel, Patrick, and Philippe Lemaire. *Le Sourire du tiki.* Pīra'e, Tahiti: Au vent des îles, 1985.

Chaze, Ra'i. *Vai: La Rivière au ciel sans nuages.* Pape'ete, Tahiti: Self-published, CreateSpace, 1990.

Chesneaux, Jean, ed. *Tahiti après la bombe: Quel avenir pour la Polynésie?* Paris: L'Harmattan, 1995.

Chesneaux, Jean, and Nic Maclellan. *La France dans le Pacifique: De Bougainville à Moruroa.* Paris: La découverte, 1992.

Choi, Shine, and Catherine Eschle. "Rethinking Global Nuclear Politics, Rethinking Feminism." *International Affairs* 98, no. 4 (2022): 1129–47.

Chomsky, Noam. *Radical Priorities.* Oakland, CA: AK, 1981.

Cizeron, Marc. *Tonton Grand-Frère*. Pape'ete, Tahiti: Haere Pō, 2006.

Cohen, Stanley. *States of Denial: Knowing about Atrocities and Suffering*. Cambridge: Polity, 2001.

Colebrook, Claire. *Essays on Extinction*. Vol. 1, *Death of the PostHuman*. Ann Arbor, MI: Open Humanities, 2014.

Commissariat à l'énergie atomique (CEA). *Les Atolls de Mururoa et Fangataufa, le milieu vivant et son évolution*. Paris: Masson, 1993.

Commission d'Enquête sur les conséquences des essais nucléaires (CESCEN). "Les Polynésiens et les essais nucléaires: Indépendance nationale et dépendance polynésienne." Pape'ete, Tahiti: Assemblée de la Polynésie française, 2006.

Committee on Energy and Natural Resources. "Military Build-Up on Guam: Hearing before the Committee on Energy and Natural Resources, Unites States Senate 110th Congress." US Government Printing Office, May 1, 2008. https://www.govinfo.gov/content/pkg/CHRG-110shrg44544/html/CHRG-110shrg44544.htm.

Cook, James. *The Journals of Captain James Cook on His Voyages of Discovery*. Vol. 2, *The Voyage of the Resolution and Adventure 1772-1775*. Edited by John Beaglehole. Cambridge: Hakluyt Society, 1955.

Crook, Tony, and Peter Rudiak-Gould. *Pacific Climate Cultures: Living Climate Change in Oceania*. Warsaw: De Gruyter, 2018.

Crosby, Alfred W. *Ecological Imperialism: The Biological Expansion of Europe, 900-1900*. New York: Cambridge University Press, 2004.

Danielsson, Bengt. "Under a Cloud of Secrecy: The French Nuclear Tests in the Southeastern Pacific." In *French Polynesia: A Book of Selected Readings*, 338-59. Suva, Fiji: Institute of Pacific Studies of the University of the South Pacific, 1988.

Danielsson, Bengt, and Marie-Thérèse Danielsson. *Moruroa, notre bombe coloniale: Histoire de la colonisation nucléaire de la Polynésie française*. Paris: L'Harmattan, 1993.

Davies, John. *The History of the Tahitian Mission, 1799-1830*. Cambridge: Hakluyt Society at the University Press, 1961.

Davis, Sasha. *The Empires' Edge: Militarization, Resistance, and Transcending Hegemony in the Pacific*. Athens: University of Georgia Press, 2015.

De Bovis, Edmond. *État de la société tahitienne à l'arrivée des Européens*. Paris: Revue coloniale, 1855.

De Frutos, David Atienza, and Alexandre Coello De la Rosa. "Death Rituals and Identity in Contemporary Guam (Mariana Islands)." *Journal of Pacific History* 47, no. 4 (2012): 459-73.

De Jung, Marco, Nic Maclellan, Carla Cantagallo, Dimity Hawkins, and Pam Kingfisher. "Challenging Nuclear Secrecy: A Discussion of Ethics, Hierarchies, and Barriers to Access in Nuclear Archives." Nuclear Truth Project, July 31, 2023. https://nucleartruthproject.org/resources/.

De La Vega, Bernard. *Angélus en terre lointaine*. Pīra'e, Tahiti: Au vent des îles, 2013.

DeLoughrey, Elizabeth. *Allegories of the Anthropocene*. Durham, NC: Duke University Press, 2019.

DeLoughrey, Elizabeth. "Heliotropes: Solar Ecologies and Pacific Radiations." In *Postcolonial Ecologies: Literatures of the Environment*, edited by Elizabeth DeLoughrey and George B. Handley, 235-53. New York: Oxford University Press, 2011.

DeLoughrey, Elizabeth. "Postcolonialism." In *The Oxford Handbook of Ecocriticism*, edited by Greg Garrard, 321–40. Oxford: Oxford University Press, 2014.

DeLoughrey, Elizabeth. *Routes and Roots: Navigating Caribbean and Pacific Island Literatures*. Honolulu: University of Hawai'i Press, 2007.

DeLoughrey, Elizabeth. "The Spiral Temporality of Patricia Grace's 'Potiki.'" *ARIEL: A Review of International English Literature* 30, no. 1 (1999): 59–83.

DeLoughrey, Elizabeth. "Toward a Critical Ocean Studies for the Anthropocene." *English Language Notes* 57, no. 1 (2019): 21–36.

Deming, Alison Hawthorne. *Zoologies: On Animals and the Human Spirit*. Minneapolis: Milkweed, 2014.

De Vries, Pieter, and Han Seur. *Moruroa and Us: Polynesians' Experiences during Thirty Years of Nuclear Testing in the French Pacific*. Lyon: Centre de documentation et de recherche sur la paix et les conflits, 1997.

Diagne, Souleymane Bachir. *Bergson postcolonial: L'Élan vital dans la pensée de Léopold Sédar Senghor et de Mohamed Iqbal*. Paris: CNRS éditions, 2011.

Diagne, Souleymane Bachir. "Négritude." In *The Stanford Encyclopedia of Philosophy*, edited by Edward N. Zalta. Stanford, CA: Metaphysics Research Lab, Stanford University, 2018. https://plato.stanford.edu/archives/sum2018/entries/negritude/.

Diagne, Souleymane Bachir. "Senghor et la Révolution de 1889." *Romanic Review* 100, nos. 1–2 (March 2009): 103–11.

Diamond, Jared M. *Collapse: How Societies Choose to Fail or Succeed*. New York: Viking, 2005.

Diaz, Vicente M., and J. Kēhaulani Kauanui. "Native Pacific Cultural Studies on the Edge." *Contemporary Pacific* 13, no. 2 (2001): 315–42.

Diderot, Denis. *Supplément au voyage de Bougainville*. 1772. Reprint, Paris: Pocket, 2004.

Dirlik, Arif. "Asia-Pacific Studies in an Age of Global Modernity." In *Remaking Area Studies: Teaching and Learning across Asia and the Pacific*, edited by Terence Wesley-Smith and Jon Goss, 5–23. Honolulu: University of Hawai'i Press, 2010.

Doom, John Taroanui. *A he'e noa i te tau: Mémoires d'une vie partagée*. Pape'ete, Tahiti: Haere Pō, 2016.

Drayton, Richard Harry. *Nature's Government: Science, Imperial Britain, and the "Improvement" of the World*. New Haven, CT: Yale University Press, 2000.

Dubois, Alain. *Jean Rostand, un biologiste contre le nucléaire*. Paris: Berg International, 2012.

Dunn, Robert R., Nyeema C. Harris, Robert K. Colwell, Lian Pin Koh, and Navjot S. Sodhi. "The Sixth Mass Coextinction: Are Most Endangered Species Parasites and Mutualists?" *Proceedings of the Royal Society B: Biological Sciences* 276, no. 1670 (2009): 3037–45.

Dunsford, Cathie. *Manawa Toa: Heart Warrior*. Melbourne: Spinifex, 2000.

Dvorak, Greg. *Coral and Concrete: Remembering Kwajalein Atoll between Japan, America, and the Marshall Islands*. Honolulu: University of Hawai'i Press, 2018.

Edmond, Rod, and Vanessa Smith, eds. *Islands in History and Representation*. New York: Routledge, 2003.

Ellis, William. *Polynesian Researches, during a Residence of Nearly Eight Years in the Society and Sandwich Islands*. New York: J. and J. Harper, 1833.

Emmett, Robert S., and David E. Nye. *The Environmental Humanities: A Critical Introduction*. Cambridge, MA: MIT Press, 2017.

Estes, Nick. *Our History Is the Future: Standing Rock versus the Dakota Access Pipeline, and the Long Tradition of Indigenous Resistance*. New York: Verso, 2019.

Farbotko, Carol. "Wishful Sinking: Disappearing Islands, Climate Refugees and Cosmopolitan Experimentation." *Asia Pacific Viewpoint* 51, no. 1 (2010): 47–60.

Fenn, Elizabeth A. "Biological Warfare in Eighteenth-Century North America: Beyond Jeffery Amherst." *Journal of American History* 86, no. 4 (2000): 1552–80.

Fifita, Ruha. "Kathy Jetñil-Kijiner: A Spoken-Word Poet for Resilience and Hope." *QAGOMA Blog*, May 9, 2019. https://blog.qagoma.qld.gov.au/apt9-kathy-jetnil-kijiner-a-spoken-word-poet/.

Figiel, Sia, ed. *Where We Once Belonged*. Illustrated ed. New York: Kaya, 1996.

Firth, Stewart. *Nuclear Playground*. Honolulu: University of Hawai'i Press, 1987.

Firth, Stewart, and Karin Von Strokirch. "A Nuclear Pacific." In *The Cambridge History of the Pacific Islanders*, edited by Donald Denoon, Stewart Firth, Jocelyn Linnekin, Malama Meleisea, and Karen Nero, 324–58. Cambridge: Cambridge University Press, 1998.

Fletcher, Robert. "The Art of Forgetting: Imperialist Amnesia and Public Secrecy." *Third World Quarterly* 33, no. 3 (2012): 423–39.

Flores, Evelyn. "The Caregiver's Story." *The Missing Slate*, October 1, 2017.

Fontin, Moira. "The Performance of Memory in Rapanui Theatre." *Pacific Dynamics: Journal of Interdisciplinary Research* 2, no. 2 (2018): 105–19.

Forchtner, Bernhard, ed. *The Far Right and the Environment: Politics, Discourse and Communication*. Routledge Studies in Fascism and the Far Right. New York: Routledge, 2020.

Foucault, Michel. *Il faut défendre la société: Cours au Collège de France, 1975–1976*. Paris: Gallimard/Seuil, 1997.

Frémy, Marc. *Te Pō rumaruma: Les Histoires de la terrasse*. Pape'ete, Tahiti: Marc Frémy, 2003.

Frémy, Marc. *Trois papiers aux clous, un amour chinois*. Pīra'e, Tahiti: Au vent des îles, 2000.

Frengs, Julia. *Corporeal Archipelagos: Writing the Body in Francophone Oceanian Women's Literature*. Lanham, MD: Lexington, 2017.

Fujikane, Candace. "Introduction: Asian Settler Colonialism in the U.S. Colony of Hawai'i." In *Asian Settler Colonialism: From Local Governance to the Habits of Everyday Life in Hawai'i*, edited by Candace Fujikane and Jonathan Y. Okamura, 1–42. Honolulu: University of Hawai'i Press, 2008.

Fujikane, Candace. *Mapping Abundance for a Planetary Future: Kanaka Maoli and Critical Settler Cartographies in Hawai'i*. Durham, NC: Duke University Press, 2021.

Gabbard, Tulsi. "Ua Mau Ke Ea o Ka 'āina i Ka Pono." Twitter, July 19, 2019. https://twitter.com/TulsiGabbard/status/1152350291481595905.

Galilea, Marisol. "Rapa Nui, isla histórica: Una lectura de *La Rosa separada* de Pablo Neruda." *Alpha (Osorno)*, no. 46 (2018): 9–31.

Ganivet, Mililani, and Marie-Hélène Villierme. *Nu/Clear Stories* (Onesia S/pacific Storytellers, 2023). Podcast, episodes 1 and 2, May and June 2023.

Ganivet, Mililani, and Marie-Hélène Villierme. "Re-membering Nuclear Stories from a Maohi Lens." *Experiment* (blog), December 13, 2021. https://experiment.com/projects /re-membering-nuclear-stories-from-a-maohi-lens.

Gardissat, Paul, and Nicolas Mezzalira. *Nabanga: An Illustrated Anthology of the Oral Traditions of Vanuatu*. Port Vila: Vanuatu National Cultural Council, 2005.

Gauguin, Paul. *Lettres de Paul Gauguin à Georges-Daniel de Monfreid*. Paris: Éditions Georges Crès et Cᵢₑ, 1918.

Gauguin, Paul. *Noa Noa*. 1901. Reprint, Paris: A. Balland, 1966.

Gay, Jean-Christophe. "Les Îles du Pacifique dans le monde du tourisme." *Hermès, La Revue*, no. 65 (2013): 84–88.

Génaédig, Émilie, and Emma Faua-Tufariua. *Les Champignons de Paris — Te mau tupurupua a Paris*. Pape'ete, Tahiti: Haere Pō, 2017.

George, James. *Ocean Roads*. Wellington: Huia, 2007.

Gerrard, Michael B. "America's Forgotten Nuclear Waste Dump in the Pacific." *SAIS Review of International Affairs* 35, no. 1 (2015): 87–97.

Ghosh, Amitav. *The Great Derangement: Climate Change and the Unthinkable*. Chicago: University of Chicago Press, 2016.

Giesen, Klaus-Gerd. "Autonomies politiques et dépendances économiques en Océanie." In *L'Océanie convoitée: Actes des colloques*, edited by Sémir Al Wardi and Jean-Marc Regnault, 328–33. Pape'ete, Tahiti: Self-published, CreateSpace, 2017.

Gillis, John R. *Islands of the Mind: How the Human Imagination Created the Atlantic World*. New York: Palgrave Macmillan, 2004.

Gillis, John R. "Taking History Offshore: Atlantic Islands in European Minds, 1400–1800." In *Islands in History and Representation*, edited by Rod Edmond and Vanessa Smith, 19–32. New York: Routledge, 2003.

Giraudoux, Jean. *Supplément au voyage de Cook; pièce en un acte*. Paris: Grasset, 1936.

Giraudoux, Jean. *Suzanne et le Pacifique*. Paris: Grasset, 1921.

Gobrait, Valérie. *Matari'i: La Légende de Matari'i*. Pape'ete, Tahiti: Valérie Gobrait, 2008.

Grace, Patricia. "Sun's Marbles." In *The Sky People*, 10–16. London: Penguin, 1994.

Grand, Alfred René. "Pouvanaa a Oopa et nationalisme à Tahiti." Thèse de 3e cycle, Université Paris 1 Panthéon-Sorbonne, Paris, 1981.

Grove, Richard. *Green Imperialism: Colonial Expansion, Tropical Island Edens and the Origins of Environmentalism, 1600–1860*. New York: Cambridge University Press, 1995.

Guam Legislature Archives. "30th Guam Legislature — Resolutions." List of resolutions in electronic format. December 30, 2010. http://www.guamlegislature.com/30th_res .htm.

Guerrini, Anita. *Experimenting with Humans and Animals: From Galen to Animal Rights*. Baltimore: Johns Hopkins University Press, 2003.

Guiart, Jean. *Le Bêtisier océanien: Ce qu'il faut savoir de l'Océanie et dictionnaire des erreurs accumulées*. Nouméa, New Caledonia: Le Rocher-à-la-Voile; Pape'ete, Tahiti: Te pito o te fenua, 2012.

Guirao, Patrice. *Lyao-Ly*. Pīra'e, Tahiti: Au vent des îles, 2013.

Haupert, Yves. *Francis Sanford à cœur ouvert*. Pīra'e, Tahiti: Au vent des iles, 1998.

Hau'ofa, Epeli. "Our Sea of Islands." *Contemporary Pacific* 6, no. 1 (1994): 148–61.

Hau'ofa, Epeli. *We Are the Ocean: Selected Works*. Honolulu: University of Hawai'i Press, 2008.

Heim, Otto. "How (Not) to Globalize Oceania: Ecology and Politics in Contemporary Pacific Island Performance Arts." *Commonwealth Essays and Studies* 41, no. 1 (2018): 131–45.

Heise, Ursula K. *Imagining Extinction: The Cultural Meanings of Endangered Species*. Chicago: University of Chicago Press, 2016.

Hejnol, Andreas. "Ladders, Trees, Complexity, and Other Metaphors in Evolutionary Thinking." In *Arts of Living on a Damaged Planet: Ghosts and Monsters of the Anthropocene*, 87–102. Minneapolis: University of Minnesota Press, 2017.

Henry, Teuira, and John Muggridge Orsmond. *Ancient Tahiti*. Honolulu: Bernice P. Bishop Museum, 1928.

Hereniko, Vilsoni. *Woven Gods: Female Clowns and Power in Rotuma*. Honolulu: University of Hawai'i Press, 1995.

Hereniko, Vilsoni, and David Hanlon. "An Interview with Albert Wendt." In *Inside Out: Literature, Cultural Politics, and Identity in the New Pacific*, edited by Vilsoni Hereniko and Rob Wilson, 85–103. Lanham, MD: Rowman and Littlefield, 1999.

Hiro, Henri. *Pehepehe i taù nūnaa / Message poétique*. Pape'ete, Tahiti: Haere Pō, 2004.

Hobart, Hi'ilei Julia. "At Home on the Mauna: Ecological Violence and Fantasies of Terra Nullius on Maunakea's Summit." *Native American and Indigenous Studies* 6, no. 2 (2019): 30–50.

Hoffheimer, Michael H. "Hegel, Race, Genocide." *Southern Journal of Philosophy* 39, no. S1 (2001): 35–62.

Hogue, Rebecca H. "Decolonial Memory and Nuclear Migration in Albert Wendt's *Black Rainbow*." *Modern Fiction Studies* 66, no. 2 (2020): 325–48.

Hogue, Rebecca H. "Nuclear Normalizing and Kathy Jetñil-Kijiner's 'Dome Poem.'" *Amerasia Journal* 47, no. 2 (2021): 208–29.

Hugo, Victor. "La Fille d'O-Taïti." In *Les Orientales*, 200–202. Paris: Ollendorf, 1829.

Hulme, Keri. *Stonefish*. Wellington: Huia, 2007.

Hulme, Keri. "Te Rapa, Te Tuhi, Me Te Uira (or Playing with Fire)." In *Below the Surface: Words and Images in Protest at French Testing on Moruroa*, edited by Ambury Hall, 52–55. Auckland: Random House New Zealand, 1995.

Hulme, Peter. *Colonial Encounters: Europe and the Native Caribbean, 1492–1797*. New York: Methuen, 1986.

Hurley, Jessica. *Infrastructures of Apocalypse: American Literature and the Nuclear Complex*. Minneapolis: University of Minnesota Press, 2020.

Husband, Dale. "Teresia Teaiwa: You Can't Paint the Pacific with Just One Brush Stroke." *E-Tangata* (blog), October 24, 2015. https://e-tangata.co.nz/korero/you-cant -paint-the-pacific-with-just-one-brush-stroke/.

Huxley, Aldous. *Island*. New York: Harper Perennial Modern Classics, 1962.

Hyvernat, Christian. *Opération TNT*. Pīra'e, Tahiti: Au vent des îles, 2005.

Ihimaera, Witi. *The Whale Rider*. Orlando: Harcourt, 1987.

Ihimaera, Witi. "Wiwi (or, If New Zealand Was the Center of the World)." In *Below the Surface: Words and Images in Protest at French Testing on Moruroa*, edited by Ambury Hall, 2:62–64. Auckland: Random House New Zealand, 1995.

Immerwahr, Daniel. *How to Hide an Empire: A History of the Greater United States*. New York: Farrar, Straus and Giroux, 2019.

Jacques, Claudine. *Le Cri de l'acacia*. Pīra'e, Tahiti: Au vent des iles, 2007.

Jacques, Claudine. *L'Homme-lézard*. Nîmes, France: HB éditions, 2002.

Jacques, Claudine. *Nouméa mangrove*. Pīra'e, Tahiti: Au vent des îles, 2010.

Jancovici, Jean-Marc. *Dormez tranquilles jusqu'en 2100: Et autres malentendus sur le climat et l'énergie*. Paris: Éditions Odile Jacob, 2015.

Jetñil-Kijiner, Kathy. "Bulldozed Reefs and Blasted Sands: Rituals for Artificial Islands." *Kathy Jetñil-Kijiner* (blog), February 7, 2019. https://www.kathyjetnilkijiner.com /bulldozed-reefs-and-blasted-sands-rituals-for-artificial-islands/.

Jetñil-Kijiner, Kathy. "'Butterfly Thief' and Complex Narratives of Disappearing Islands." *Kathy Jetñil-Kijiner* (blog), April 30, 2017. https://www.kathyjetnilkijiner.com /butterfly-thief-and-complex-narratives-of-disappearing-islands/.

Jetñil-Kijiner, Kathy. "Dome Poem Part II: Of Islands and Elders." *Kathy Jetñil-Kijiner* (blog), March 2, 2018. https://www.kathyjetnilkijiner.com/dome-poem-part-ii-of -islands-and-elders/.

Jetñil-Kijiner, Kathy. "Iep Jāltok: A History of Marshallese Literature." Master's thesis, University of Hawai'i at Mānoa, 2014.

Jetñil-Kijiner, Kathy. *Iep Jāltok: Poems from a Marshallese Daughter*. Tucson: University of Arizona Press, 2017.

Jetñil-Kijiner, Kathy. "A Moment of Clarity—Why I'm Going to Paris COP21." *Kathy Jetñil-Kijiner* (blog), November 22, 2015, https://jkijiner.wordpress.com/2015/11/22 /a-moment-of-clarity-why-im-going-to-paris-cop21/.

Jetñil-Kijiner, Kathy, dir. *Monsters*. Genbaku Dome, Hiroshima, 2017.

Jetñil-Kijiner, Kathy. "New Year, New Monsters, New Poems." *Kathy Jetñil-Kijiner* (blog), January 25, 2018. https://www.kathyjetnilkijiner.com/new-year-new-monsters-and -new-poems/.

Jetñil-Kijiner, Kathy. "A Word about My Mother." *Kathy Jetñil-Kijiner* (blog), February 20, 2014. https://jkijiner.wordpress.com/2014/02/20/a-word-about-my-mother/.

Jetñil-Kijiner, Kathy, and Lin Dan, dirs. *Anointed*. Runit Dome, Marshall Islands, 2017.

Jetñil-Kijiner, Kathy, Aka Niviâna, and Lin Dan, dirs. *Rise: From One Island to Another*. Greenland, Marshall Islands, 2018.

Johnston, Barbara Rose, and Holly M. Barker. *Consequential Damages of Nuclear War: The Rongelap Report*. Walnut Creek, CA: Left Coast, 2008.

Kahn, Miriam. *Tahiti beyond the Postcard: Power, Place, and Everyday Life*. Seattle: University of Washington Press, 2011.

Kahn, Miriam. "Tahiti Intertwined: Ancestral Land, Tourist Postcard, and Nuclear Test Site." *American Anthropologist* 102, no. 1 (2000): 7–26.

Keever, Beverly. *News Zero: The New York Times and the Bomb*. Monroe, ME: Common Courage, 2004.

Keju-Johnson, Darlene. "Micronesia." In *Pacific Women Speak: Why Haven't You Known?*, edited by Women Working for an Independent and Nuclear-Free Pacific (WWINFP), 6–10. Oxford: Green Line, 1987.

Keown, Michelle. *Pacific Islands Writing: The Postcolonial Literatures of Aotearoa / New Zealand and Oceania*. New York: Oxford University Press, 2007.

Kerdiles, Chantal. *Voyance sous les tropiques*. Pīra'e, Tahiti: Au vent des îles, 1997.

Khalili, Laleh. *Sinews of War and Trade: Shipping and Capitalism in the Arabian Peninsula*. New York: Verso, 2020.

Kimmerer, Robin Wall. *Braiding Sweetgrass: Indigenous Wisdom, Scientific Knowledge and the Teachings of Plants*. Minneapolis: Milkweed, 2015.

Klein, Naomi. *No Is Not Enough: Resisting Trump's Shock Politics and Winning the World We Need*. Chicago: Haymarket, 2017.

Klein, Naomi. *This Changes Everything: Capitalism vs. the Climate*. Toronto: Vintage Canada, 2014.

Kuletz, Valerie. "The Movement for Environmental Justice in the Pacific Islands." In *The Environmental Justice Reader: Politics, Poetics, and Pedagogy*, edited by Joni Adamson, Mei Mei Evans, and Rachel Stein, 125–37. Tucson: University of Arizona Press, 2002.

Kurtovitch, Nicolas. *Good night friend*. Pīra'e, Tahiti: Au vent des îles, 2006.

Labriola, Monica. "Marshall Islands." *Contemporary Pacific* 28, no. 1 (2016): 193–202.

Lacy, Ciara, dir. *American Masters | Jamaica Heolimeleikalani Osorio: This Is the Way We Rise*. Firelight Media, 2020. https://www.pbs.org/video/jamaica-heolimeleikalani-osorio-this-is-the-way-we-rise-ndwixe/.

Lai, Paul. "Discontiguous States of America: The Paradox of Unincorporation in Craig Santos Perez's Poetics of Chamorro Guam." *Journal of Transnational American Studies* 3, no. 2 (2011): 1–28.

Lama, Jean-Claude. *Regards: Une vie polynésienne*. Pīra'e, Tahiti: Au vent des îles, 1999.

Lambert, Léopold. *États d'urgence: Une histoire spatiale du continuum colonial français*. Toulouse: Premiers matins de novembre, 2021.

La Parisienne Libérée. *Le Nucléaire, c'est fini*. Paris: La fabrique éditions, 2019.

Latour, Bruno. *Où atterrir? Comment s'orienter en politique*. Paris: La découverte, 2017.

Laval, Honoré. *Mémoires pour servir à l'histoire de Mangareva, ère chrétienne, 1834–1871*. Paris: Musée de l'homme, 1968.

Le Clézio, J.-M. G. *Raga: Approche du continent invisible*. Paris: Éditions du seuil, 2006.

Leem, Selina Neirok. "More Than Just a Blue Passport." In *Effigies III*, edited by Allison Adelle Hedge Coke, Brandy Nālani McDougall, and Craig Santos Perez, 98–101. Norfolk, UK: Salt, 2019.

Le Goupils, Marc. *Comment on cesse d'être colon: Six années en Nouvelle-Calédonie*. Paris: Grasset, 1910.

Lévi-Strauss, Claude. *Tristes tropiques*. Paris: Plon, 1955.

Lini, Walter. *Beyond Pandemonium: From the New Hebrides to Vanuatu*. Wellington: Asia Pacific, 1980.

Liston, Jolie, and Melson Miko. "Oral Tradition and Archaeology: Palau's Earth Architecture." In *Pacific Island Heritage: Archaeology, Identity and Community*, edited by Jolie Liston, Geoffrey Clark, and Dwight Alexander, 181–204. Canberra: ANU Press, 2011.

London, Jack. *South Sea Tales*. New York: Macmillan, 1911.

Looser, Diana. "A Piece 'More Curious Than All the Rest': Re-encountering Pre-colonial Pacific Island Theatre, 1769–1855." *Theatre Journal* 63, no. 4 (2011): 521–40.

Loti, Pierre. *Le Mariage de Loti*. Paris: Calmann Lévy, 1878.

Lousley, Cheryl. "Ecocriticism and the Politics of Representation." In *The Oxford Handbook of Ecocriticism*, edited by Greg Garrard, 155–71. Oxford: Oxford University Press, 2014.

Lutts, Ralph H. "Chemical Fallout: Rachel Carson's *Silent Spring*, Radioactive Fallout, and the Environmental Movement." In *No Birds Sing: Rhetorical Analyses of Rachel Carson's "Silent Spring,"* edited by Craig Waddell, 17–42. Carbondale: Southern Illinois University Press, 2000.

Maclellan, Nic. *Grappling with the Bomb: Britain's Pacific H-Bomb Tests*. Canberra: ANU Press, 2017.

Maclellan, Nic. "Nuclear Testing and Racism in the Pacific Islands." In *The Palgrave Handbook of Ethnicity*, edited by Steven Ratuva, 1–21. London: Palgrave Macmillan, 2019.

Maile, David Uahikeaikalei'ohu. "Science, Time, and Mauna a Wākea: The Thirty-Meter Telescope's Capitalist-Colonialist Violence, Part I." *Red Nation* (blog), May 13, 2015. http://therednation.org/science-time-and-mauna-a-wakea-the-thirty-meter-telescopes-capitalist-colonialist-violence-an-essay-in-two-parts/.

Maile, David Uahikeaikalei'ohu. "Science, Time, and Mauna a Wākea: The Thirty-Meter Telescope's Capitalist-Colonialist Violence, Part II." *Red Nation* (blog), May 20, 2015. http://therednation.org/science-time-and-mauna-a-wakea-the-thirty-meter-telescopes-capitalist-colonialist-violence/.

Mākua, Sunnie Kaikala, Manulani Aluli Meyer, and Lynette Lokelani Wakinekona. "Mo'olelo: Continuity, Stories, and Research in Hawai'i." In *Applying Indigenous Research Methods*, edited by Sweeney Windchief and Timothy San Pedro, 138–49. New York: Routledge, 2019.

Mangioni, Talei Luscia. "Fighting for a Nuclear Free Pacific." *Funambulist: Politics of Space and Bodies* 39, no. 1 (2022): 42–47.

Manu-Tahi, Charles Teriiteanuanua. *Te parau itea ore hia: Pehepehe: Poèmes*. Pape'ete, Tahiti: Te hiroa maohi tumu, 1979.

Marshallese People, "Petition from the Marshallese People concerning the Pacific Islands: Complaint regarding Explosions of Lethal Weapons within Our Home Islands to United Nations Trusteeship Council." United Nations Trusteeship Council, April 20, 1954. https://www.osti.gov/opennet/servlets/purl/16364835.pdf.

Martin, Brice, and Carine Heitz. "Un 'tsunami d'eau radioactive'? Réalité et perception des risques sismiques." In *Des bombes en Polynésie: Les Essais nucléaires français dans le Pacifique*, edited by Renaud Meltz and Alexis Vrignon, 37–90. Paris: Éditions vendémiaire, 2022.

Massau, Serge. *Paroles d'un autochtone: Entretiens avec le sénateur Richard Ariihau Tuheiava*. Pape'ete, Tahiti: Haere Pō, 2011.

Matsuda, Matt K. *Pacific Worlds: A History of Seas, Peoples, and Cultures*. New York: Cambridge University Press, 2012.

Maugham, W. Somerset. *The Moon and Sixpence*. New York: Viking Penguin, 1919.

Maurer, Anaïs. "Nukes and Nudes: Counter-hegemonic Identities in the Nuclearized Pacific." *French Studies: A Quarterly Review* 72, no. 3 (2018): 394-411.

Maurer, Anaïs. "Océanitude: Repenser le tribalisme occidental au prisme des nationalismes océaniens." *Francosphères* 8, no. 2 (2019): 109-25.

Maurer, Anaïs. "'Qui ne mourrait pas de cancer dans nos îles?' La créativité poétique des océaniens antinucléaires." In *Des Bombes en Polynésie: Les Essais nucléaires français dans le Pacifique*, edited by Renaud Meltz and Alexis Vrignon, 549-67. Paris: Éditions vendémiaire, 2022.

Maurer, Anaïs. "Snaring the Nuclear Sun: Decolonial Ecologies in Titaua Peu's *Mutismes: E 'Ore te Vāvā*." *Contemporary Pacific* 32, no. 2 (2020): 371-97.

Maurer, Anaïs, and Rebecca H. Hogue. "Introduction: Transnational Nuclear Imperialisms." *Journal of Transnational American Studies* 11, no. 2 (2020): 25-43.

Mawyer, Alexander. "The Maladie du Secret: Witnessing the Nuclear State in French Polynesia." Lecture presented to the Pacific Islands Political Science Association, Mānoa, June 2014.

Mayer, Raymond. "'Convoitise mondialisée et réactivité océanienne d'après les actualités chantées et dansées à Wallis et Futuna.'" In *L'Océanie convoitée: Actes des colloques, Paris, septembre 2015, Punaauia (UPF), novembre 2016*, 309-12. Paris: CNRS éditions, 2017.

Mayer, Raymond, Malino Nau, Eric Pambrun, and Christophe Laurent. "Chanter la guerre à Wallis ('Uvea)." *Journal de la Société des Océanistes*, nos. 122-23 (December 2006): 153-71.

McCall, Grant. "El pasado en el presente de Rapanui (Isla de Pascua)." In *Etnografía: Sociedades indígenas contemporáneas y su ideología*, edited by Jorge Hidalgo, 17-46. Santiago: Editorial A. Bello, 1996.

McClintock, Anne. *Imperial Leather: Race, Gender, and Sexuality in the Colonial Conquest*. New York: Routledge, 1995.

McDougall, Brandy Nālani. *Finding Meaning: Kaona and Contemporary Hawaiian Literature*. Tucson: University of Arizona Press, 2016.

McDougall, Brandy Nālani. "Water Remembers." *Missing Slate*, October 1, 2017.

Meillassoux, Claude. *Femmes, greniers et capitaux*. Paris: F. Maspero, 1975.

Melde, Susanne. "Data on Environmental Migration: How Much Do We Know?" International Organization for Migration: Knowledge Platform on People on the Move in a Changing Climate, 2016. https://environmentalmigration.iom.int/data-environmental-migration-how-much-do-we-know.

Meltz, Renaud. "Pourquoi la Polynésie?" In *Des Bombes en Polynésie: Les Essais nucléaires français dans le Pacifique*, edited by Renaud Meltz and Alexis Vrignon, 37-90. Paris: Éditions vendémiaire, 2022.

Melville, Herman. *Mardi, and a Voyage Thither*. Boston: Page, 1949.

Melville, Herman. *Omoo: Adventures in the South Seas*. Project Gutenberg Online Catalog, 1847.

Melville, Herman. *Typee: A Peep at Polynesian Life*. London: J. Murray, 1846.

Merle, Isabelle. *Expériences coloniales: La Nouvelle-Calédonie, 1853-1920*. Paris: Belin, 1995.

Meyer, Manulani Aluli. "Ekolu Mea Nui: Three Ways to Experience the World." *Canadian Journal of Native Studies* 31, no. 2 (2017): 11–18.

Meyer, Manulani Aluli. "Written Direct Testimony of Dr. Manulani Aluli Meyer as a Witness at the Conservation District Use Application for Permit of the Thirty Meter Telescope (TMT)." Available at *Sacred Mauna Kea* blog, November 7, 2017. https://dlnr .hawaii.gov/mk/files/2016/10/B.05a-wdt-Meyer.pdf.

Meyer, Manulani Aluli, Ngahiraka Mason, and Luana Busby-Neff. "Manulani Aluli Meyer: Kapu Aloha for Maunakea, a Discipline of Compassion." UH Hilo Stories, University of Hawaiʻi, April 13, 2015. https://hilo.hawaii.edu/chancellor/stories/2015 /04/13/kapu-aloha/.

Mikhailov, Viktor, ed. *Catalog of Worldwide Nuclear Testing*. New York: Begell House, 1999.

Moerenhout, J.-A. *Voyages aux îles du Grand océan*. Paris: Arthus-Bertrand, 1837.

Morgant-Cross, Hinamoeura, Anaïs Duong-Pédicat, and Roselyne Makalu. "Le Militantisme anti-nucléaire à Māʻohi Nui." In *La Pause décoloniale*. Podcast, episode 17, October 6, 2022. YouTube video, 1:04:11. https://www.youtube.com/watch?v =iYgPkoaL8eI.

Moser, Susanne. "Getting Real about It: Meeting the Psychological and Social Demands of a World in Distress." In *Environmental Leadership: A Reference Handbook*, edited by Deborah Rigling Gallagher, 900–908. Thousand Oaks, CA: SAGE, 2012.

Mou Sang Teinauri, Béatrice. *Je m'appelle Airuarii*. Papeʻete: Publication indépendante, 2022.

Muñoz Azócar, Diego. "Diaspora Rapanui (1871–2015): L'Île de Pâques, le Chili continental et la Polynésie française." PhD diss., École des Hautes Etudes en Sciences Sociales, Paris, 2017.

Myers, Ransom A., and Boris Worm. "Rapid Worldwide Depletion of Predatory Fish Communities." *Nature* 423, no. 6937 (2003): 280–83.

Natuman, Losana. "The Bitterness of Sugar Cane." In *Sista, Stanap Strong! A Vanuatu Women's Anthology*, edited by Mikaela Nyman and Rebecca Tobo Olul-Hossen, 19–24. Wellington: Victoria University Press, 2021.

Neruda, Pablo. *La Rosa separada*. Buenos Aires: Editorial Losada, 1973.

Neumann, Klaus. "'In Order to Win Their Friendship': Renegotiating First Contact." In *Voyaging through the Contemporary Pacific*, edited by Geoffrey M. White and David Hanlon, 173–91. Lanham, MD: Rowman and Littlefield, 2000.

Nicole, Robert. *The Word, the Pen, and the Pistol: Literature and Power in Tahiti*. Albany: State University of New York Press, 2001.

Niheu, Kalamaʻokaina. "Reclaiming the Sacred ʻAina (Land)." In *Pacific Women Speak Out for Independence and Denuclearization*, edited by Zohl dé Ishtar, 7–14. Annandale: Raven, 1998.

Nixon, Rob. *Slow Violence and the Environmentalism of the Poor*. Cambridge, MA: Harvard University Press, 2011.

Nogues, Collier. "'With [Our] Entire Breath': The US Military Buildup on Guåhan (Guam) and Craig Santos Perez's Literature of Resistance." *Shima* 12, no. 1 (2018): 21–34.

Nuclear Free and Independent Pacific Conference and Pacific Concerns Resource Centre. *No Te Parau Tia, No Te Parau Mau, No Te Tiamaraa = For Justice, Truth and Independence: Report of the 8th Nuclear Free and Independent Pacific (NFIP) Conference,*

Arue, Tahiti, Te Ao Maohi (French Polynesia), 20–24 September 1999. Suva, Fiji: Pacific Concerns Resource Centre, 2000.

Nuunja, Kahina. "Free People: The Imazighen of North Africa." *Intercontinental Cry* (blog), March 12, 2013. https://intercontinentalcry.org/free-people-the-imazighen-of-north-africa/.

Osorio, Jamaica Heolimeleikalani. *Remembering Our Intimacies: Moʻolelo, Aloha ʻĀina, and Ea.* Minneapolis: University of Minnesota Press, 2021.

Paeamara, Lucas. *Mangareva: Taku Akaereere.* Pīraʻe, Tahiti: Au vent des îles, 2005.

Pambrun, Jean-Marc Teraʼituatini. *L'Allégorie de la natte, ou, Le Tahu'a-parau-tumu-fenua dans son temps.* Papeʻete, Tahiti: Ed. by author, 1993.

Pambrun, Jean-Marc Teraʼituatini. *Henri Hiro, héros polynésien: biographie.* Moorea: Puna Honu, 2010.

Pambrun, Jean-Marc Teraʼituatini. *L'Île aux anthropologues.* Paris: Le manuscrit, 2010.

Parly, Florence. "Communiqué de presse: Inauguration du système Telsite 2." Ministère des armées, Salle de presse, June 21, 2018. Accessed January 17, 2019. https://www.defense.gouv.fr/salle-de-presse/communiques/communiques-de-florence-parly/cp_inauguration-du-systeme-telsite-2.

Pashley, Alex. "Climate Change Migration Is 'Genocide,' Says Marshall Islands Minister." *Climate Home News,* October 5, 2015. https://climatechangenews.com/2015/10/05/climate-change-migration-is-genocide-says-marshall-islands-minister/.

Pélopidas, Benoît. *Repenser les choix nucléaires: La Séduction de l'impossible.* Paris: Les presses de Sciences Po, 2022.

Peltzer, Louise. *Lettre à Poutaveri.* Pīraʻe, Tahiti: Au vent des îles, 1995.

Penny, Laurie. *Sexual Revolution: Modern Fascism and the Feminist Fightback.* London: Bloomsbury, 2022.

Peralto, Leon Noʻeau. "Mauna a Wakea: Hanau Ka Mauna, the Piko of Our Ea." In *A Nation Rising: Hawaiian Movements for Life, Land, and Sovereignty,* edited by Noelani Goodyear-Kaʻōpua, Ikaika Hussey, and Erin Kahunawaikaʼala Wright, 232–44. Durham, NC: Duke University Press, 2014.

Perez, Craig Santos. *From Unincorporated Territory [Guma'].* Richmond, CA: Omnidawn, 2014.

Perez, Craig Santos. *Habitat Threshold.* Oakland, CA: Omnidawn, 2020.

Perez, Craig Santos. "Habitat Threshold Book Talk." Book talk series at the Greenhouse: An environmental humanities research group at the University of Stavanger, Stavanger, Norway, November 17, 2020.

Perez, Craig Santos. *Navigating CHamoru Poetry: Indigeneity, Aesthetics, and Decolonization.* Tucson: University of Arizona Press, 2022.

Perez, Craig Santos, and Justyn Ah Chong, dirs. "Praise Song for Oceania." Honolulu: Olanā Media, 2017.

Perkins, ʻUmi. "Moʻokūʻauhau and Mana." In *The Past before Us: Moʻokūʻauhau as Methodology,* edited by Nālani Wilson-Hokowhitu, 69–80. Honolulu: University of Hawaiʻi Press, 2019.

Perkins, ʻUmi. "Pono and the Koru: Toward Indigenous Theory in Pacific Island Literature." *Hūlili* 4, no. 1 (2007): 59–89.

Peu, Titaua. *Pina*. Pīra'e, Tahiti: Au vent des îles, 2016.

Plumwood, Val. *Environmental Culture: The Ecological Crisis of Reason*. New York: Routledge, 2001.

Poncet, Alexandre. *Histoire de l'île Wallis*. Vol. 2, *Le Protectorat français*. Paris: Société des océanistes, 2013.

Priestley, Rebecca. *Mad on Radium: New Zealand in the Atomic Age*. Auckland: Auckland University Press, 2012.

Pule, John Puhiatau. "100 Love Poems." Mana Moana Pasifika Voices. Sharm El Sheikh, Egypt: United Nations Framework Convention of Climate Change COP-26, 2022. https://www.manamoana.co.nz/artwork/100-love-poems/.

Quigg, Agnes. "History of the Pacific Islands Studies Program at the University of Hawaii: 1950–1986." Master's thesis, University of Hawai'i at Mānoa, 1987.

Quilès, Paul, Jean-Marie Collin, and Michel Drain. *L'Illusion nucléaire: La Face cachée de la bombe atomique*. Paris: Éditions Charles Léopold Mayer, 2018.

Raapoto, Turo a. *Te pinaìnaì o te àau*. Puna'auia, Tahiti: Tupuna éditions, 1990.

Ramírez, Susan Berry Brill de. *Contemporary American Indian Literatures and the Oral Tradition*. Tucson: University of Arizona Press, 1999.

Regnault, Jean-Marc, and Catherine Vannier. *Le Metua et le Général: Un combat inégal*. Moorea: Les éditions de Tahiti, 2009.

Regnault, Jean-Marc. *Le Pouvoir confisqué en Polynésie française: L'Affrontement Temaru-Flosse*. Paris: Les Indes savantes, 2005.

Reich, Moemoe Malietoa von. "Floating Face Down." In *Sustainable Development or Malignant Growth? Perspectives of Pacific Island Women*, edited by 'Atu Emberson-Bain, 43. Suva, Fiji: Marama, 1994.

Representatives of Pacific Countries and Territories, Aotearoa–New Zealand, Australia, Cook Islands, Federated States of Micronesia, Fiji, French Polynesia, Hawaii, Kiribati, Niue, New Caledonia, Palau, Papua New Guinea, Rapa Nui, Samoa, Solomon Islands, and Tonga. "The Ocean Declaration of Maupiti." UNESCO World Heritage Workshop of the Pacific Islands, Maupiti, November 7, 2009.

Reverzy, Jean. *Le Passage*. 1954. Reprint, Paris: Les éditions du sonneur, 2014.

Reynolds, Pauline, and Vehia Wheeler. "Mā'ohi Methodologies and Frameworks for Conducting Research in Mā'ohi Nui." *AlterNative* 18, no. 4 (2022).

Roberts, Callum. *The Ocean of Life: The Fate of Man and the Sea*. New York: Penguin, 2013.

Robin, Maxime. "Aux États-Unis, des écologistes séduits par le nucléaire." *Le Monde diplomatique*, August 1, 2022, 20–21.

Robinson, Angela L. "Of Monsters and Mothers: Affective Climates and Human-Nonhuman Sociality in Kathy Jetñil-Kijiner's 'Dear Matafele Peinam.'" *Contemporary Pacific* 32, no. 2 (2020): 311–39.

Rodman, Margaret. "Boundary and a Bridge: Women's Pig Killing as a Border-Crossing between Spheres of Exchange in East Aoba." In *Vanuatu: Politics, Economics and Ritual in Island Melanesia*, edited by Michael Allen, 72–74. New York: Academic Press, 1981.

Rossero, Roland. *Corps à corps*. Nouméa, New Caledonia: Éditions humanis, 2015.

Rostand, Jean. "Avant-Propos." In *Folie nucléaire*, 25–38. Paris: Éditions de l'Épi, 1966.

Rousseau, Jean-Jacques. *Émile, ou de l'éducation*. Francfort: Cengage Gale London, 1762.

Ruff, Tilman A. "The Humanitarian Impact and Implications of Nuclear Test Explosions in the Pacific Region." *International Review of the Red Cross* 97, no. 899 (2015): 775–813.

Said, Edward W. *Reflections on Exile and Other Essays*. Cambridge, MA: Harvard University Press, 2000.

Saraf, Aanchal. "'We'd Rather Eat Rocks': Contesting the Thirty Meter Telescope in a Struggle over Science and Sovereignty in Hawai'i." *Journal of Transnational American Studies* 11, no. 1 (2020): 151–75.

Saura, Bruno. *Des Tahitiens, des Français: Leurs représentations réciproques aujourd'hui*. Pīra'e, Tahiti: Au vent des îles, 2011.

Saura, Bruno. *Des Tahitiens, des Français*. Vol. 2, *Essai sur l'assimilation culturelle en situation coloniale consentie*. Pīra'e, Tahiti: Au vent des îles, 2021.

Saura, Bruno. *Histoire et mémoire des temps coloniaux en Polynésie française*. Pīra'e, Tahiti: Au vent des îles, 2015.

Saura, Bruno. *Mythes et usages des mythes: Autochtonie et idéologie de la Terre Mère en Polynésie*. Paris: Peeters, 2013.

Saura, Bruno. *Pouvanaa a Oopa: Père de la culture politique tahitienne*. Pīra'e, Tahiti: Au vent des îles, 2012.

Saura, Bruno. *Un poisson nommé Tahiti: Mythes et pouvoirs aux temps anciens polynésiens*. Pīra'e, Tahiti: Au vent des îles, 2020.

Saura, Bruno, and Dorothy Levy. *Bobby: L'Enchanteur du Pacifique*. Pīra'e, Tahiti: Au vent des îles, 2013.

Scales, Helen. *The Brilliant Abyss: Exploring the Majestic Hidden Life of the Deep Ocean, and the Looming Threat That Imperils It*. New York: Atlantic Monthly Press, 2021.

Scranton, Roy. *Learning to Die in the Anthropocene: Reflections on the End of a Civilization*. San Francisco: City Lights, 2015.

Seasteading Institute. "Floating City Project." September 17, 2018. https://www .seasteading.org/floating-city-project/.

Seasteading Institute and the Government of French Polynesia. "Memorandum of Understanding." January 13, 2017. https://firebasestorage.googleapis.com/v0/b/blue -frontiers.appspot.com/o/docs%2FMemorandum_of_Understanding.pdf?alt =media&token=9509af2a-643d-470f-9e2a-7538d61b1a15.

Segalen, Victor. *Les Immémoriaux*. Paris: Librairie générale française, 1907.

Senghor, Léopold Sédar. *Liberté I: Négritude et humanisme*. Paris: Éditions du seuil, 1964.

Service Mixte de Sécurité Radiologique. "Rapport Secret SMSR 2720." 1966.

Servigne, Pablo, and Gauthier Chapelle. *L'Entraide: L'Autre loi de la jungle*. Paris: Les liens qui libèrent, 2019.

Servigne, Pablo, and Raphaël Stevens. *Comment tout peut s'effondrer: Petit manuel de collapsologie à l'usage des générations présentes*. Paris: Éditions du seuil, 2015.

Servigne, Pablo, Raphaël Stevens, and Gauthier Chapelle. *Une autre fin du monde est possible*. Paris: Éditions du seuil, 2018.

Shah, Sonia. "Contre les pandémies, l'écologie." *Le Monde diplomatique*, March 1, 2020.

Sharrad, Paul. *Albert Wendt and Pacific Literature: Circling the Void*. Manchester: Manchester University Press, 2003.

Shewry, Teresa. *Hope at Sea: Possible Ecologies in Oceanic Literature*. Minneapolis: University of Minnesota Press, 2015.

Shilliam, Robbie. *The Black Pacific: Anti-colonial Struggles and Oceanic Connections*. London: Bloomsbury Academic, 2015.

Siagatonu, Terisa Tinei. "Atlas." Poem recited for the COP21, Paris, December 10, 2015. https://www.youtube.com/watch?v=mZMgGzD1−g&ab_channel=FastforClimate.

Siagatonu, Terisa Tinei. "Layers." *The Missing Slate*, October 1, 2017.

Simenon, Georges. *Touriste de bananes*. Paris: Folio, 1938.

Simmons, David R. *Ta Moko: The Art of Maori Tattoo*. Rosedale, NZ: Raupo, 2009.

Sinavaiana-Gabbard, Caroline. "Literature and the Wheel of Time: Cartographies of Vā." *Sympokē* 26, no. 1 (2018): 33–49.

Sinavaiana-Gabbard, Caroline. "Where the Spirits Laugh Last: Comic Theater in Samoa." In *Inside Out: Literature, Cultural Politics, and Identity in the New Pacific*, edited by Vilsoni Hereniko and Rob Wilson, 183–205. Lanham, MD: Rowman and Littlefield, 1999.

Smith, Kev. "Ecofascism: Deep Ecology and Right-Wing Co-optation." *Synthesis/Regeneration* 2, no. 21 (2003): 1–25.

Smith, Linda Tuhiwai. *Decolonizing Methodologies: Research and Indigenous Peoples*. London: Zed, 2012.

Soga, Masashi, and Kevin J. Gaston. "Extinction of Experience: The Loss of Human–Nature Interactions." *Frontiers in Ecology and the Environment* 14, no. 2 (2016): 94–101.

Sope, Mildred, and Mikaela Nyman. "A Conversation about Poetry and Politics." In *Sista, Stanap Strong! A Vanuatu Women's Anthology*, edited by Mikaela Nyman and Rebecca Tobo Olul-Hossen, 30–36. Wellington: Victoria University Press, 2021.

Soulé, Marc. "Relations coutume, État, Église à Wallis et Futuna 1837–1961." *Outre-Mers. Revue d'histoire* 92, no. 348 (2005): 117–25.

Spitz, Chantal T. "Cannibalisme identitaire." *Littérama'ohi*, no. 23 (2016): 35–40.

Spitz, Chantal T. *et la mer pour demeure*. Pīra'e, Tahiti: Au vent des îles, 2022.

Spitz, Chantal T. *L'Île des rêves écrasés*. Pīra'e, Tahiti: Au vent des îles, 1991.

Spitz, Chantal T. "J'eus un pays." *Littérama'ohi*, no. 24 (2018): 43–47.

Spitz, Chantal T. *Pensées insolentes et inutiles*. Pape'ete, Tahiti: Éditions Te Ite, 2006.

Steiner, Candice Elanna. "A Sea of Warriors: Performing an Identity of Resilience and Empowerment in the Face of Climate Change in the Pacific." *Contemporary Pacific* 27, no. 1 (2015): 147–80.

Stephan, Marc. *Pakepakeha: Le Fantôme du Hauraki golf*. Pīra'e, Tahiti: Au vent des îles, 2013.

Stevenson, Robert Louis. *The Beach of Falesà*. North Hollywood: Aegypan, 1892.

Stevenson, Robert Louis. *The Ebb-Tide*. London: Penguin Classics, 1894.

Stevenson, Robert Louis. *South Sea Tales*. New York: Oxford University Press, 1893.

Subramani. "A Promise of Renewal: An Interview with Epeli Hau'ofa." In *Inside Out: Literature, Cultural Politics, and Identity in the New Pacific*, edited by Vilsoni Hereniko and Rob Wilson, 39–53. Lanham, MD: Rowman and Littlefield, 1999.

Suzuki, Erin. *Ocean Passages: Navigating Pacific Islander and Asian American Literatures*. Philadelphia: Temple University Press, 2021.

Swan, Quito. *Pasifika Black: Oceania, Anti-colonialism, and the African World*. New York: New York University Press, 2022.

Sylvain, Adolphe. *Sylvain's Tahiti*. Cologne: Taschen, 2001.

Tabe, Tammy. "Climate Change Migration and Displacement: Learning from Past Relocations in the Pacific." *Social Sciences* 8, no. 7 (2019): 1–18.

Taillemite, Etienne, ed. *Bougainville et ses compagnons autour du monde: 1766–1769, journaux de navigation*. Paris: Imprimerie nationale, 1977.

Tau, Te Maire. *The Oral Traditions of Ngāi Tahu: Ngā Pikitūroa o Ngāi Tahu*. Dunedin: University of Otago Press, 2003.

Taubenberger, Jeffery K., Johan V. Hultin, and David M. Morens. "Discovery and Characterization of the 1918 Pandemic Influenza Virus in Historical Context." *Antiviral Therapy* 12, no. 4, pt. B (2007): 581–91.

Tavo, Paul. *L'Âme du kava*. Port Vila: Alliance française du Vanuatu, 2011.

Tavo, Paul. *Quand le cannibale ricane*. Port Vila: Alliance française du Vanuatu, 2015.

Tcherkézoff, Serge. *Tahiti 1768: Jeunes filles en pleurs, la face cachée des premiers contacts et la naissance du mythe occidental*. Pira'e, Tahiti: Au vent des îles, 2004.

Teaiwa, Katerina Martina. *Consuming Ocean Island: Stories of People and Phosphate from Banaba*. Bloomington: Indiana University Press, 2014.

Teaiwa, Katerina Martina, April K. Henderson, and Terence Wesley-Smith. Introduction to *Sweat and Salt Water: Selected Works*, edited by Katerina Teaiwa, April K. Henderson, and Terence Wesley-Smith, xv–xxii. Honolulu: University of Hawai'i Press, 2021.

Teaiwa, Teresia K. "Bikinis and Other S/Pacific N/Oceans." *Contemporary Pacific* 6, no. 1 (1994): 87–109.

Teaiwa, Teresia K. "Fear of an Estuary." In *Terenesia: Amplified Poetry and Songs*, by Teresia K. Teaiwa and Sia Figiel. Hawai'i Dub Machine. Honolulu: 'Elepaio, 2000.

Teaiwa, Teresia K. "For or before an Asia Pacific Studies Agenda? Specifying Pacific Studies." In *Remaking Area Studies: Teaching and Learning across Asia and the Pacific*, edited by Terence Wesley-Smith and Jon Goss, 110–24. Honolulu: University of Hawai'i Press, 2010.

Teaiwa, Teresia K. "Militarism, Tourism and the Native: Articulations in Oceania." PhD diss., University of California, Santa Cruz, 2001.

Teaiwa, Teresia K. "Reading Gauguin's *Noa Noa* with Hau'ofa's *Kisses in the Nederends*: 'Militourism,' Feminism, and the 'Polynesian' Body." In *Inside Out: Literature, Cultural Politics, and Identity in the New Pacific*, 249–63. Lanham, MD: Rowman and Littlefield, 1999.

Teaiwa, Teresia K. *Sweat and Salt Water: Selected Works*. Edited by Katerina Teaiwa, April K. Henderson, and Terence Wesley-Smith. Honolulu: University of Hawai'i Press, 2021.

Teaiwa, Teresia K. "What Remains to Be Seen: Reclaiming the Visual Roots of Pacific Literature." *PMLA* 125, no. 3 (2010): 730–36.

Teaiwa, Teresia K. "Yaqona/Yagoqu: Roots and Routes of a Displaced Native." *Cultural Studies and New Writing* 4, no. 2 (1998): 92–106.

Teaiwa, Teresia K., and Sia Figiel. *Terenesia: Amplified Poetry and Songs.* Hawai'i Dub Machine. Honolulu: 'Elepaio, 2000.

Te Awekotuku, Ngahuia. "Mururoa/Moruroa." In *Below the Surface: Words and Images in Protest at French Testing on Moruroa,* edited by Ambury Hall, 6–7. Auckland: Random House New Zealand, 1995.

Tetiarahi, Gabriel. "The Society Islands: Squeezing Out the Polynesians." In *Land Tenure in the Pacific,* 45–58. 3rd ed. Suva, Fiji: University of the South Pacific Press, 1987.

Thomas, Nicholas. *Islanders: The Pacific in the Age of Empire.* New Haven, CT: Yale University Press, 2012.

Tjibaou, Jean-Marie. *La Présence kanak.* Paris: Éditions Odile Jacob, 1996.

Tobin, Jack A. *Stories from the Marshall Islands: Bwebwenato Jan Aelon Kein.* Honolulu: University of Hawai'i Press, 2001.

Trask, Haunani-Kay. *From a Native Daughter: Colonialism and Sovereignty in Hawai'i.* Honolulu: University of Hawai'i Press, 1999.

Trask, Haunani-Kay. "Writing in Captivity: Poetry in a Time of De-colonization." *Wasafiri* 12, no. 25 (1997): 42–43.

Trouillot, Michel-Rolph. *Silencing the Past: Power and the Production of History.* Boston: Beacon, 1995.

Tsing, Anna Lowenhaupt, Nils Bubandt, Elaine Gan, and Heather Anne Swanson, eds. *Arts of Living on a Damaged Planet: Ghosts and Monsters of the Anthropocene.* Minneapolis: University of Minnesota Press, 2017.

Turiano-Reea, Goenda. "Le Comique dans la tradition orale et la littérature contemporaine tahitiennes—vision du rire, vision du monde." PhD diss., Université de la Polynésie française, 2016.

Tuwhare, Hone. *Mihi: Collected Poems.* Auckland: Penguin, 1987.

Tuwhare, Hone. *No Ordinary Sun: Poems.* Auckland: Blackwood and J. Paul, 1962.

Tuwhare, Hone. "Three Poems by Hone Tuwhare." *Te Ao Hou,* September 1959, 17.

Vargas Llosa, Mario. *El paraíso en la otra esquina.* Bogotá: Alfaguara, 2003.

Veran, Christina. "Oceania Rising." *Cultural Survival Quarterly Magazine* 37, no. 2 (2013): 12–13.

Vibart, Eric. *Tahiti: Naissance d'un paradis.* Brussels: Éditions complexe, 1987.

Vigier, Stéphanie. *La Fiction face au passé: Histoire, mémoire et espace-temps dans la fiction littéraire océanienne contemporaine.* Limoges, France: Presses universitaires de Limoges et du Limousin, 2012.

Vimalassery, Manu, Juliana Hu Pegues, and Alyosha Goldstein. "Introduction: On Colonial Unknowing." *Theory and Event* 19, no. 4 (2016).

Voyles, Traci Brynne. *Wastelanding: Legacies of Uranium Mining in Navajo Country.* Minneapolis: University of Minnesota Press, 2015.

Vu, Béatrice Le, Florent de Vathaire, Cécile Challeton de Vathaire, John Paofaite, Laurent Roda, Gilles Soubiran, François Lhoumeau, and François Laudon. "Cancer Incidence in French Polynesia 1985–95." *Tropical Medicine and International Health* 5, no. 10 (2000): 722–31.

Waddell, Eric. *Jean-Marie Tjibaou, Kanak Witness to the World: An Intellectual Biography.* Honolulu: Pacific Islands Development Program, East-West Center, 2008.

Wallerstein, Immanuel. *European Universalism: The Rhetoric of Power*. New York: W. W. Norton, 2006.

Warren, Joyce Lindsay Pualani. "Theorizing Pō: Embodied Cosmogony and Polynesian National Narratives." PhD diss., University of California, Los Angeles, 2017.

Wélépane, Wanir. *Aux vents des îles*. Nouméa, New Caledonia: Agence de développement de la culture Kanak, 1993.

Wendt, Albert. *Black Rainbow*. Honolulu: University of Hawai'i Press, 1995.

Wendt, Albert. "Novelists and Historians and the Art of Remembering." In *Class and Culture in the South Pacific*, edited by Anthony Hooper, 78–92. Suva, Fiji: Centre for Pacific Studies, University of Auckland, and Institute of Pacific Studies, University of the South Pacific, 1987.

Wendt, Albert, ed. *Nuanua: Pacific Writing in English since 1980*. Honolulu: University of Hawai'i Press, 1995.

Wendt, Albert. "Tatauing the Post-colonial Body." In *Inside Out: Literature, Cultural Politics, and Identity in the New Pacific*, edited by Vilsoni Hereniko and Rob Wilson, 399–412. Lanham, MD: Rowman and Littlefield, 1999.

Wendt, Albert. "Towards a New Oceania." In *Writers in East-West Encounter: New Cultural Bearings*, edited by Guy Amirthanayagam, 202–15. London: Palgrave Macmillan UK, 1982.

Wenzel, Jennifer. "Reading Fanon Reading Nature." In *What Postcolonial Theory Doesn't Say*, edited by Anna Bernard, Ziad Elmarsafy, and Stuart Murray, 185–98. New York: Routledge, 2015.

Wheeler, Vehia Jennifer. "Climate Change, Watershed Management, and Resiliency to Flooding: A Case Study of Papeno'o Valley, Tahiti Nui (French Polynesia)." Master's thesis, University of Hawai'i at Mānoa, 2018.

Whyte, Kyle Powys. "Indigenous Science (Fiction) for the Anthropocene: Ancestral Dystopias and Fantasies of Climate Change Crises." *Environment and Planning E: Nature and Space* 1, nos. 1–2 (2018): 224–42.

Whyte, Kyle Powys. "Our Ancestors' Dystopia Now: Indigenous Conservation and the Anthropocene." In *The Routledge Companion to the Environmental Humanities*, edited by Ursula Heise, Jon Christensen, and Michelle Niemann, 206–15. New York: Routledge, 2017.

Williams, Madi. *Polynesia, 900–1600*. Leeds, UK: Arc Humanities, 2021.

Wilson-Hokowhitu, Nālani, and Manulani Aluli Meyer. "I Ka Wā Mamua, The Past before Us." In *The Past before Us: Moʻokūʻauhau as Methodology*, edited by Nālani Wilson-Hokowhitu, 1–8. Honolulu: University of Hawai'i Press, 2019.

Women Working for an Independent and Nuclear-Free Pacific (WWINFP). *Pacific Women Speak: Why Haven't You Known?* Oxford: Green Line, 1987.

Woodward, Valerie Solar. "'I Guess They Didn't Want Us Asking Too Many Questions': Reading American Empire in Guam." *Contemporary Pacific* 25, no. 1 (2013): 67–91.

World Economic Forum. "The New Plastics Economy: Rethinking the Future of Plastics." January 19, 2016. https://www.weforum.org/reports/the-new-plastics -economy-rethinking-the-future-of-plastics/.

World Health Organization. "Antibiotic Resistance." World Health Organization.

Accessed July 31, 2020. https://www.who.int/news-room/fact-sheets/detail
/antibiotic-resistance.

Worster, Donald. *Nature's Economy: A History of Ecological Ideas*. Cambridge: Cambridge
University Press, 1994.

Young, Forrest Wade. "Rapa Nui." *Contemporary Pacific* 29, no. 1 (2017): 173–81.

Zalasiewicz, Jan, et al. "When Did the Anthropocene Begin? A Mid-Twentieth Century
Boundary Level Is Stratigraphically Optimal." *Quaternary International* 383 (October
2015): 196–203.

Zimmerman, Michael E. "The Threat of Ecofascism." *Social Theory and Practice* 21, no. 2
(1995): 207–38.

Index

apocalypse: already experienced by Indigenous peoples, 7–9, 14–15, 20, 76, 135–36; circularity of episodes, 124–25; epidemic population loss as, 37; Māori encounter with colonizers, 97; Pacific peoples' survival of, 8–9, 25–29. *See also* (post)apocalyptic literature, Pacific

Ariirau (Stéphanie Ariirau Richard-Vivi), 63

Ari'oi comical theater (Tahiti), 30, 108–19; images, *109, 113, 115, 117, 118, 119; Maititi Haere Mai*, 113; as religious political satire, 111–12; sexuality in, 112–13; *115*

Aristotle, 66, 72

Arvin, Maile Renee, 54

Ata, Alexandre Moeava, 30, 108, 120–25

"Atlas" (Siagatonu), 53, 134–36

Atomic Energy Commission (US), 139, 141

Atomic Fish (THS!), *84*

Australia, nuclear testing in, 148

Awekotuku, Ngahuia, 53

Bachimon, Philippe, 38

Bahng, Aimee, 145–46

Bakale, Anare, 92

Banaba (island), 150

Bataillon (French missionary), 19

Bensa, Alban, 16, 32

Bergson, Henri, 65

Bhabha, Homi K., 50

Bigler, Carmen, 140

"Bikini and Other S/Pacific N/Oceans" (Teaiwa), 150

bikini bathing suit, 45, 51

biodiversity, alienation from, 29, 79, 87–89, 99, 104

biopolitics, 39

Black Atlantic, 54–55, 64–69, 76. *See also* Negritude

"blackbirding," 19, 37, 39

Black Rainbow (Hotere), 125, 129

Black Rainbow (Wendt), 125–31

Blitz, Claudine, 51

Bougainville, Louis-Antoine de, 2, 42–44, 52

Brotherson, Moetai, 21

Burn, James, 148

Busby-Neff, Luana Palapala, 75

"Butterfly Thief" (Jetñil-Kijiner), 146–48

Byrd, Jodi, 40

Cahier d'un retour au pays natal (*Notebook of a Return to My Native Land*) (Césaire), 76

Camoui, Luc Énoka, 53

Capelle, Alfred, 148

capitalism, 2–4; carbon-fueled, 8, 9, 30, 105; death spawned by, 78; disaster capitalism, 2; forced entry of Pacific people into, 59–60, 85; infinite growth logic, 69; mainstream myths of, 9–10; scarcity, economies of, 8, 70. *See also* Seasteading Institute

carbon imperialism, 13, 23, 27–28, 58, 142, 167

Caro, Niki, 91

Carson, Rachel, 11, 134

Cartesian thinking, 28–29, *68*; fight against on Mauna Kea, 71–72; Negritude's critique of, 65–67; as "reason-eye," 67, 73; and science, 65–66, 73, 162–63

Case, Pua, 70, 71, 73

Centre d'experimentation du Pacifique (CEP, Pacific Experimentation Center), 25, 154; societal destruction by, 5–6, 80–81, 85–86, 110–11, 121–24

Césaire, Aimé, 28, 57, 64–66, 76

Chailloux, Steve, 3

CHamoru people, 97–103; lisåyo mourning prayer, 29, 80, 98–99

Chappell, David A., 159

Chaze, Ra'i, 29, 80–90, 104; "Eden," 80, 82–90; *Vai: La Riviere au ciel sans nuages* (*Water: The River under the Cloudless Sky*), 81

Chilean colonization, 39, 46

Chirac, Jacques, 118

Choi, Shine, 12

ciguatera, epidemics of, 83–86

Clean Energies (NGO), 146

climate apathy, 9, 16, 162

climate crisis/collapse: collective responsibility for, 159, 162; as crisis of imagination, 24; as current reality for Oceanians, 8–9, 15; droughts, 13, 135, 149; imperial obliviousness to, 28, 40; mainstream apocalypse narratives, 8–10; salt water content, 152–53; temperature rise, 40–41, 133–34. *See also* sea level rise

"climate genocide," 41

climate porn, 15

climate refugees, 30, 58, 62, 133, 197n2

Clinton administration, 32

Club Med, 51

coconuts, 150–54

Nei Tabera Ni Kai (film company), 153
neoliberalism, 2, 29, 101
Neruda, Pablo, 28, 34, 46–50
New Zealand. *See* Aotearoa
Niheu, Kalamaʻokaina, 38
Nixon, Rob, 23
noble savage narrative, 10, 35, 42–43, 81–82; and
    contemporary tourism, 52
"No Ordinary Sun" (Tuwhare), 17, 131
No tōʻu here ia Mataiea (Out of my love for
    Mataiea) association, 2–3
nuclear and thermonuclear testing, 4–5, 174n47,
    174n50; aboveground impact of, 92; destruc-
    tion of division between rational and irratio-
    nal, 95; "end of all wars" story, 3, 11, 137; lands
    destroyed for hundreds of thousands of years,
    11, 15, 76, 97, 107, 136–37; maps of sites, *13, 16*;
    nuclearized Anthropocene, 11–13; Oceania as
    first continent to be destroyed by, 10–11; racial
    hierarchy and choice of sites, 31, 36; test yields,
    13, 13–14; unstable conditions for radioactive
    waste containment, 93, 107, 193–94n13. *See also*
    nuclear colonialism/imperialism; nuclear test-
    ing, France; nuclear testing, United Kingdom;
    nuclear testing, United States
nuclear colonialism/imperialism: animals, effect
    on, 91, 93–97; arsenals dependent on other
    nations' resources, 11–12; contradictions of,
    121; and deculturation, 161; economy of, 5–6,
    154–57; environmental collapse under, 9; guilt
    of "voluntary" survivors, 156–57; humorous
    denunciation of, 125–31; mastery and posses-
    sion of nature as ideology of, 24, 28, 127; Oce-
    ania on front lines of, 13–16; as outsourcing of
    nuclear pollution, 14; "voluntary" migration
    under, 154–62. *See also* colonialism
Nuclear Free and Independent Pacific (NFIP), 15,
    92, 108, 109, *109*, 150
nuclear morbidity, trope of, 108
Nuclear Playground (Firth), 150
Nu/Clear Stories (podcast), 85, 161
nuclear testing, France, 3–4, 12–13, 26, 31–32,
    147nn47, 50; Aldebaran (1966), 155; Cano-
    pus, 161; In Ekker, 12; largest series of nuclear
    tests, 49, 182n79; site selection based on myth
    of Tahitian vahine, 110; *Telsite 2*, 107; "under-
    ground," 92–93, 107. *See also* Fangataufa atoll;
    Moruroa atoll
nuclear testing, United Kingdom, 13, 31–32,

174n47, 174n50; Grapple Y, 149; Operation
    Grapple, 148–49, 151
nuclear testing, United States, 31; Castle Bravo,
    11, 14, 23, 138, 142; "Ivy Mike" bomb, 138; Opera-
    tion Crossroad, 137, 198n19; Operation Home-
    coming, 139. *See also* Pikinni (Bikini) Atoll;
    United States
Nukuatea, leprosarium on, 38–39

obliviousness, imperial, 28, 36–41, 43, 149
ocean: as frontier to be trespassed, 4; living with
    versus building walls, 62; no longer a meta-
    phor, 63; as pathway to each other, 63; as
    relationship/identity, 56, 63–64; tears, rela-
    tionship to, 63. *See also* Pacific Ocean
Ocean Declaration of Maupiti, 56
Oceania: condemned to submersion by UN sus-
    tainable development goals, 40–41; as dump-
    ing grounds for nuclear and radioactive waste,
    14, 138, 142, 175n53; first continent to be de-
    stroyed by nuclear fire, 10–11; on front line of
    nuclear imperialism, 13–16; geopolitical mar-
    ginalization of, 22; as "isolated," 31–32, 137,
    178n19; as preferred term, 54; size of, 44
Oceanians: ahistoricity/prehistoricity attributed
    to, 16, 28, 35, 40; compensation for victims of
    nuclear testing, 93, 166–67, 205nn7–8; fu-
    sional relationship with ocean and world, 58,
    62–64; "future threats" already experienced
    by, 7–9, 14–15, 20, 76, 135–36; removed from
    global public consciousness, 32, 33–34; victim
    discourse about, 22, 62, 146–47, 159
Oceanitude: coined by Tavo, 53, 54, 56, 60, 75–76;
    as collective identity, 28–29, 52, 54–56, 76; as foil
    to globalization, 60–61; genealogy of, 57, 64–69;
    genesis of, 57–64; global spread of, 62–63; impor-
    tance of for non-Pacific peoples, 56–57; as philos-
    ophy of the future, 64; reason-fusion in literature
    of, 75–76; as replacement for "extinction of ex-
    perience," 62; valuing-the-living together, 52, 56,
    64; "vegetal" way of life, 67–68, *68*
O'Keefe, John, 43
ʻōlelo noʻeau (proverbs), 74, 166
Omai: A Voyage 'Round the World (O'Keefe), 43
"One fish, Two fish, Plastics, Dead fish" (Perez),
    98, 99
Oopa, Céline, 157
Operation Grapple, 148–49
oral traditions, 8, 20, 89, 149; kantan chamorrita